STAR WARS®

KNIGHTS OF THE OLD REPUBLIC

VOLUME SEVEN
DUELING AMBITIONS

THE OLD REPUBLIC
(25,000–1,000 YEARS BEFORE THE BATTLE OF YAVIN)

The Old Republic was the legendary government that united a galaxy under the rule of the Senate. In this era, the Jedi are numerous, and serve as guardians of peace and justice. The **Tales of the Jedi** *comics series takes place in this era, chronicling the immense wars fought by the Jedi of old, and the ancient Sith.*

The events in this story take place approximately 3,963 years before the Battle of Yavin.

STAR WARS

KNIGHTS OF THE OLD REPUBLIC

VOLUME SEVEN
DUELING AMBITIONS

SCRIPT JOHN JACKSON MILLER

ART BRIAN CHING, BONG DAZO & DEAN ZACHARY

COLORS MICHAEL ATIYEH

LETTERING MICHAEL HEISLER

FRONT COVER ART DAN SCOTT

BACK COVER ART DARYL MANDRYK

Dark Horse Books®

PUBLISHER MIKE RICHARDSON

COLLECTION DESIGNER STEPHEN REICHERT

ASSISTANT EDITOR FREDDYE LINS

EDITOR DAVE MARSHALL

*Special thanks to Elaine Mederer, Jann Moorhead, David Anderman, Leland Chee,
Sue Rostoni, and Carol Roeder at Lucas Licensing.*

STAR WARS: KNIGHTS OF THE OLD REPUBLIC VOLUME SEVEN—DUELING AMBITIONS

This volume collects issues #36–#41 of the Dark Horse
comic-book series *Star Wars: Knights of the Old Republic*.

Published by
Dark Horse Books
A division of Dark Horse Comics, Inc.
10956 SE Main Street
Milwaukie, OR 97222

darkhorse.com
starwars.com

To find a comics shop in your area,
call the Comic Shop Locator Service toll-free at 1-888-266-4226

First edition: November 2009
ISBN 978-1-59582-348-9

1 3 5 7 9 10 8 6 4 2
Printed in China

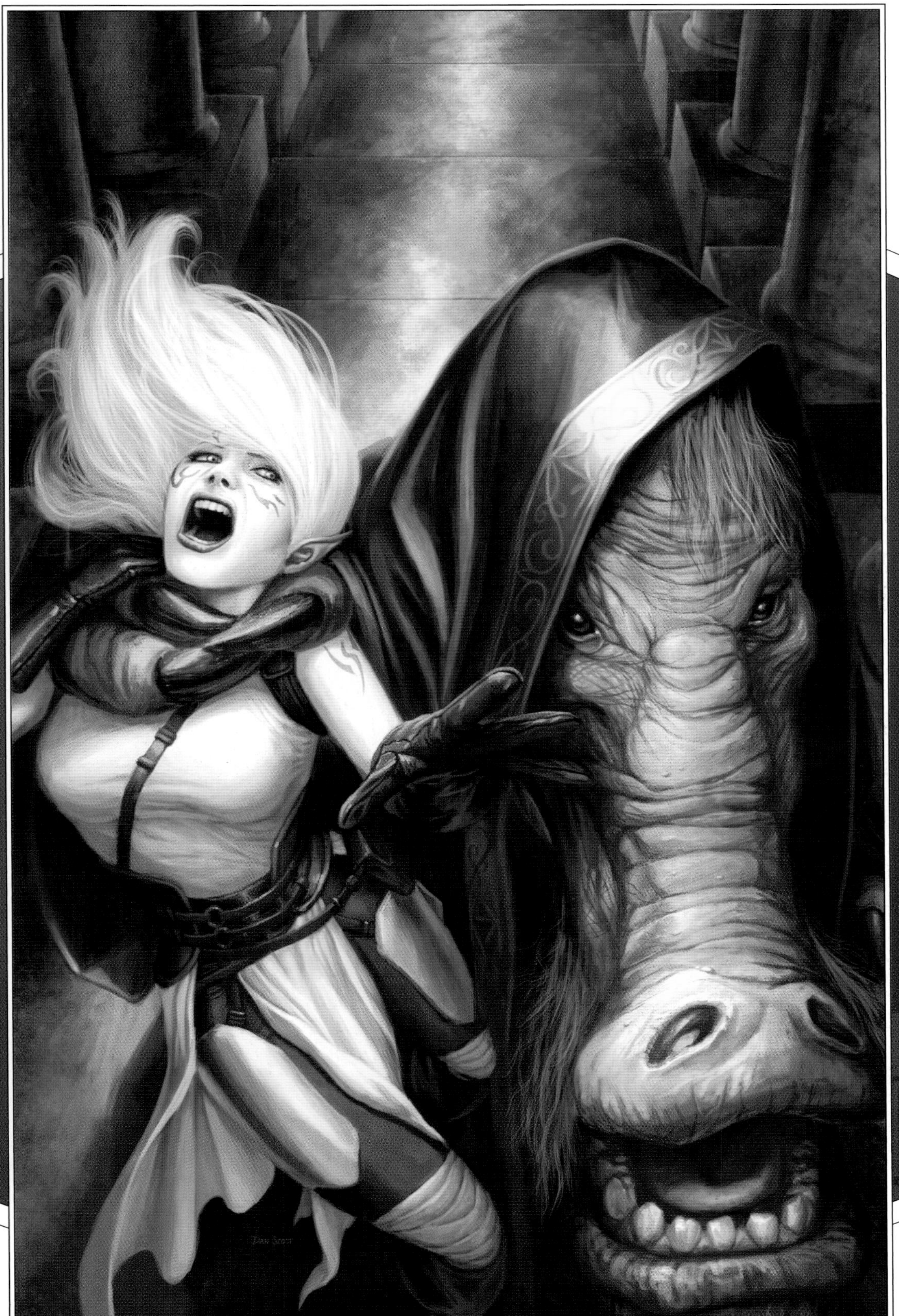

ILLUSTRATION BY DAN SCOTT

PROPHET MOTIVE

art by Bong Dazo

With the Galactic Republic warring with the nomadic Mandalorians on the frontier, life in the Core Worlds continues as usual for many—even for those who live on the wrong side of the law, such as swindler Marn "The Gryph" Hierogryph and his friends.

Cleared of murder charges in the hushed-up Covenant Affair, Gryph sets his sights on fortune. His band includes the fierce Jarael; Rohlan, a Mandalorian deserter; Slyssk, his inept pilot; and Elbee, a stubborn loading droid. With their help, he sees only opportunities ahead.

But freedom to move may not be freedom to act—for his one-time henchman, Zayne Carrick, is now his full partner in crime. The former Jedi student has clashed before with Gryph over the morality of their trade. The only certainty is that from here on out, nothing will be easy . . .

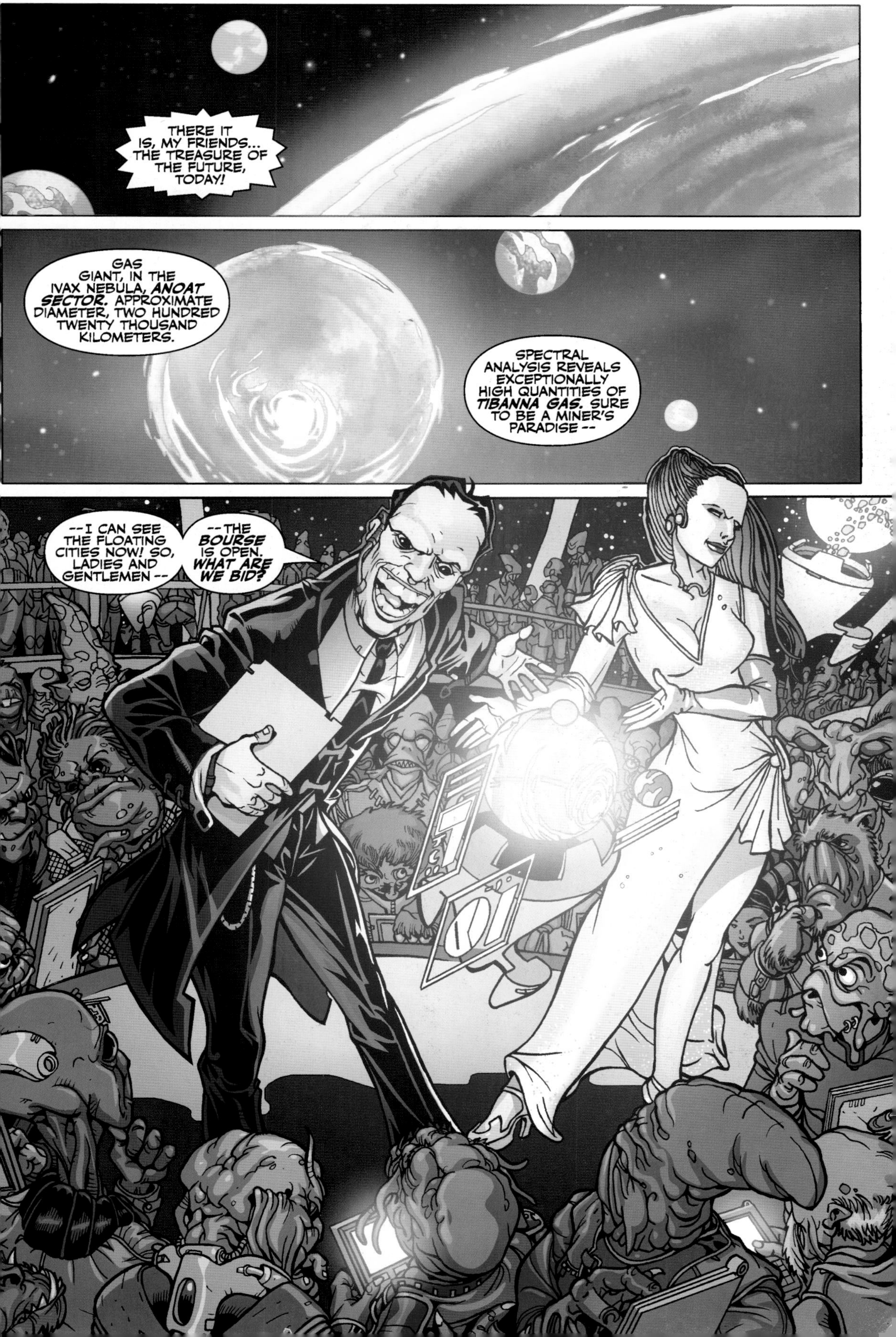
THERE IT IS, MY FRIENDS... THE TREASURE OF THE FUTURE, TODAY!
GAS GIANT, IN THE IVAX NEBULA, ANOAT SECTOR. APPROXIMATE DIAMETER, TWO HUNDRED TWENTY THOUSAND KILOMETERS.
SPECTRAL ANALYSIS REVEALS EXCEPTIONALLY HIGH QUANTITIES OF TIBANNA GAS. SURE TO BE A MINER'S PARADISE --
--I CAN SEE THE FLOATING CITIES NOW! SO, LADIES AND GENTLEMEN --
--THE BOURSE IS OPEN. WHAT ARE WE BID?

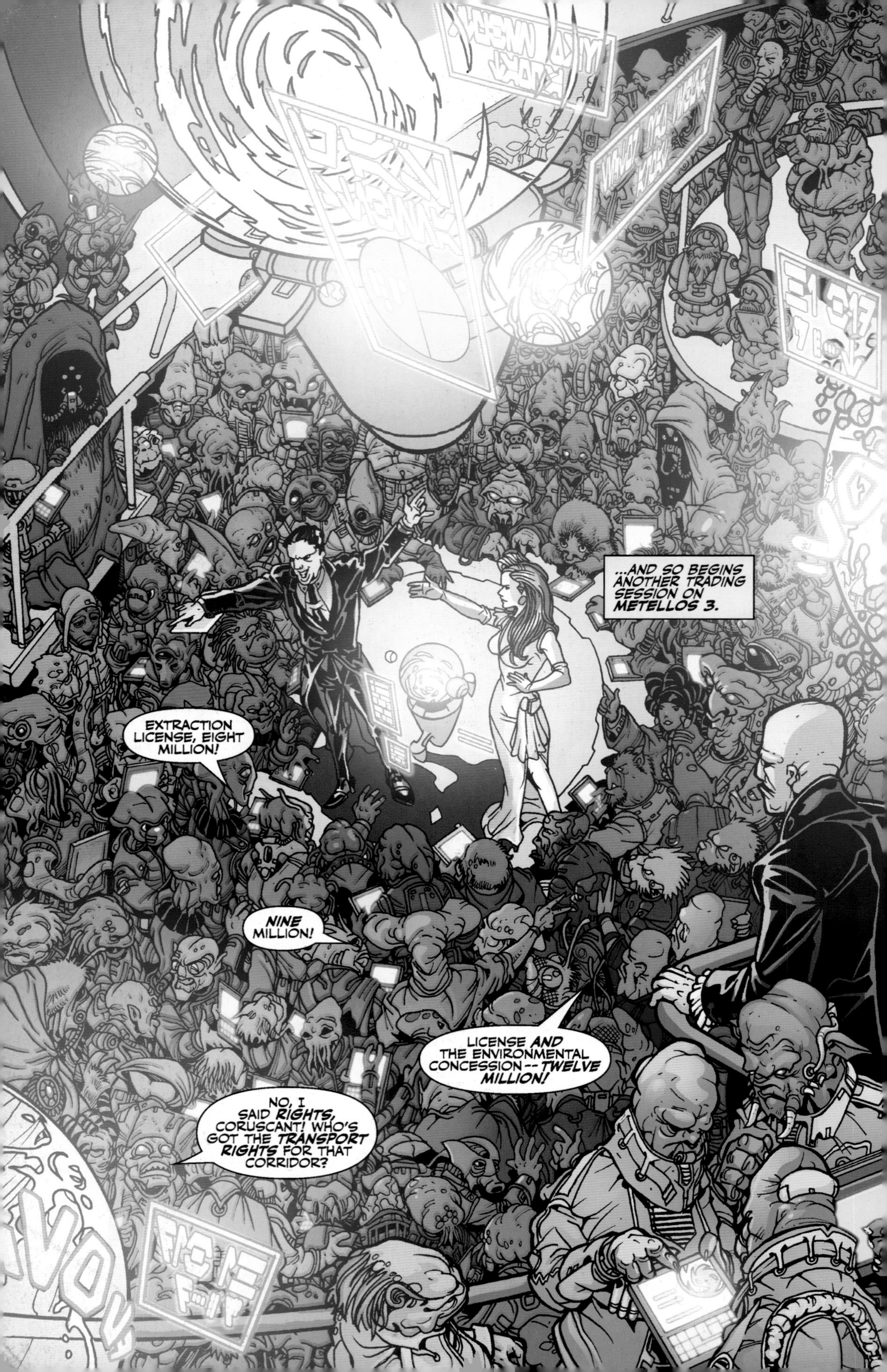
...AND SO BEGINS ANOTHER TRADING SESSION ON METELLOS 3.
EXTRACTION LICENSE, EIGHT MILLION!
NINE MILLION!
LICENSE AND THE ENVIRONMENTAL CONCESSION--TWELVE MILLION!
NO, I SAID RIGHTS, CORUSCANT! WHO'S GOT THE TRANSPORT RIGHTS FOR THAT CORRIDOR?

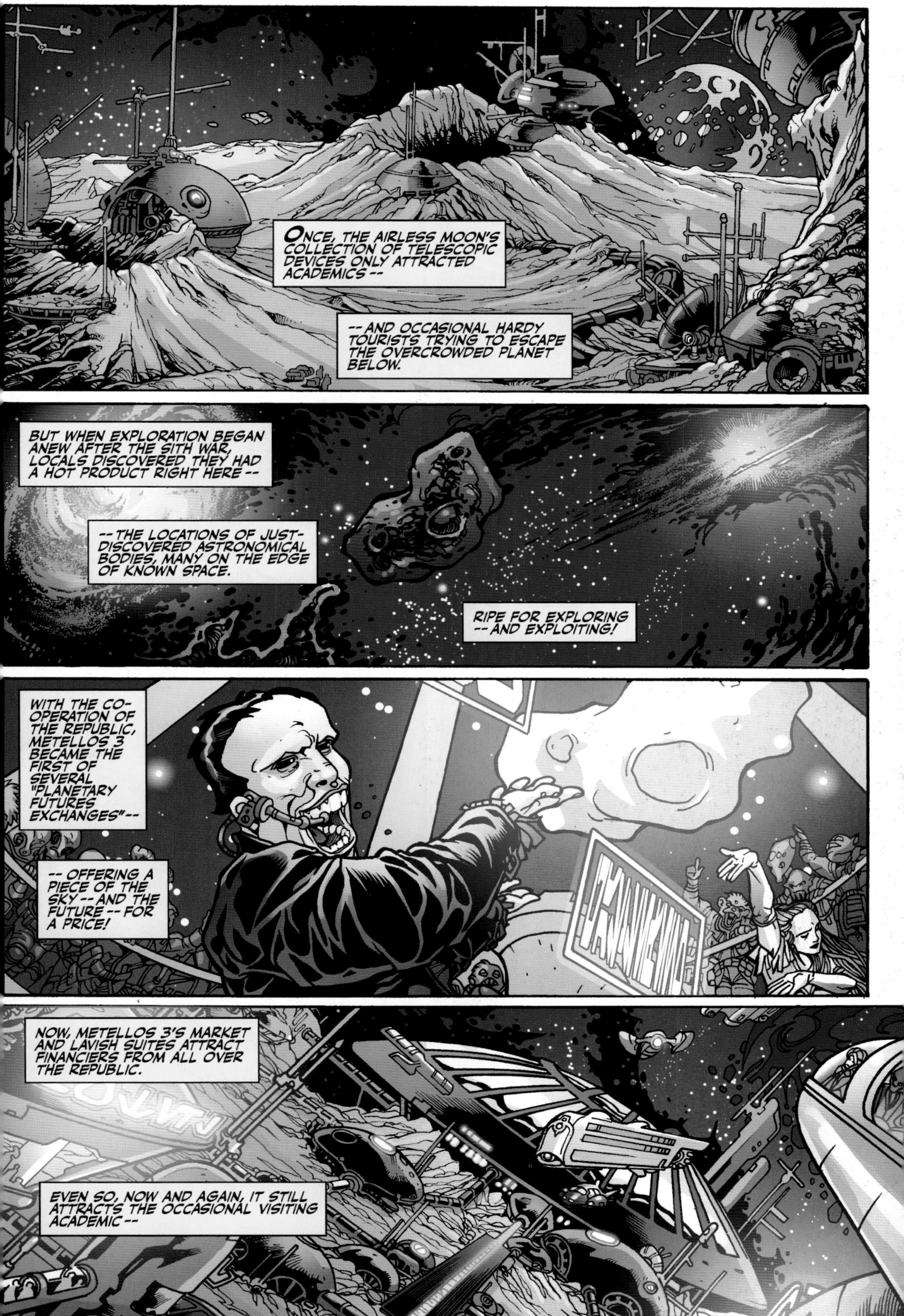
ONCE, THE AIRLESS MOON'S COLLECTION OF TELESCOPIC DEVICES ONLY ATTRACTED ACADEMICS --
-- AND OCCASIONAL HARDY TOURISTS TRYING TO ESCAPE THE OVERCROWDED PLANET BELOW.
BUT WHEN EXPLORATION BEGAN ANEW AFTER THE SITH WAR, LOCALS DISCOVERED THEY HAD A HOT PRODUCT RIGHT HERE --
-- THE LOCATIONS OF JUST-DISCOVERED ASTRONOMICAL BODIES, MANY ON THE EDGE OF KNOWN SPACE.
RIPE FOR EXPLORING -- AND EXPLOITING!
WITH THE CO-OPERATION OF THE REPUBLIC, METELLOS 3 BECAME THE FIRST OF SEVERAL "PLANETARY FUTURES EXCHANGES"--
-- OFFERING A PIECE OF THE SKY -- AND THE FUTURE -- FOR A PRICE!
NOW, METELLOS 3'S MARKET AND LAVISH SUITES ATTRACT FINANCIERS FROM ALL OVER THE REPUBLIC.
EVEN SO, NOW AND AGAIN, IT STILL ATTRACTS THE OCCASIONAL VISITING ACADEMIC --

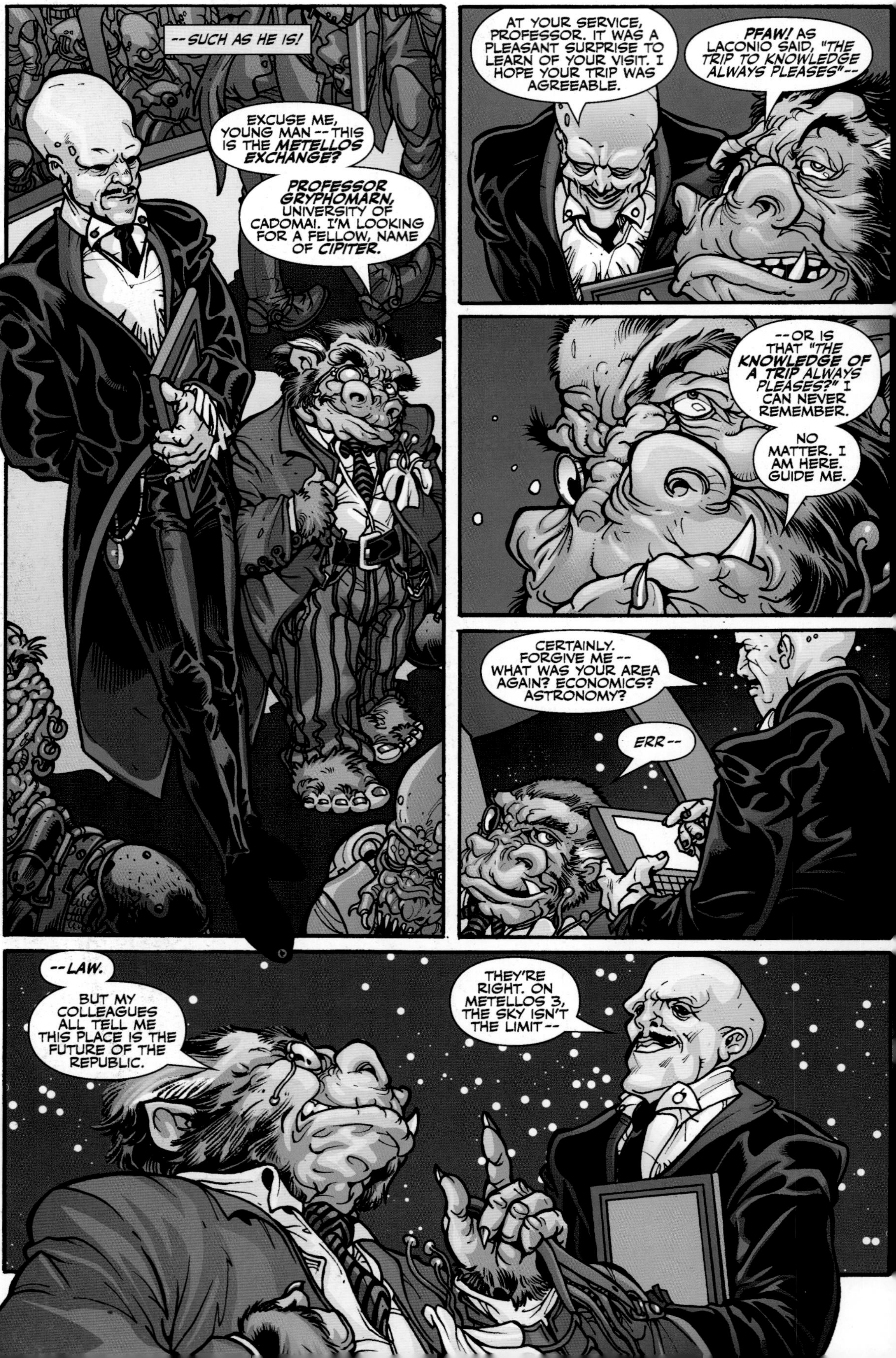
--SUCH AS HE IS!
EXCUSE ME, YOUNG MAN--THIS IS THE METELLOS EXCHANGE?
PROFESSOR GRYPHOMARN, UNIVERSITY OF CADOMAI. I'M LOOKING FOR A FELLOW, NAME OF CIPITER.
AT YOUR SERVICE, PROFESSOR. IT WAS A PLEASANT SURPRISE TO LEARN OF YOUR VISIT. I HOPE YOUR TRIP WAS AGREEABLE.
PFAW! AS LACONIO SAID, "THE TRIP TO KNOWLEDGE ALWAYS PLEASES"--
--OR IS THAT "THE KNOWLEDGE OF A TRIP ALWAYS PLEASES?" I CAN NEVER REMEMBER.
NO MATTER. I AM HERE. GUIDE ME.
CERTAINLY. FORGIVE ME--WHAT WAS YOUR AREA AGAIN? ECONOMICS? ASTRONOMY?
ERR--
--LAW.
BUT MY COLLEAGUES ALL TELL ME THIS PLACE IS THE FUTURE OF THE REPUBLIC.
THEY'RE RIGHT. ON METELLOS 3, THE SKY ISN'T THE LIMIT--

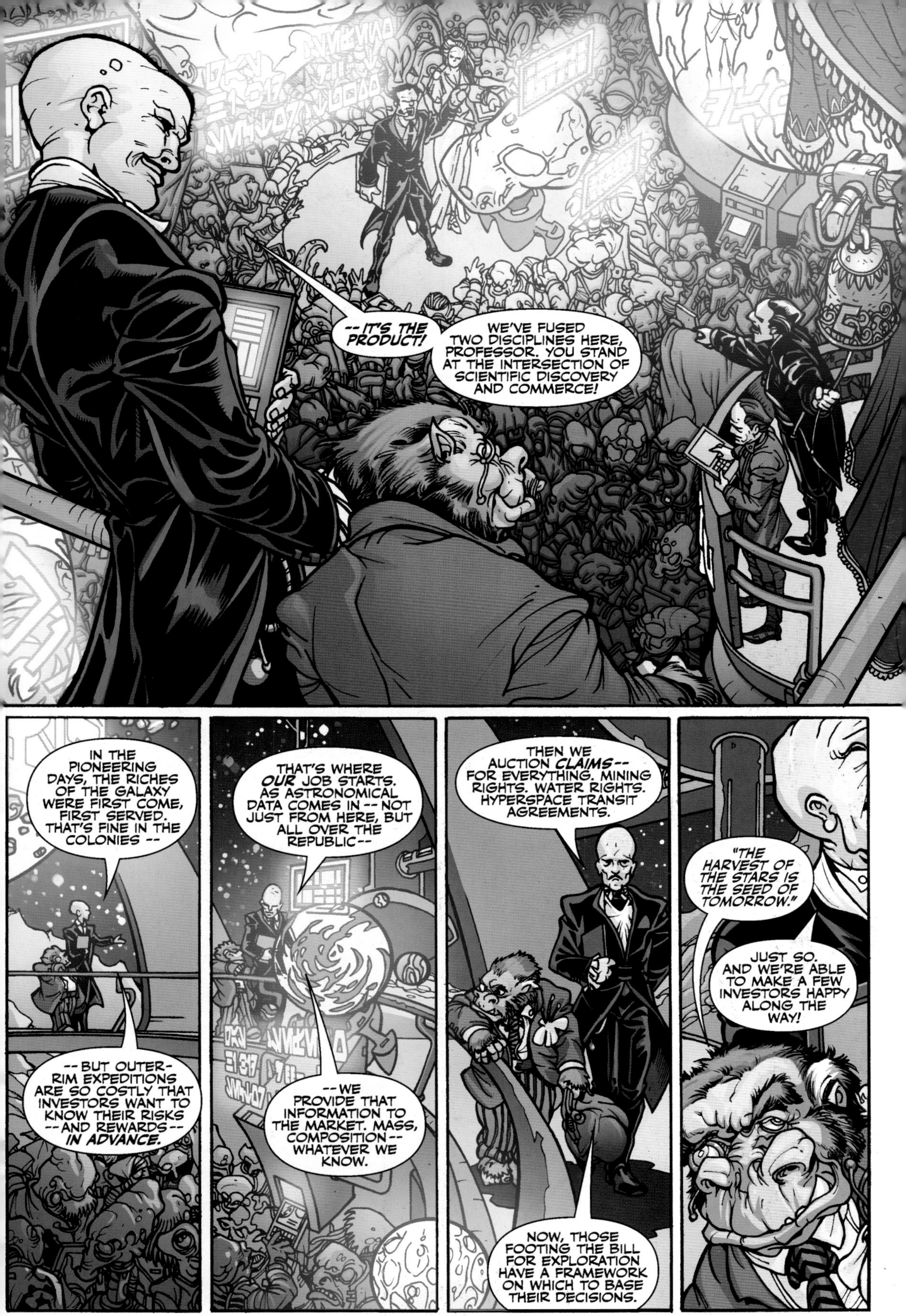
--IT'S THE PRODUCT!
WE'VE FUSED TWO DISCIPLINES HERE, PROFESSOR. YOU STAND AT THE INTERSECTION OF SCIENTIFIC DISCOVERY AND COMMERCE!
IN THE PIONEERING DAYS, THE RICHES OF THE GALAXY WERE FIRST COME, FIRST SERVED. THAT'S FINE IN THE COLONIES --
-- BUT OUTER-RIM EXPEDITIONS ARE SO COSTLY THAT INVESTORS WANT TO KNOW THEIR RISKS --AND REWARDS-- IN ADVANCE.
THAT'S WHERE OUR JOB STARTS. AS ASTRONOMICAL DATA COMES IN -- NOT JUST FROM HERE, BUT ALL OVER THE REPUBLIC--
--WE PROVIDE THAT INFORMATION TO THE MARKET. MASS, COMPOSITION-- WHATEVER WE KNOW.
THEN WE AUCTION CLAIMS-- FOR EVERYTHING. MINING RIGHTS. WATER RIGHTS. HYPERSPACE TRANSIT AGREEMENTS.
NOW, THOSE FOOTING THE BILL FOR EXPLORATION HAVE A FRAMEWORK ON WHICH TO BASE THEIR DECISIONS.
"THE HARVEST OF THE STARS IS THE SEED OF TOMORROW."
JUST SO. AND WE'RE ABLE TO MAKE A FEW INVESTORS HAPPY ALONG THE WAY!

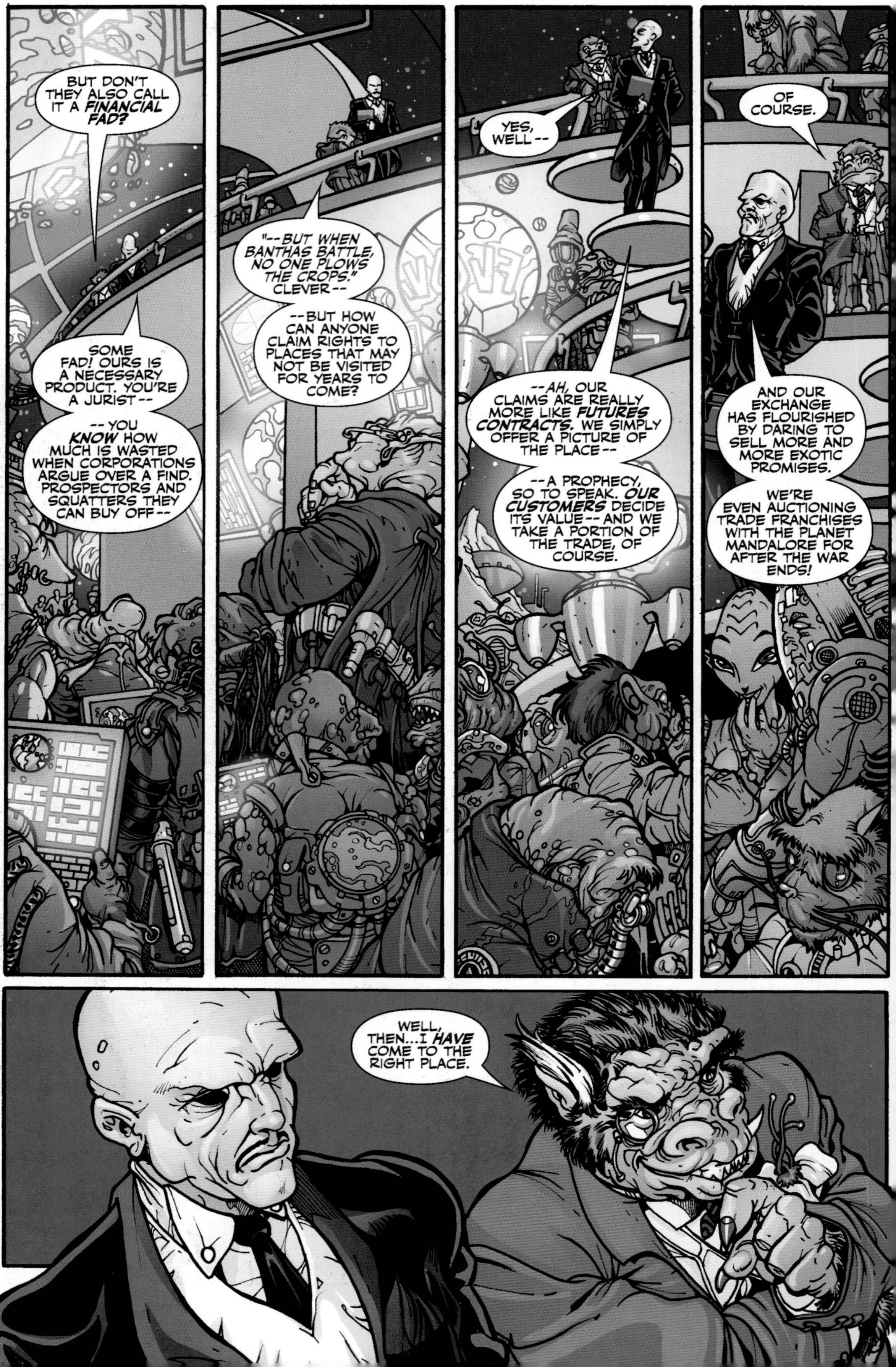
BUT DON'T THEY ALSO CALL IT A FINANCIAL FAD?
SOME FAD! OURS IS A NECESSARY PRODUCT. YOU'RE A JURIST--
--YOU KNOW HOW MUCH IS WASTED WHEN CORPORATIONS ARGUE OVER A FIND. PROSPECTORS AND SQUATTERS THEY CAN BUY OFF--
"--BUT WHEN BANTHAS BATTLE, NO ONE PLOWS THE CROPS." CLEVER--
--BUT HOW CAN ANYONE CLAIM RIGHTS TO PLACES THAT MAY NOT BE VISITED FOR YEARS TO COME?
YES, WELL--
--AH, OUR CLAIMS ARE REALLY MORE LIKE FUTURES CONTRACTS. WE SIMPLY OFFER A PICTURE OF THE PLACE--
--A PROPHECY, SO TO SPEAK. OUR CUSTOMERS DECIDE ITS VALUE-- AND WE TAKE A PORTION OF THE TRADE, OF COURSE.
OF COURSE.
AND OUR EXCHANGE HAS FLOURISHED BY DARING TO SELL MORE AND MORE EXOTIC PROMISES.
WE'RE EVEN AUCTIONING TRADE FRANCHISES WITH THE PLANET MANDALORE FOR AFTER THE WAR ENDS!
WELL, THEN...I HAVE COME TO THE RIGHT PLACE.

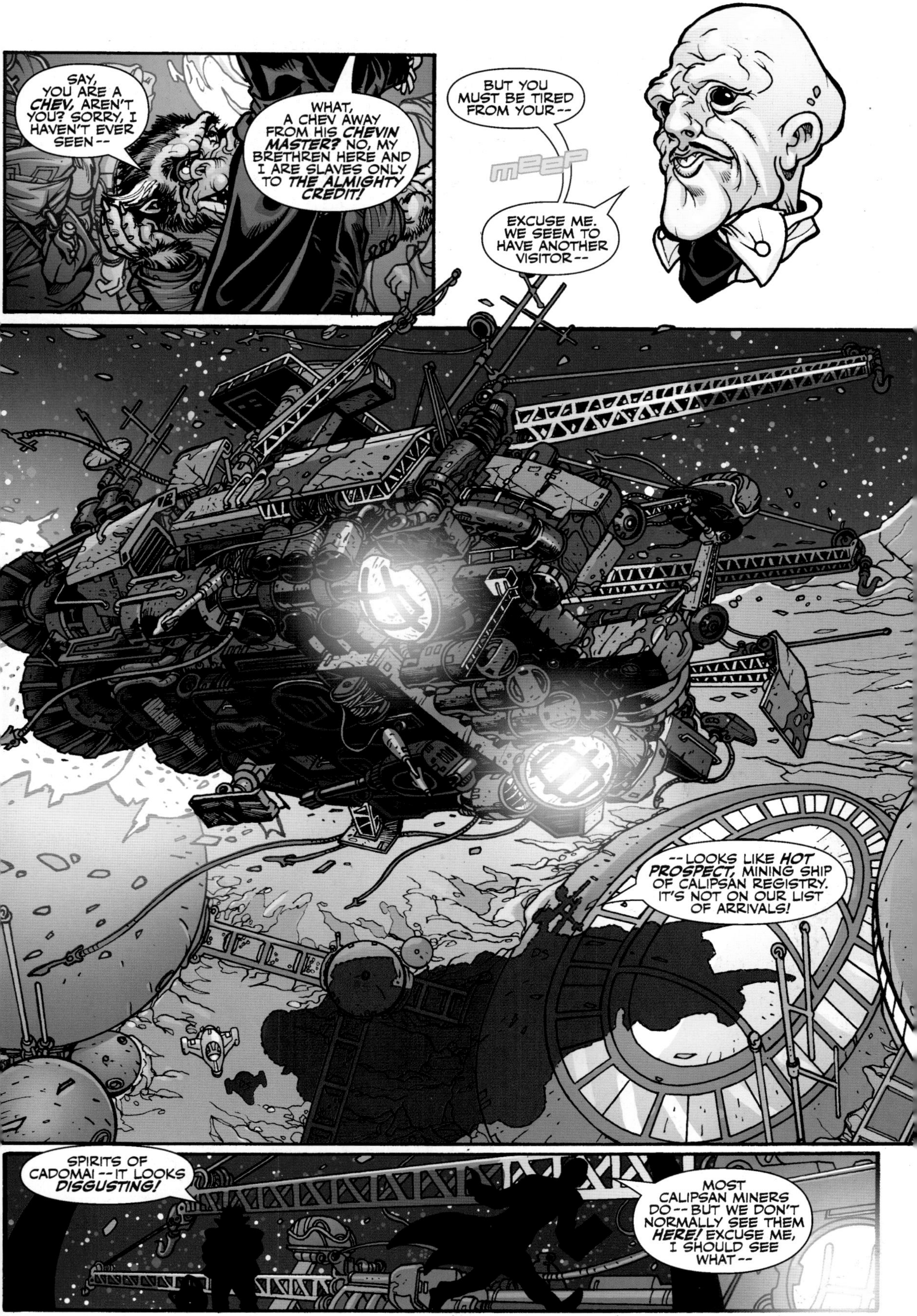
SAY, YOU ARE A CHEV, AREN'T YOU? SORRY, I HAVEN'T EVER SEEN--
WHAT, A CHEV AWAY FROM HIS CHEVIN MASTER? NO, MY BRETHREN HERE AND I ARE SLAVES ONLY TO THE ALMIGHTY CREDIT!
BUT YOU MUST BE TIRED FROM YOUR--
MEEP
EXCUSE ME. WE SEEM TO HAVE ANOTHER VISITOR--
--LOOKS LIKE HOT PROSPECT, MINING SHIP OF CALIPSAN REGISTRY. IT'S NOT ON OUR LIST OF ARRIVALS!
SPIRITS OF CADOMAI--IT LOOKS DISGUSTING!
MOST CALIPSAN MINERS DO--BUT WE DON'T NORMALLY SEE THEM HERE! EXCUSE ME, I SHOULD SEE WHAT--

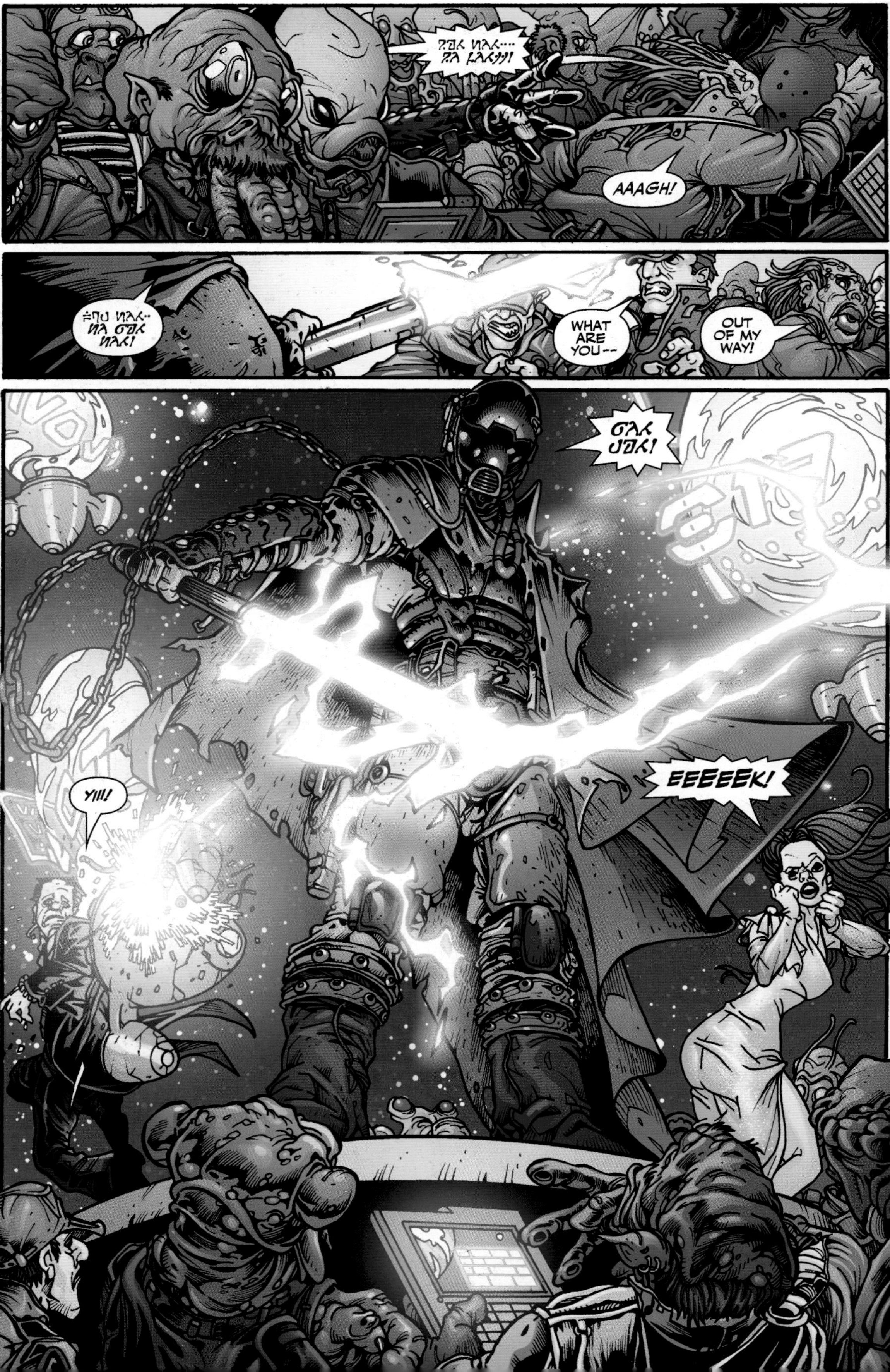

AAAGH!
WHAT ARE YOU--
OUT OF MY WAY!
EEEEEK!
YIII!

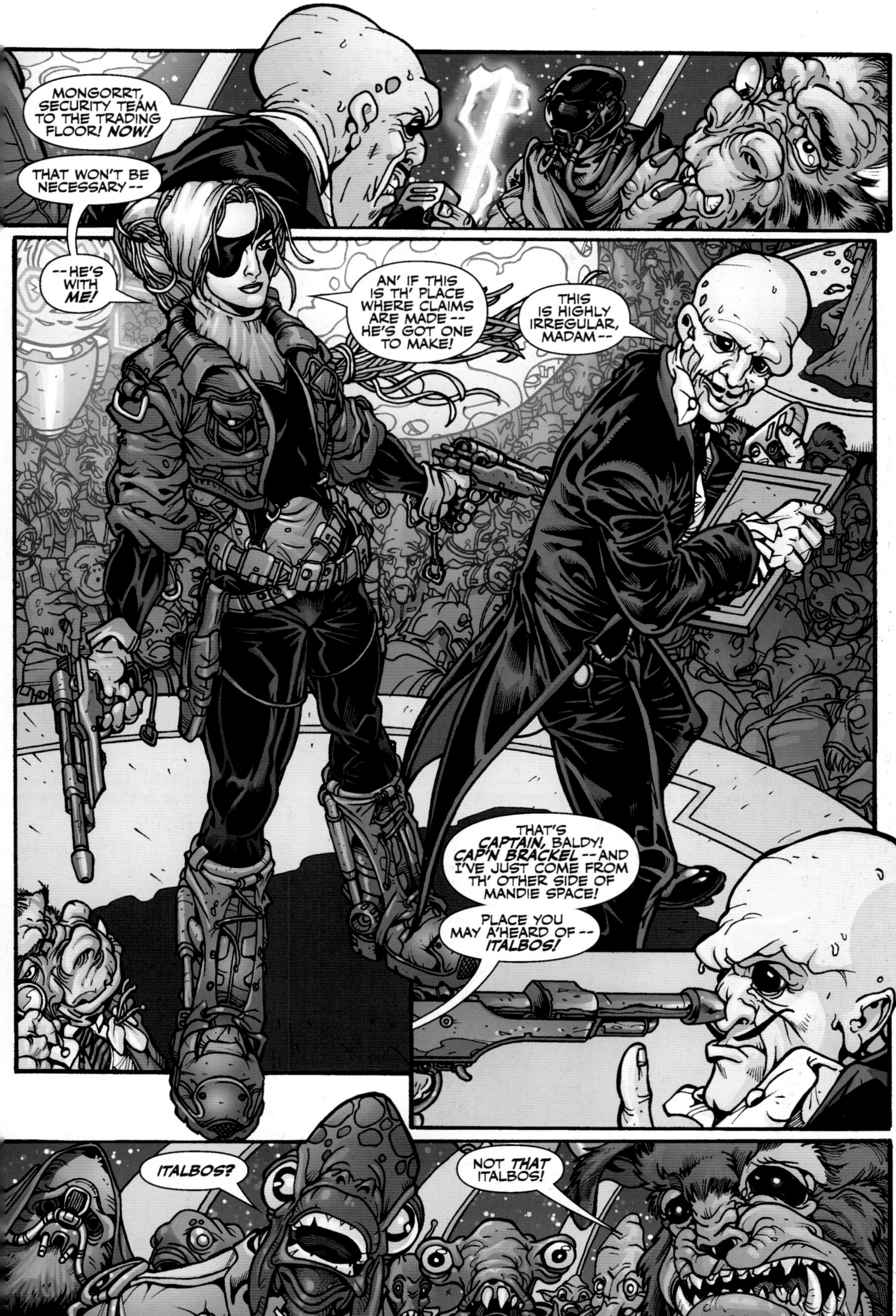
MONGORRT, SECURITY TEAM TO THE TRADING FLOOR! NOW!
THAT WON'T BE NECESSARY--
--HE'S WITH ME!
AN' IF THIS IS TH' PLACE WHERE CLAIMS ARE MADE-- HE'S GOT ONE TO MAKE!
THIS IS HIGHLY IRREGULAR, MADAM--
THAT'S CAPTAIN, BALDY! CAP'N BRACKEL--AND I'VE JUST COME FROM TH' OTHER SIDE OF MANDIE SPACE!
PLACE YOU MAY A'HEARD OF-- ITALBOS!
ITALBOS?
NOT THAT ITALBOS!

ONLY ONE THERE IS, MONEYBAGS. YOU OUGHTA KNOW-- YOU NAMED IT!

PROBLEM IS, YOU *CLAIMED* IT-- AND MY NEW BUDDY HERE AIN'T TOO HAPPY ABOUT IT!

Y'SEE, YOU GUYS SOLD TH' PLACE OFF BEFORE YOU EVER VISITED. I HAPPENED BY TO CHECK IT OUT--

-- AND FOUND THIS GUY AND HIS PEOPLE ALREADY LIVING THERE. AN' THEY DIDN'T LIKE BEING SOMEONE ELSE'S *PROPERTY!*

CAN THIS BE TRUE?

I DON'T KNOW. ITALBOS *WAS* A BIG SALE, BUT WE DIDN'T EXPECT ANYONE TO REACH THERE WHILE THE WAR WAS ON.

THIS *DOES* HAPPEN SOMETIMES. BUT WE HAVE A DISPUTE RESOLUTION PROCESS IN PLACE --

WONDERFUL! YOUNG LADY, I SHOULD LIKE TO REPRESENT YOU!

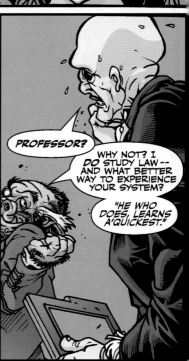

PROFESSOR?

WHY NOT? I *DO* STUDY LAW -- AND WHAT BETTER WAY TO EXPERIENCE YOUR SYSTEM?

"HE WHO DOES, LEARNS A' QUICKEST."

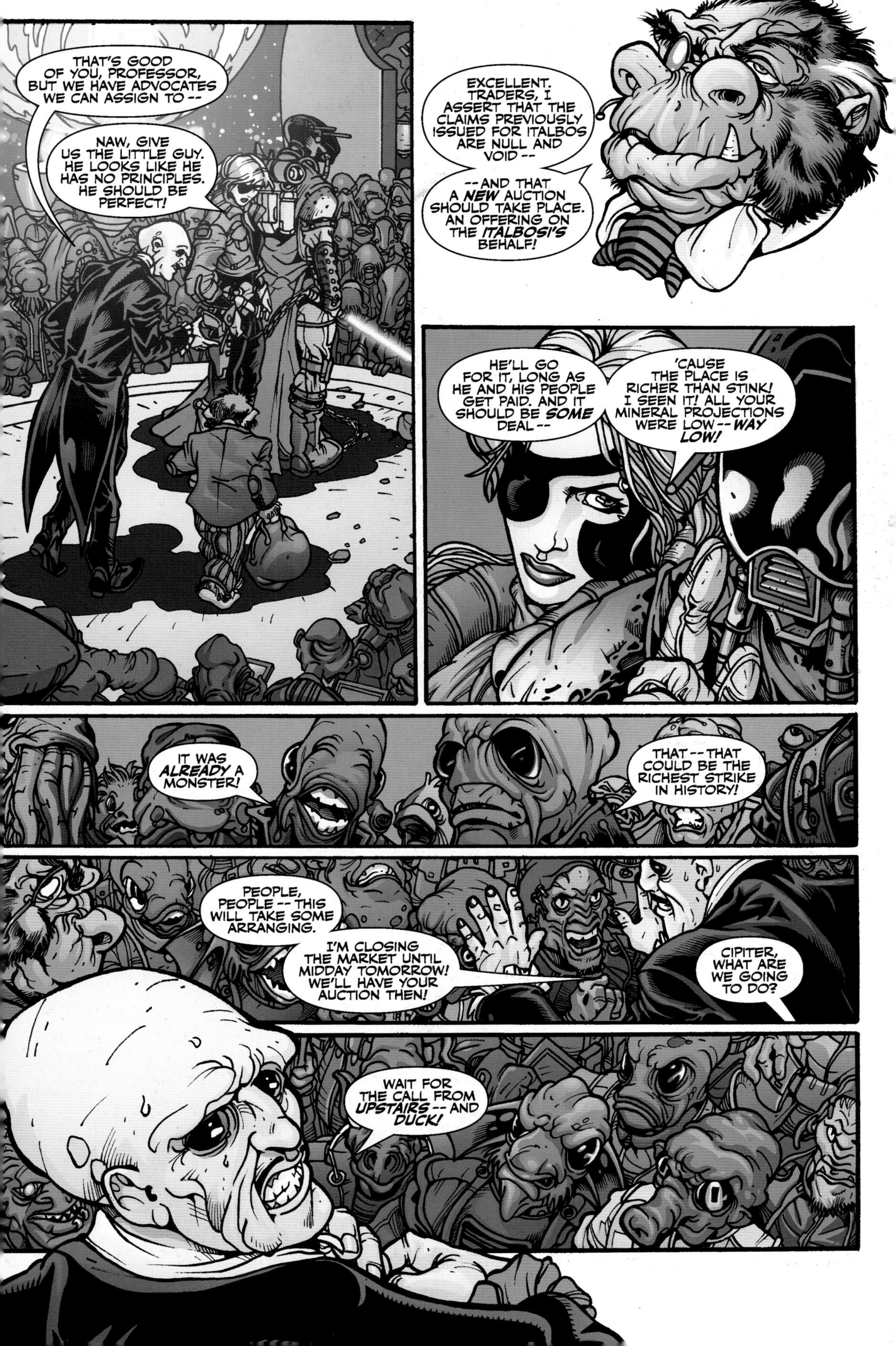
THAT'S GOOD OF YOU, PROFESSOR, BUT WE HAVE ADVOCATES WE CAN ASSIGN TO --
NAW, GIVE US THE LITTLE GUY. HE LOOKS LIKE HE HAS NO PRINCIPLES. HE SHOULD BE PERFECT!
EXCELLENT. TRADERS, I ASSERT THAT THE CLAIMS PREVIOUSLY ISSUED FOR ITALBOS ARE NULL AND VOID --
-- AND THAT A NEW AUCTION SHOULD TAKE PLACE. AN OFFERING ON THE ITALBOSI'S BEHALF!
HE'LL GO FOR IT, LONG AS HE AND HIS PEOPLE GET PAID. AND IT SHOULD BE SOME DEAL --
'CAUSE THE PLACE IS RICHER THAN STINK! I SEEN IT! ALL YOUR MINERAL PROJECTIONS WERE LOW -- WAY LOW!
IT WAS ALREADY A MONSTER!
THAT -- THAT COULD BE THE RICHEST STRIKE IN HISTORY!
PEOPLE, PEOPLE -- THIS WILL TAKE SOME ARRANGING.
I'M CLOSING THE MARKET UNTIL MIDDAY TOMORROW! WE'LL HAVE YOUR AUCTION THEN!
CIPITER, WHAT ARE WE GOING TO DO?
WAIT FOR THE CALL FROM UPSTAIRS -- AND DUCK!

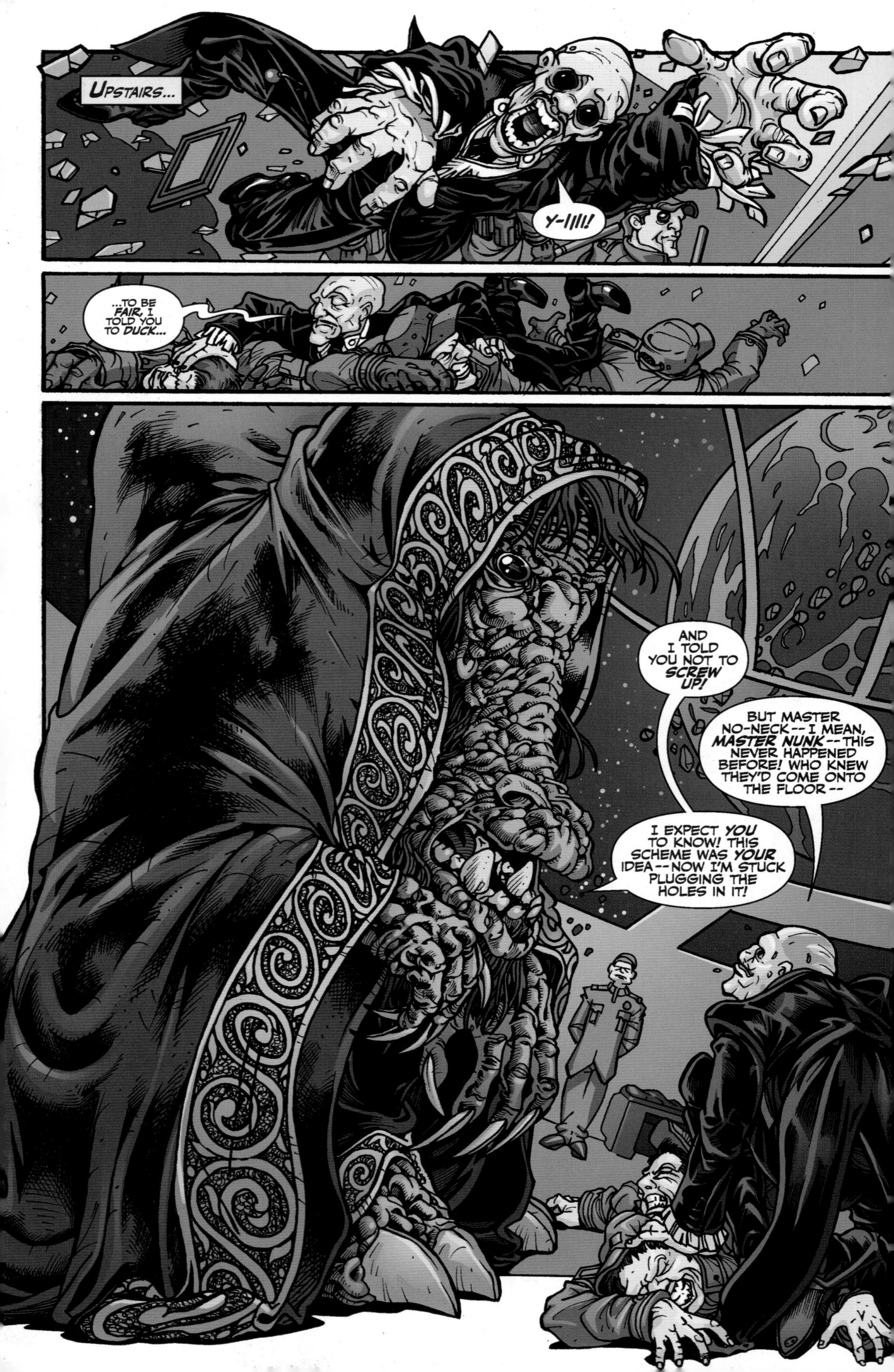
UPSTAIRS...
Y-IIII!
...TO BE FAIR, I TOLD YOU TO DUCK...
AND I TOLD YOU NOT TO SCREW UP!
BUT MASTER NO-NECK-- I MEAN, MASTER NUNK--THIS NEVER HAPPENED BEFORE! WHO KNEW THEY'D COME ONTO THE FLOOR--
I EXPECT YOU TO KNOW! THIS SCHEME WAS YOUR IDEA--NOW I'M STUCK PLUGGING THE HOLES IN IT!

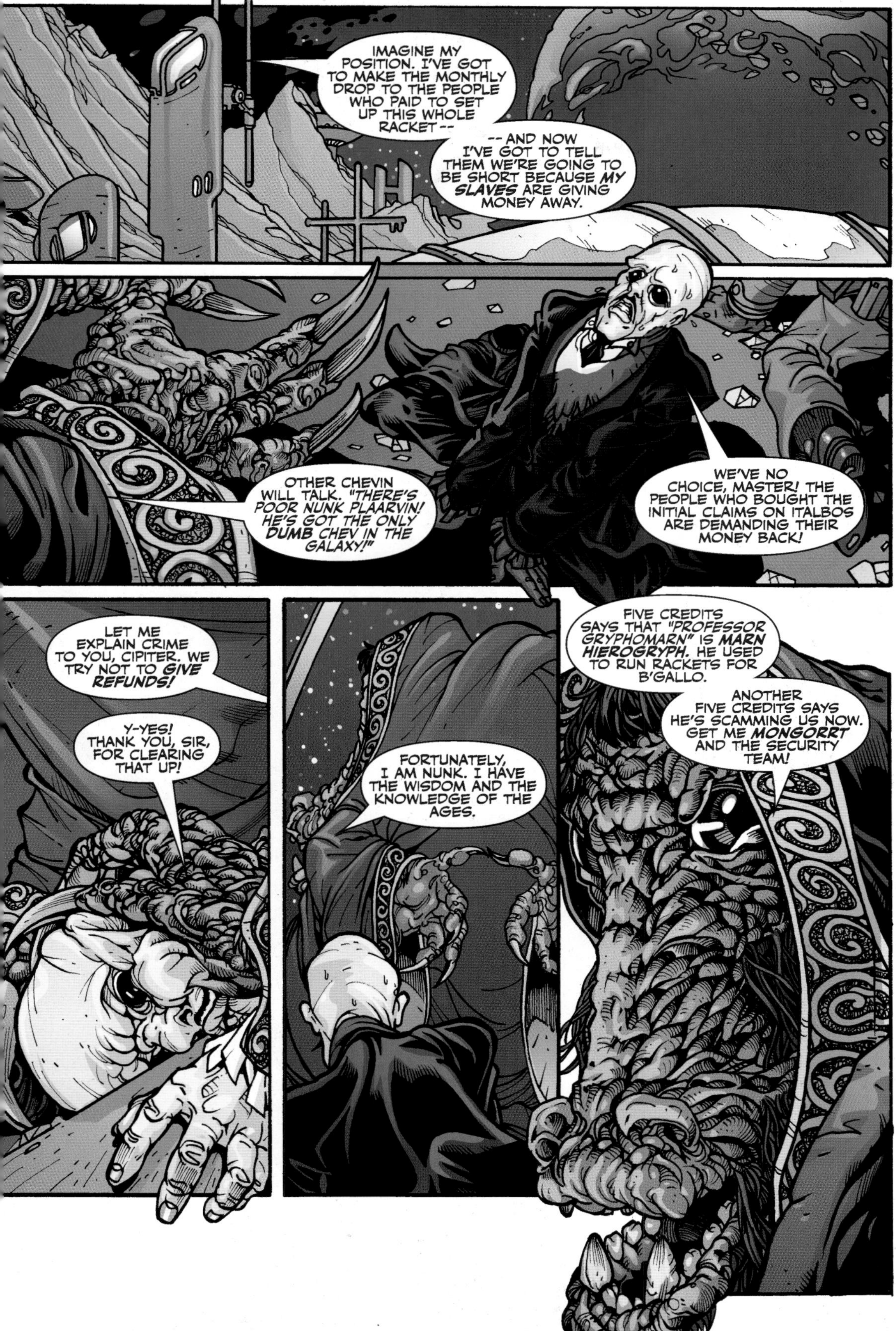
IMAGINE MY POSITION. I'VE GOT TO MAKE THE MONTHLY DROP TO THE PEOPLE WHO PAID TO SET UP THIS WHOLE RACKET--
--AND NOW I'VE GOT TO TELL THEM WE'RE GOING TO BE SHORT BECAUSE MY SLAVES ARE GIVING MONEY AWAY.
OTHER CHEVIN WILL TALK. "THERE'S POOR NUNK PLAARVIN! HE'S GOT THE ONLY DUMB CHEV IN THE GALAXY!"
WE'VE NO CHOICE, MASTER! THE PEOPLE WHO BOUGHT THE INITIAL CLAIMS ON ITALBOS ARE DEMANDING THEIR MONEY BACK!
LET ME EXPLAIN CRIME TO YOU, CIPITER. WE TRY NOT TO GIVE REFUNDS!
Y-YES! THANK YOU, SIR, FOR CLEARING THAT UP!
FORTUNATELY, I AM NUNK. I HAVE THE WISDOM AND THE KNOWLEDGE OF THE AGES.
FIVE CREDITS SAYS THAT "PROFESSOR GRYPHOMARN" IS MARN HIEROGRYPH. HE USED TO RUN RACKETS FOR B'GALLO.
ANOTHER FIVE CREDITS SAYS HE'S SCAMMING US NOW. GET ME MONGORRT AND THE SECURITY TEAM!

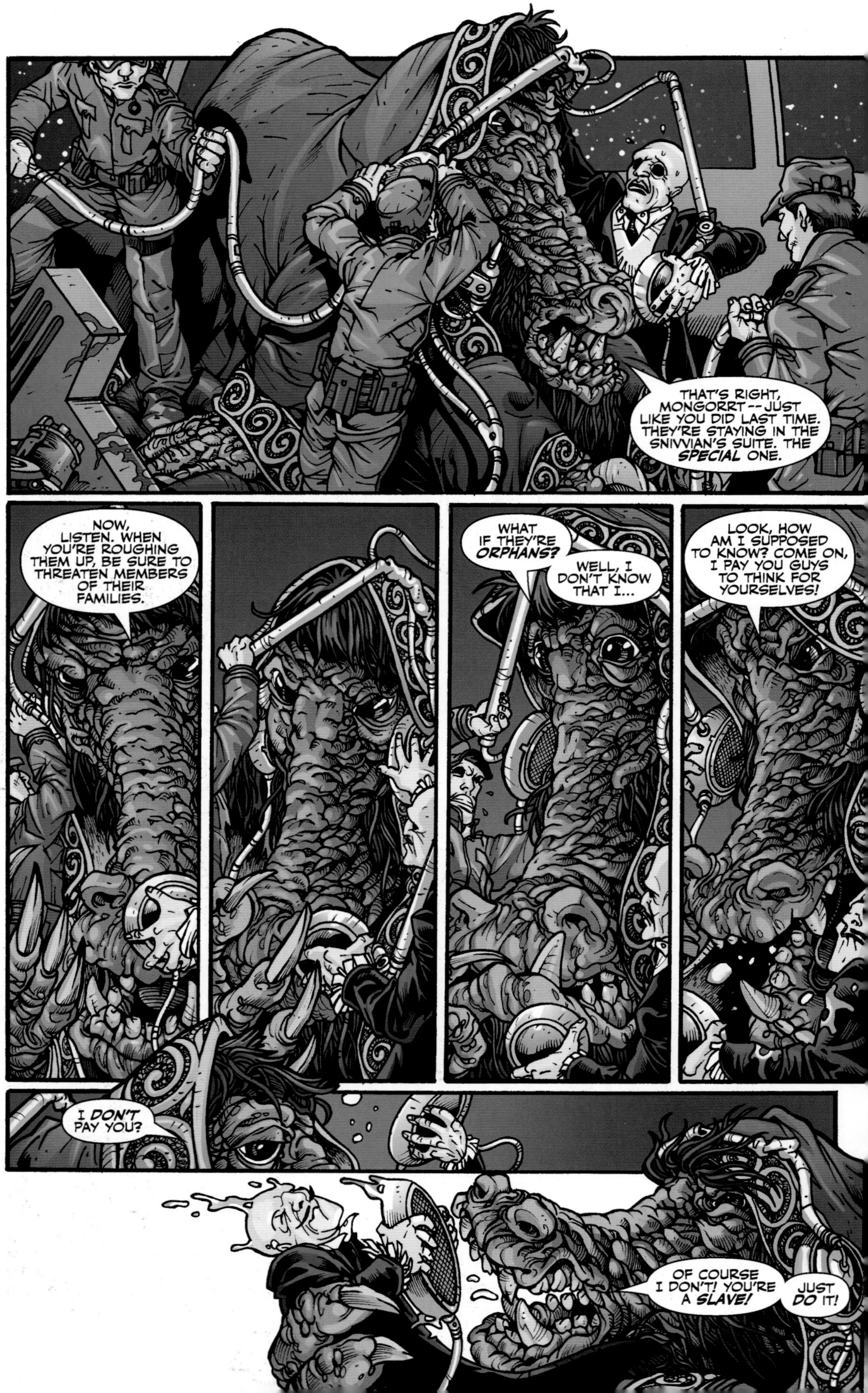
THAT'S RIGHT, MONGORRT--JUST LIKE YOU DID LAST TIME. THEY'RE STAYING IN THE SNIVVIAN'S SUITE. THE *SPECIAL* ONE.
NOW, LISTEN. WHEN YOU'RE ROUGHING THEM UP, BE SURE TO THREATEN MEMBERS OF THEIR FAMILIES.
WHAT IF THEY'RE *ORPHANS?*
WELL, I DON'T KNOW THAT I...
LOOK, HOW AM I SUPPOSED TO KNOW? COME ON, I PAY YOU GUYS TO THINK FOR YOURSELVES!
I *DON'T* PAY YOU?
OF COURSE I DON'T! YOU'RE A *SLAVE!*
JUST *DO* IT!

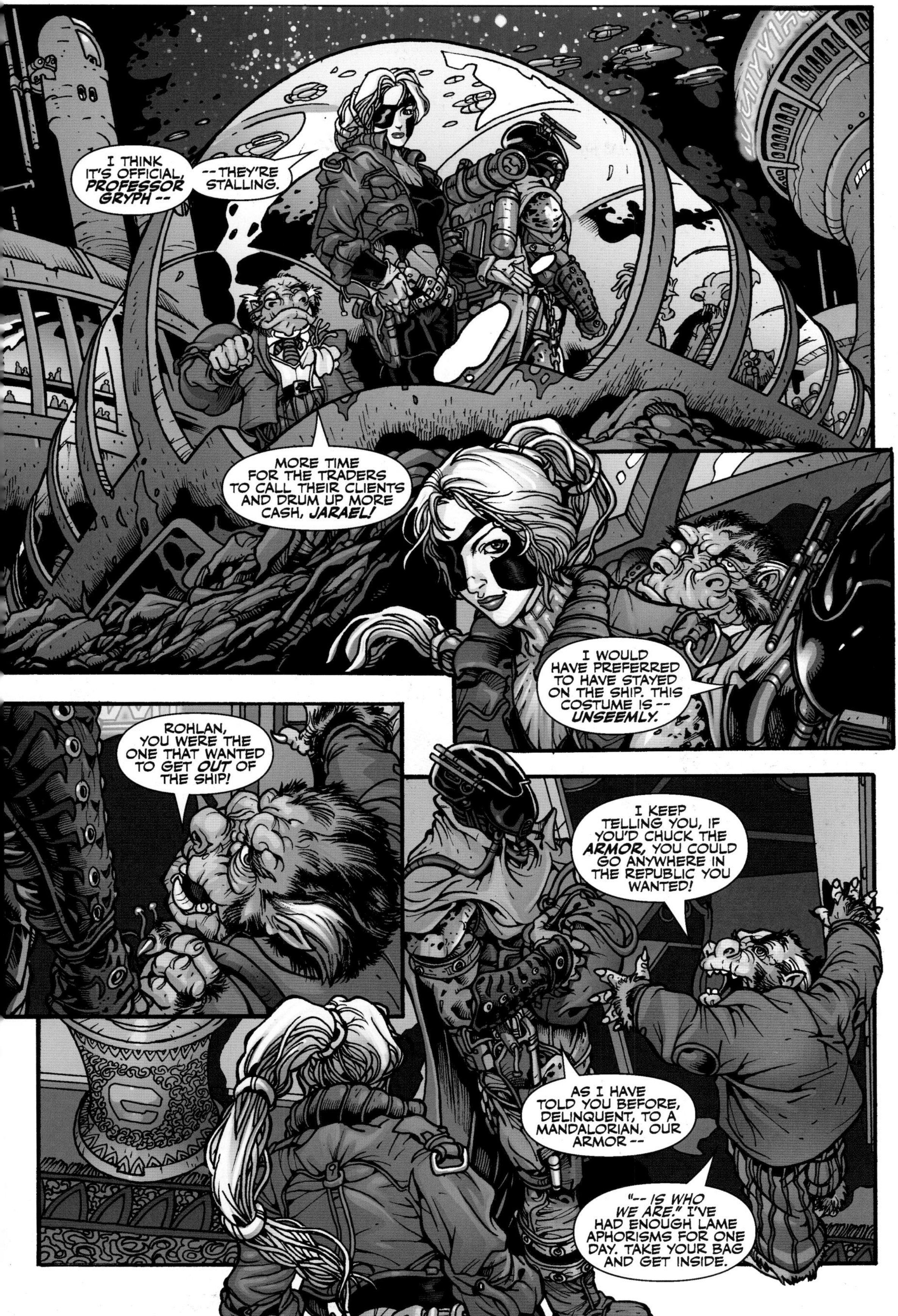
I THINK IT'S OFFICIAL, PROFESSOR GRYPH --
--THEY'RE STALLING.
MORE TIME FOR THE TRADERS TO CALL THEIR CLIENTS AND DRUM UP MORE CASH, JARAEL!
I WOULD HAVE PREFERRED TO HAVE STAYED ON THE SHIP. THIS COSTUME IS -- UNSEEMLY.
ROHLAN, YOU WERE THE ONE THAT WANTED TO GET OUT OF THE SHIP!
I KEEP TELLING YOU, IF YOU'D CHUCK THE ARMOR, YOU COULD GO ANYWHERE IN THE REPUBLIC YOU WANTED!
AS I HAVE TOLD YOU BEFORE, DELINQUENT, TO A MANDALORIAN, OUR ARMOR --
"-- IS WHO WE ARE." I'VE HAD ENOUGH LAME APHORISMS FOR ONE DAY. TAKE YOUR BAG AND GET INSIDE.

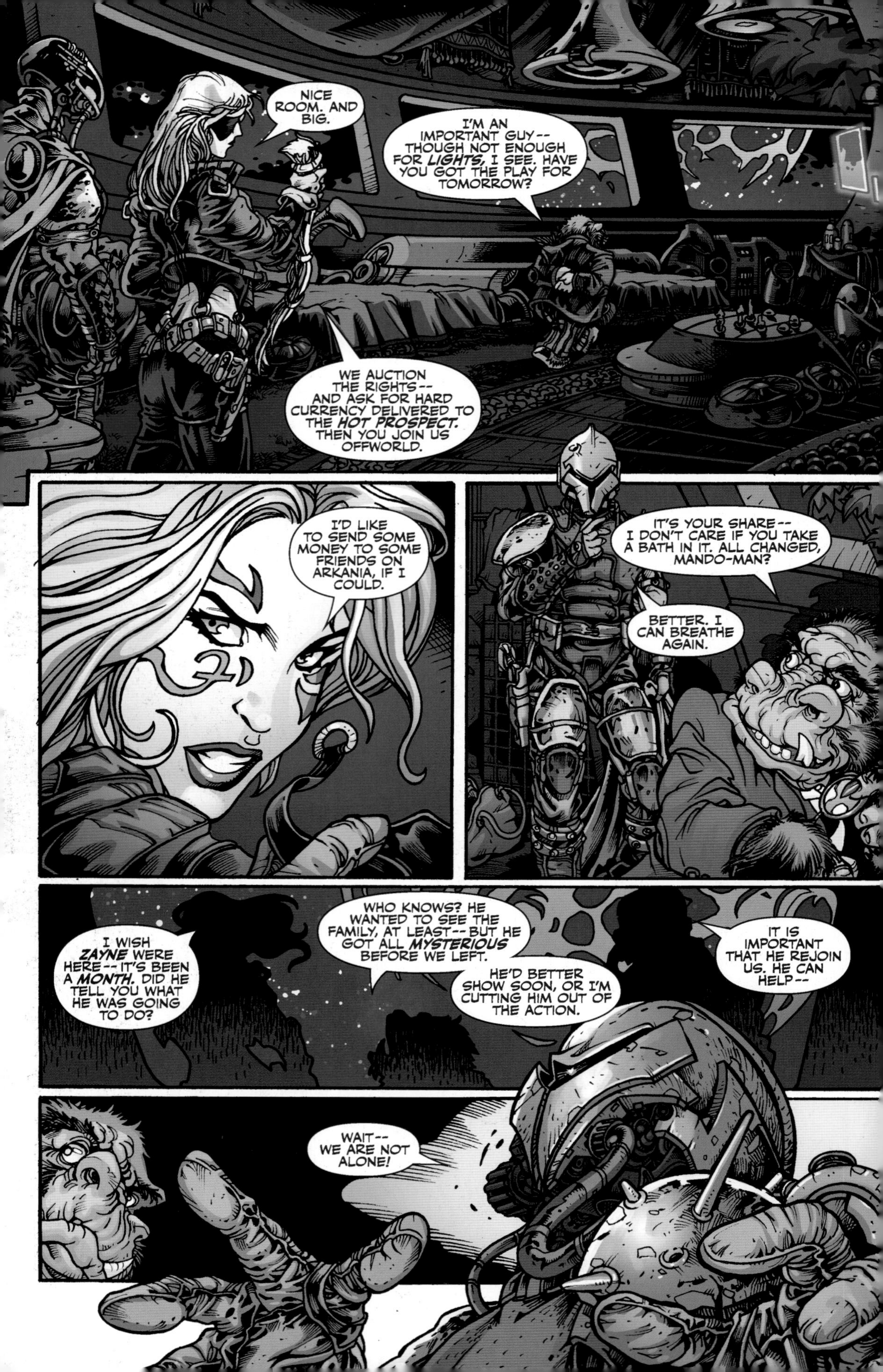
NICE ROOM. AND BIG.
I'M AN IMPORTANT GUY-- THOUGH NOT ENOUGH FOR LIGHTS, I SEE. HAVE YOU GOT THE PLAY FOR TOMORROW?
WE AUCTION THE RIGHTS-- AND ASK FOR HARD CURRENCY DELIVERED TO THE HOT PROSPECT. THEN YOU JOIN US OFFWORLD.
I'D LIKE TO SEND SOME MONEY TO SOME FRIENDS ON ARKANIA, IF I COULD.
IT'S YOUR SHARE-- I DON'T CARE IF YOU TAKE A BATH IN IT. ALL CHANGED, MANDO-MAN?
BETTER. I CAN BREATHE AGAIN.
I WISH ZAYNE WERE HERE-- IT'S BEEN A MONTH. DID HE TELL YOU WHAT HE WAS GOING TO DO?
WHO KNOWS? HE WANTED TO SEE THE FAMILY, AT LEAST-- BUT HE GOT ALL MYSTERIOUS BEFORE WE LEFT.
HE'D BETTER SHOW SOON, OR I'M CUTTING HIM OUT OF THE ACTION.
IT IS IMPORTANT THAT HE REJOIN US. HE CAN HELP--
WAIT-- WE ARE NOT ALONE!

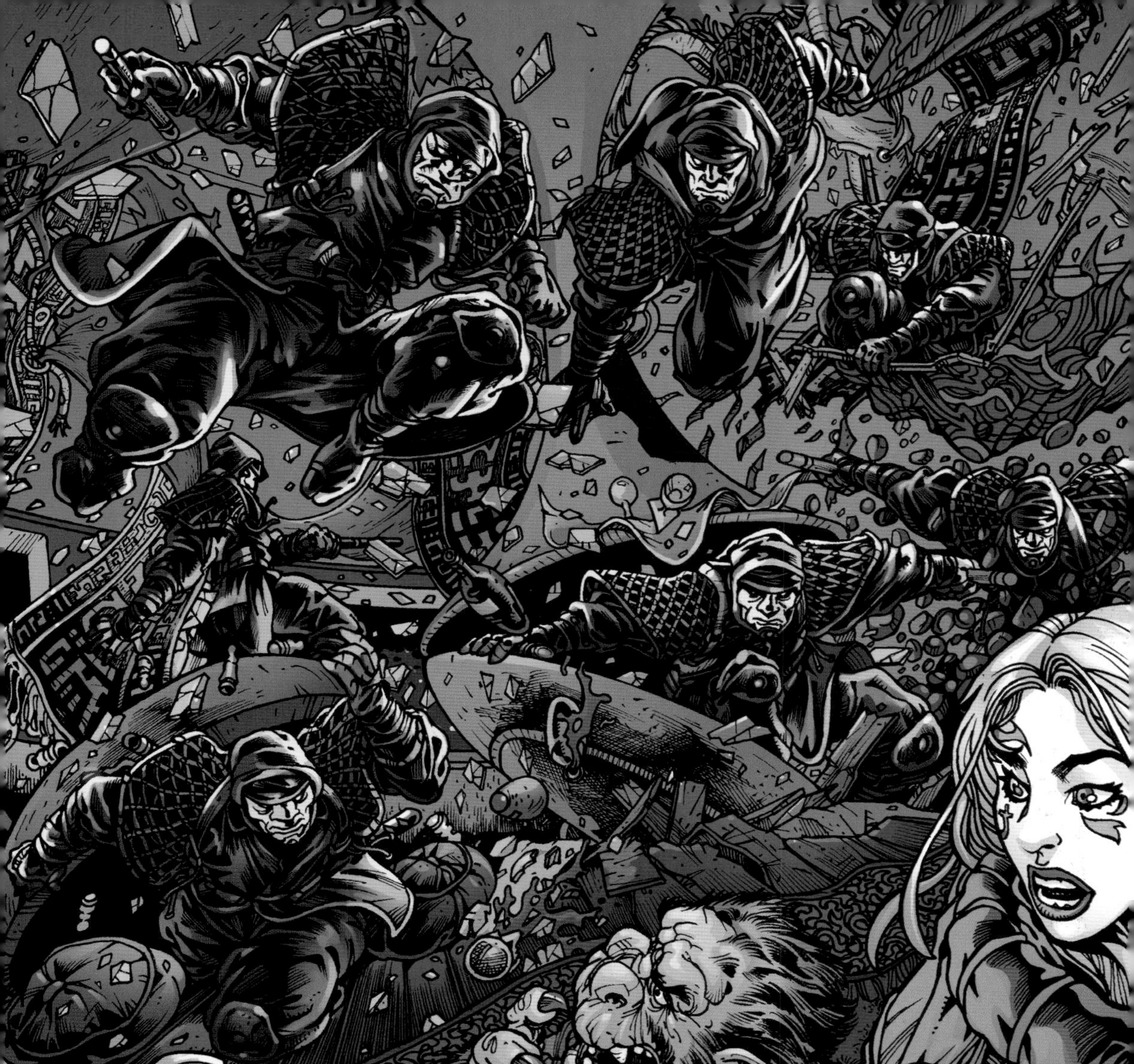

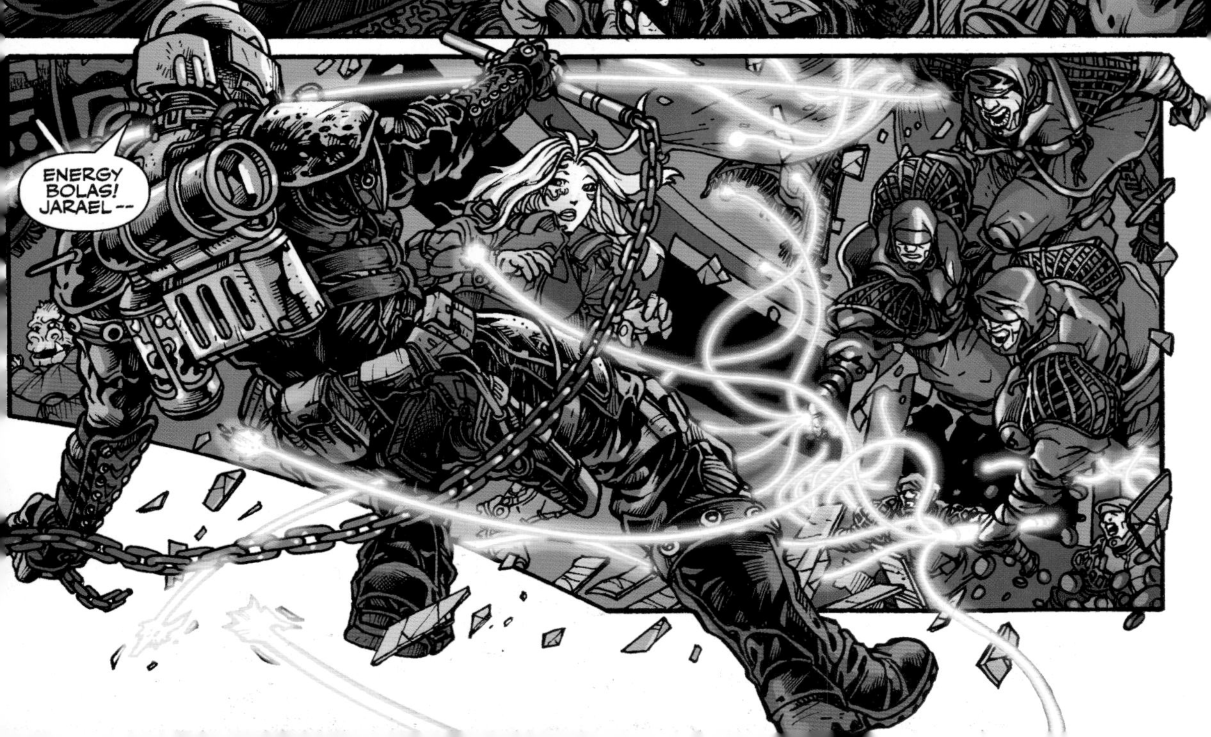
ENERGY BOLAS! JARAEL--

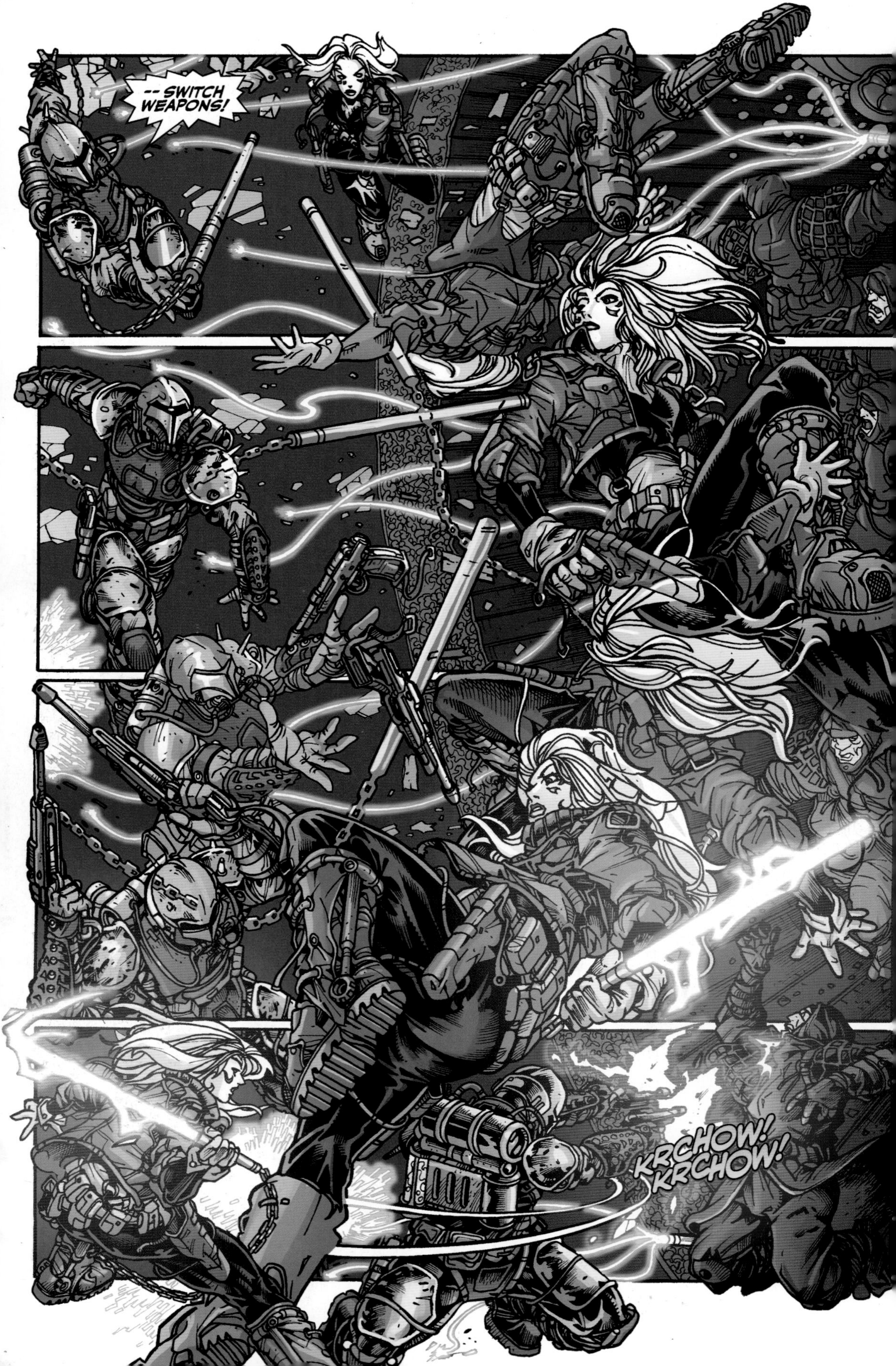
-- SWITCH WEAPONS!
KRCHOW! KRCHOW!

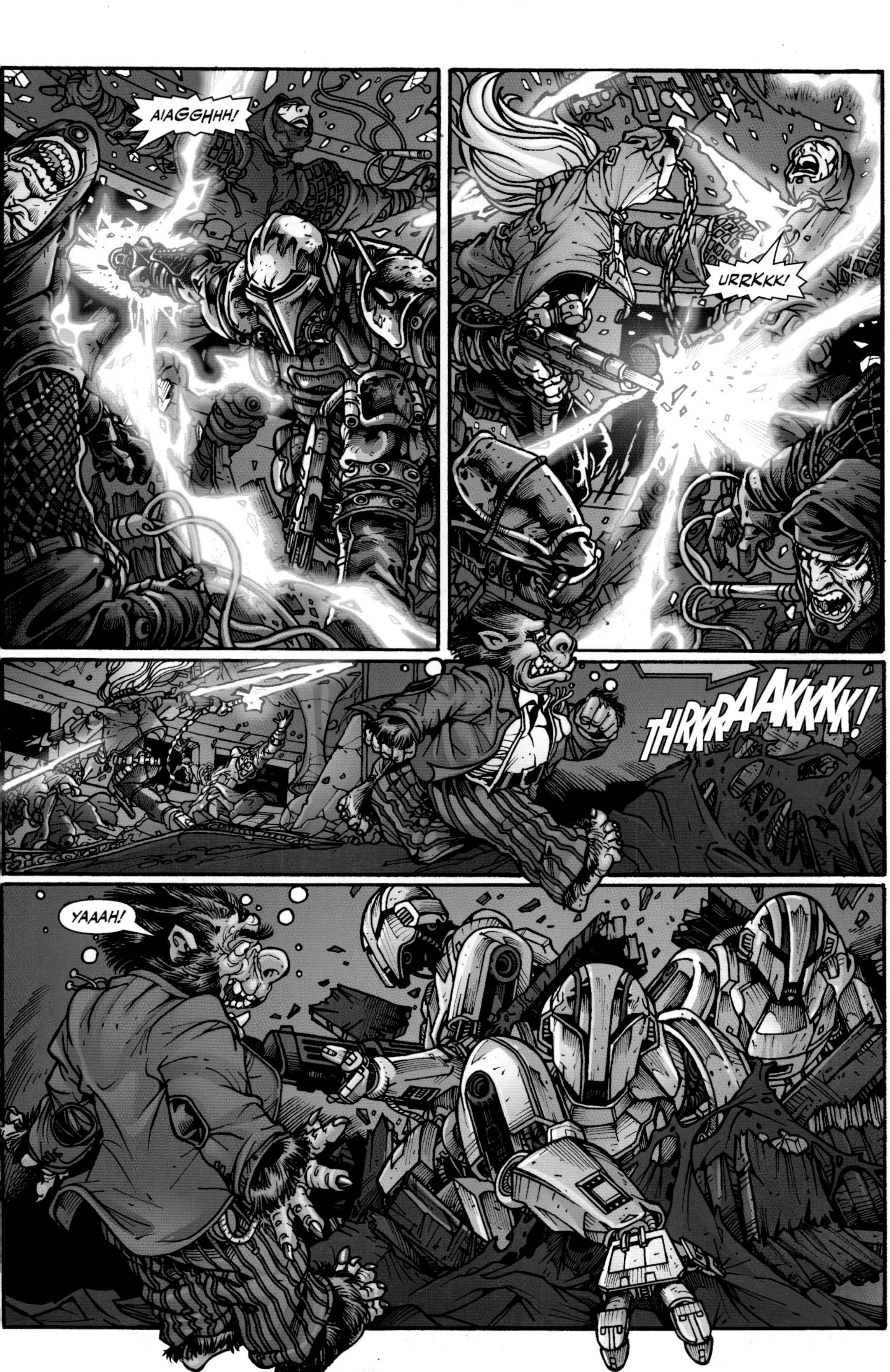
AIAGGHHH!
URRKKK!
THRKRAAKKKK!
YAAAH!

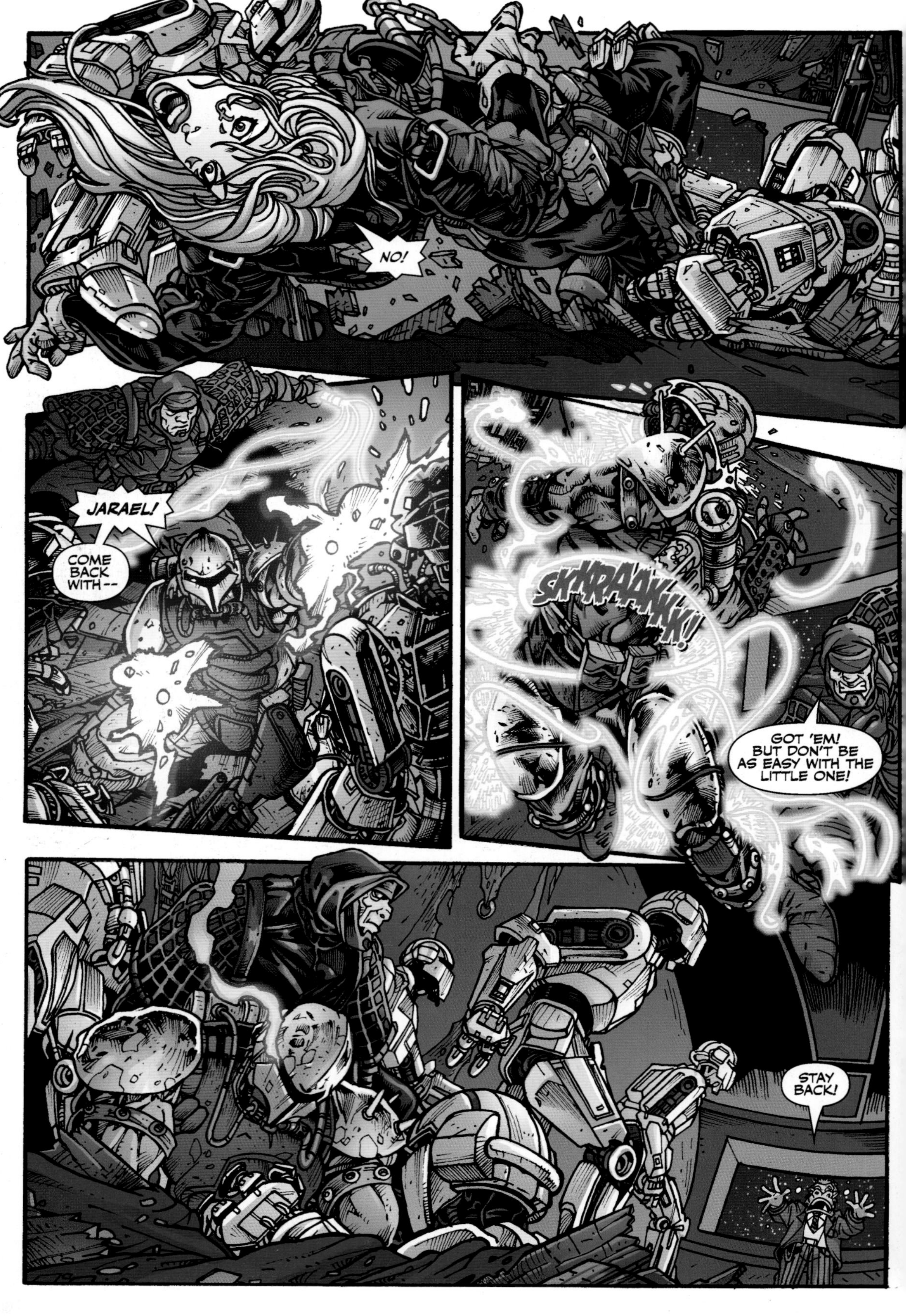
NO!
JARAEL!
COME BACK WITH--
SKKRAAAKK!
GOT 'EM! BUT DON'T BE AS EASY WITH THE LITTLE ONE!
STAY BACK!

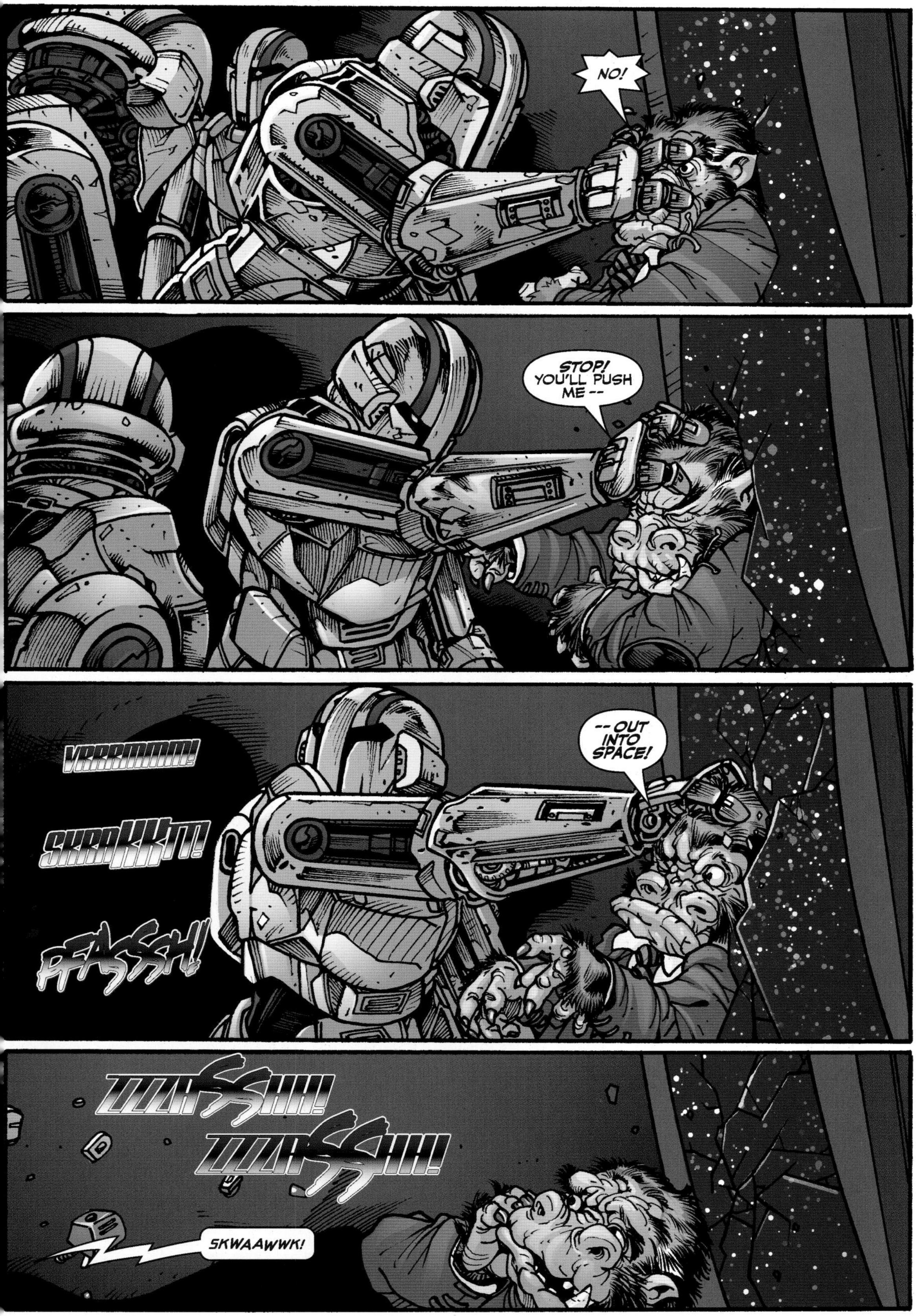
NO!
STOP! YOU'LL PUSH ME --
VRRRMMM!
SKRRKKTT!
PFASSSH!
-- OUT INTO SPACE!
ZZZASSHH!
ZZZASSHH!
SKWAAWWK!

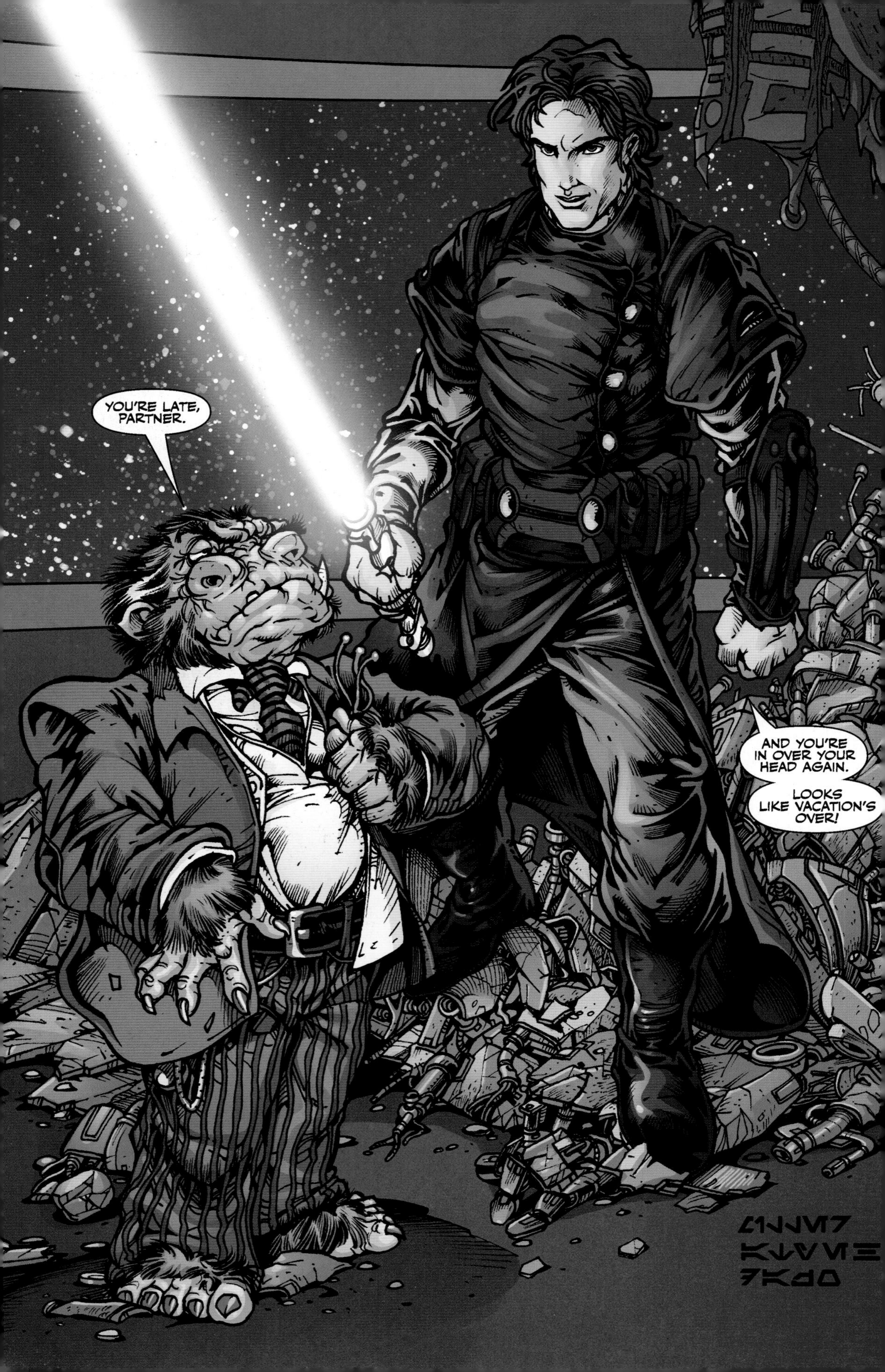
YOU'RE LATE, PARTNER.
AND YOU'RE IN OVER YOUR HEAD AGAIN.
LOOKS LIKE VACATION'S OVER!

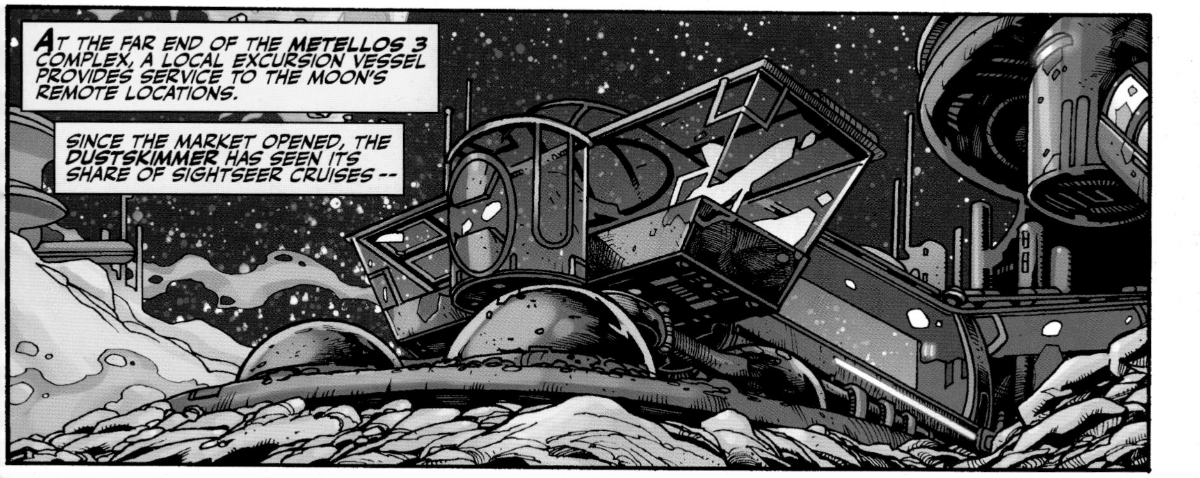
AT THE FAR END OF THE METELLOS 3 COMPLEX, A LOCAL EXCURSION VESSEL PROVIDES SERVICE TO THE MOON'S REMOTE LOCATIONS.
SINCE THE MARKET OPENED, THE DUSTSKIMMER HAS SEEN ITS SHARE OF SIGHTSEER CRUISES --

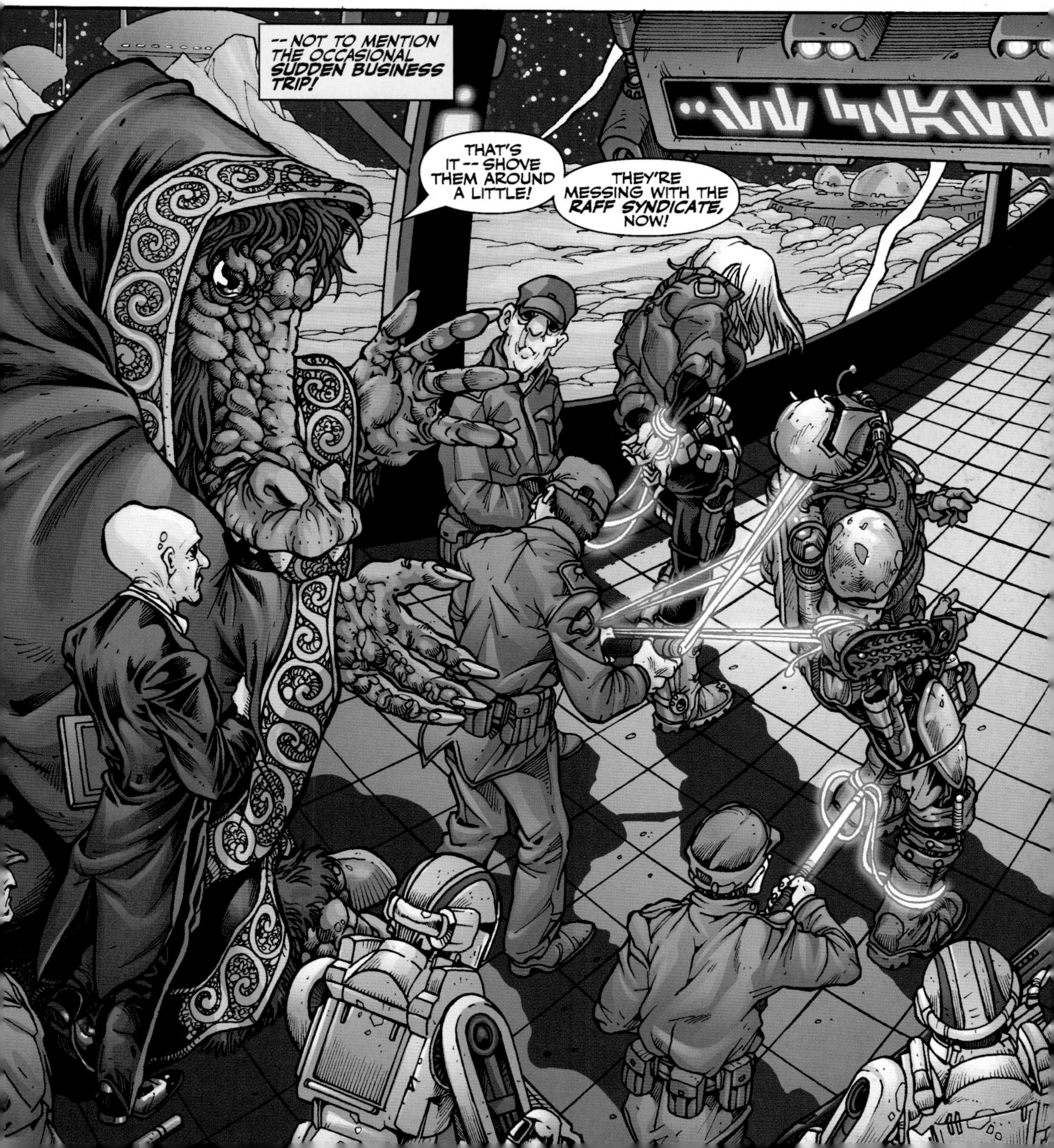
-- NOT TO MENTION THE OCCASIONAL SUDDEN BUSINESS TRIP!
THAT'S IT -- SHOVE THEM AROUND A LITTLE!
THEY'RE MESSING WITH THE RAFF SYNDICATE, NOW!

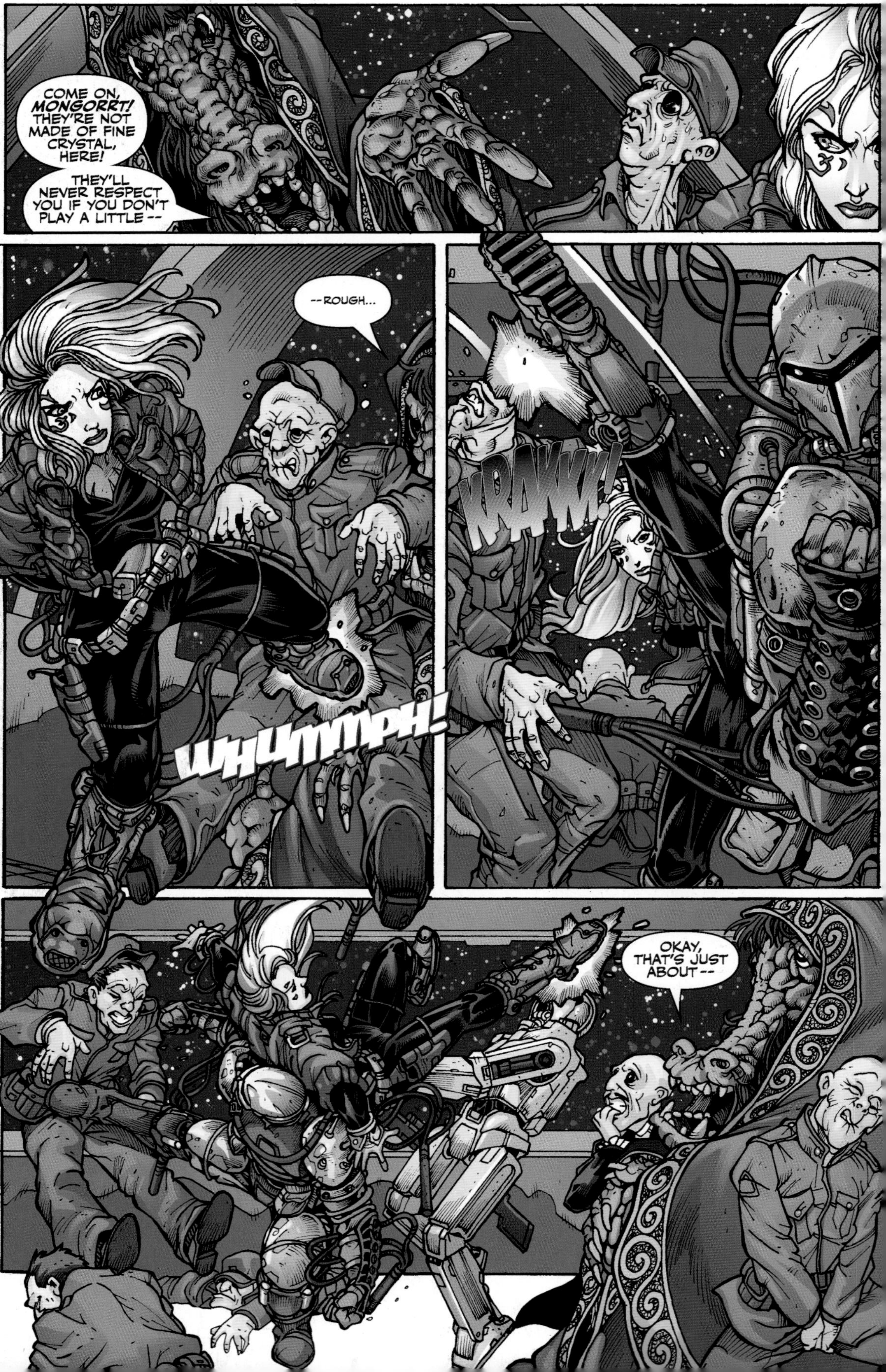
COME ON, MONGORRT! THEY'RE NOT MADE OF FINE CRYSTAL, HERE!
THEY'LL NEVER RESPECT YOU IF YOU DON'T PLAY A LITTLE --
--ROUGH...
WHUMMPH!
KRAKKK!
OKAY, THAT'S JUST ABOUT --

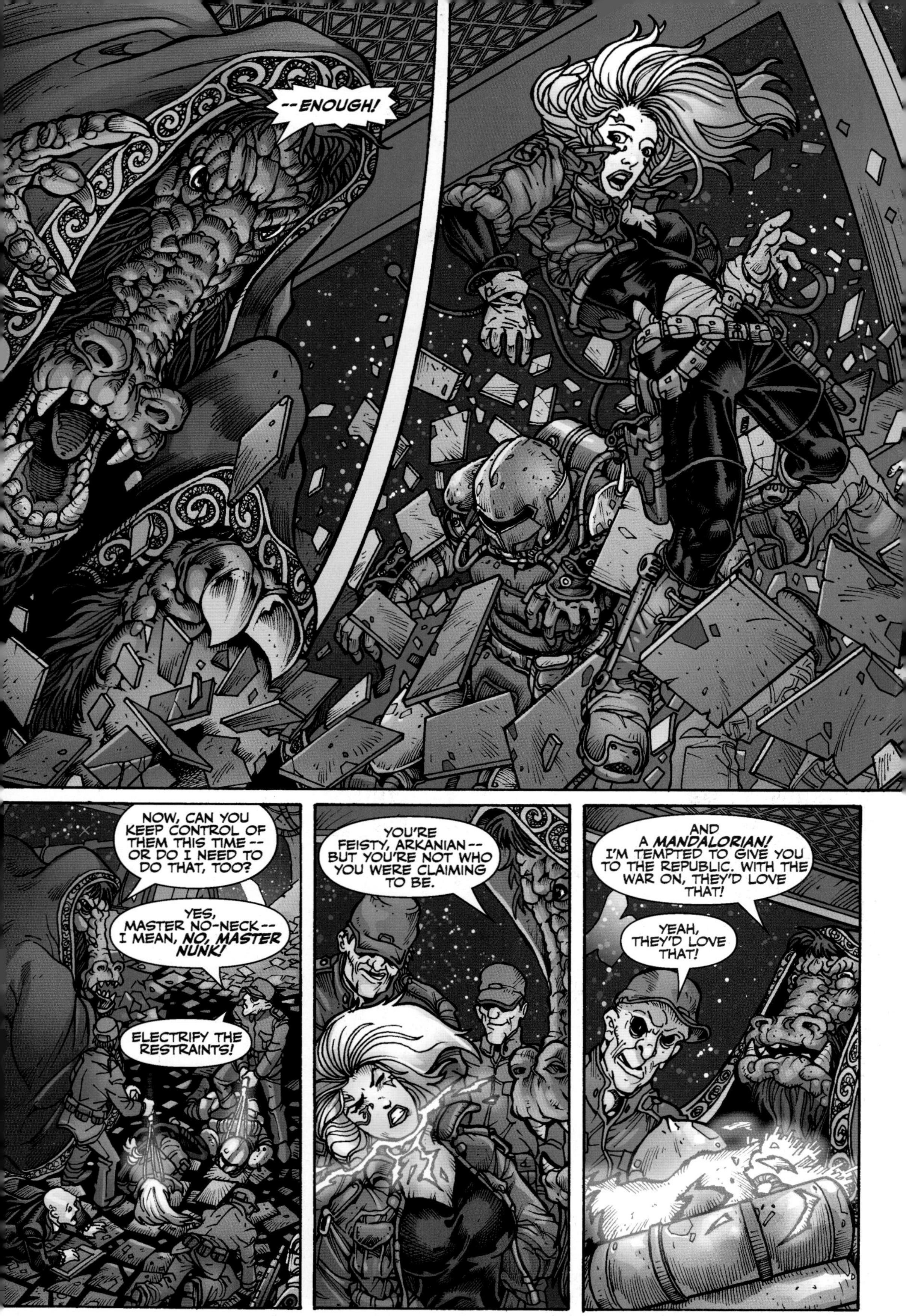
--ENOUGH!
NOW, CAN YOU KEEP CONTROL OF THEM THIS TIME -- OR DO I NEED TO DO THAT, TOO?
YES, MASTER NO-NECK-- I MEAN, NO, MASTER NUNK!
ELECTRIFY THE RESTRAINTS!
YOU'RE FEISTY, ARKANIAN-- BUT YOU'RE NOT WHO YOU WERE CLAIMING TO BE.
AND A MANDALORIAN! I'M TEMPTED TO GIVE YOU TO THE REPUBLIC. WITH THE WAR ON, THEY'D LOVE THAT!
YEAH, THEY'D LOVE THAT!

WHAT ARE YOU TALKING ABOUT? WE *CAN'T* GIVE THEM TO THE REPUBLIC. ARE YOU TRYING TO RUIN EVERYTHING?

I'M TELLING YOU, *CIPITER*, YOUR PEOPLE ARE THE WORST CHEV ANY CHEVIN EVER HAD TO TRY TO RUN.

IF WE CAN'T MAKE OUR MONTHLY KICK TO THE *RAFFS*, THEY'LL SACK ME AND THEN YOU'LL *ALL* BE IN THE STEW!

BUT THAT'S NOT GOING TO HAPPEN. I DON'T KNOW WHERE MARN HIEROGRYPH SLITHERED OFF TO --

-- BUT YOUR LITTLE *AUCTION* LATER TODAY IS DEFINITELY NOT GOING OFF AS PLANNED!

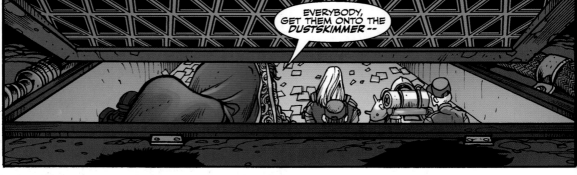

EVERYBODY, GET THEM ONTO THE *DUSTSKIMMER* --

32

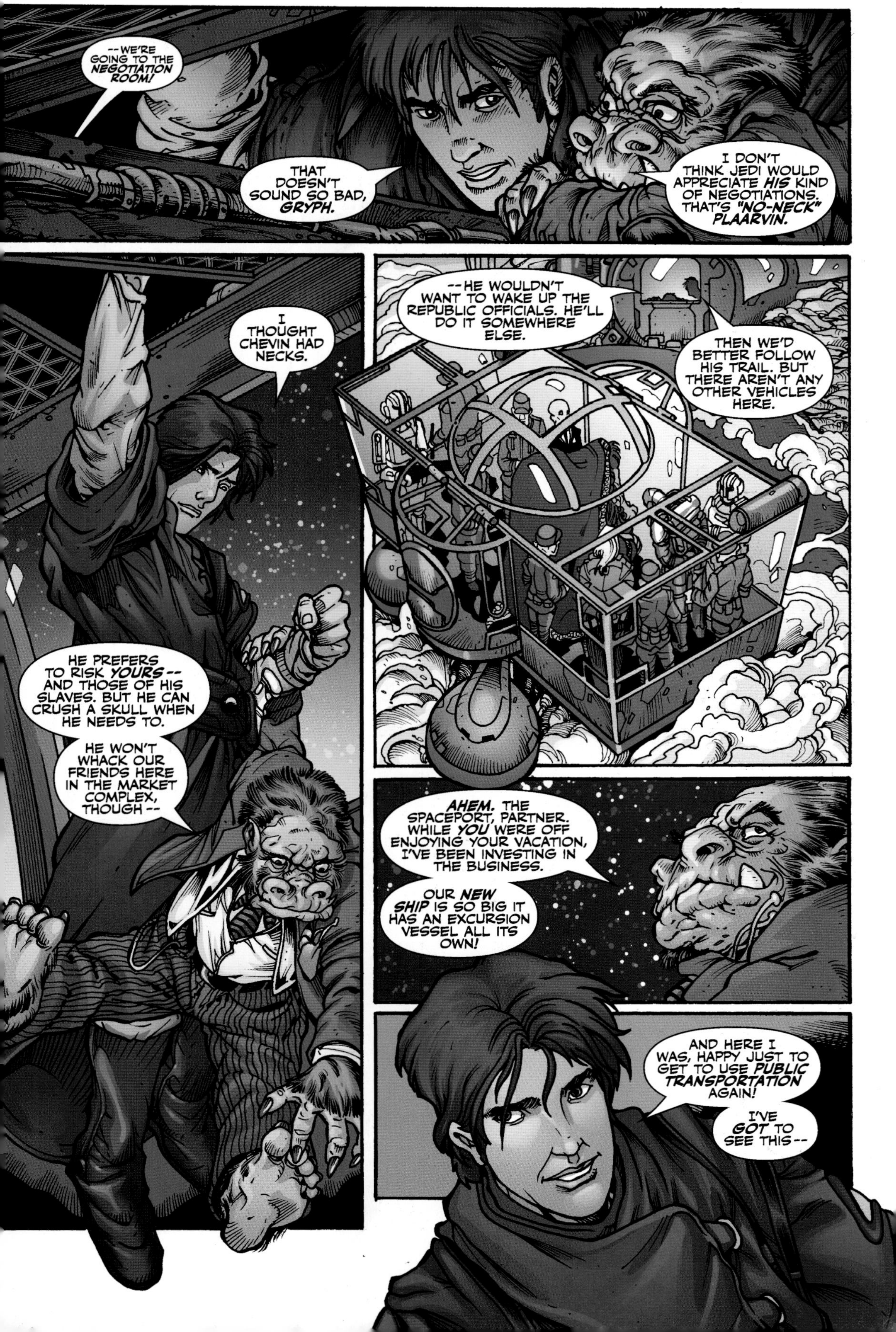
--WE'RE GOING TO THE NEGOTIATION ROOM!
THAT DOESN'T SOUND SO BAD, GRYPH.
I DON'T THINK JEDI WOULD APPRECIATE HIS KIND OF NEGOTIATIONS. THAT'S "NO-NECK" PLAARVIN.
I THOUGHT CHEVIN HAD NECKS.
HE PREFERS TO RISK YOURS-- AND THOSE OF HIS SLAVES. BUT HE CAN CRUSH A SKULL WHEN HE NEEDS TO.
HE WON'T WHACK OUR FRIENDS HERE IN THE MARKET COMPLEX, THOUGH--
--HE WOULDN'T WANT TO WAKE UP THE REPUBLIC OFFICIALS. HE'LL DO IT SOMEWHERE ELSE.
THEN WE'D BETTER FOLLOW HIS TRAIL. BUT THERE AREN'T ANY OTHER VEHICLES HERE.
AHEM. THE SPACEPORT, PARTNER. WHILE YOU WERE OFF ENJOYING YOUR VACATION, I'VE BEEN INVESTING IN THE BUSINESS.
OUR NEW SHIP IS SO BIG IT HAS AN EXCURSION VESSEL ALL ITS OWN!
AND HERE I WAS, HAPPY JUST TO GET TO USE PUBLIC TRANSPORTATION AGAIN!
I'VE GOT TO SEE THIS--

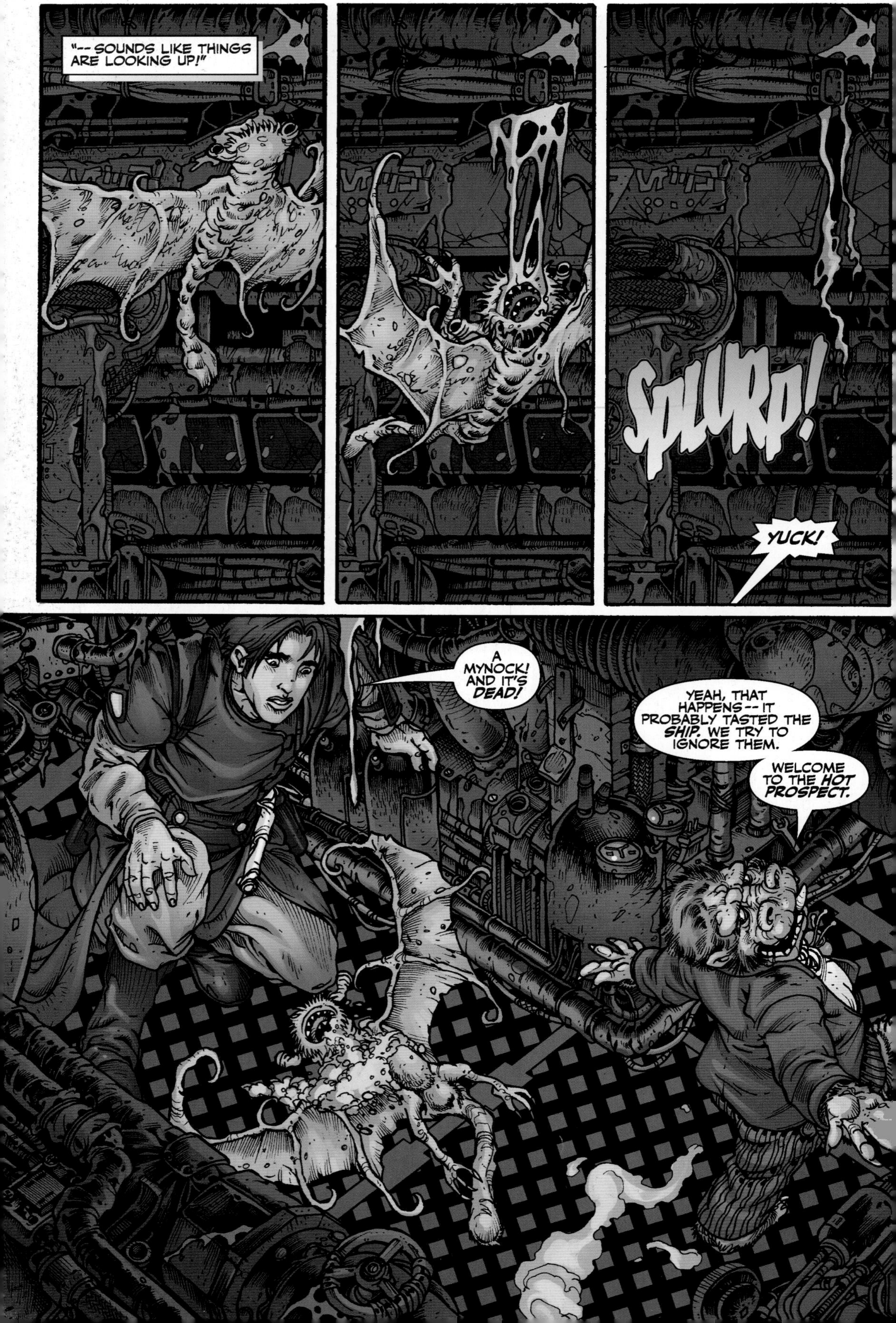
"-- SOUNDS LIKE THINGS ARE LOOKING UP!"
SPLURP!
YUCK!
A MYNOCK! AND IT'S DEAD!
YEAH, THAT HAPPENS -- IT PROBABLY TASTED THE SHIP. WE TRY TO IGNORE THEM.
WELCOME TO THE HOT PROSPECT.

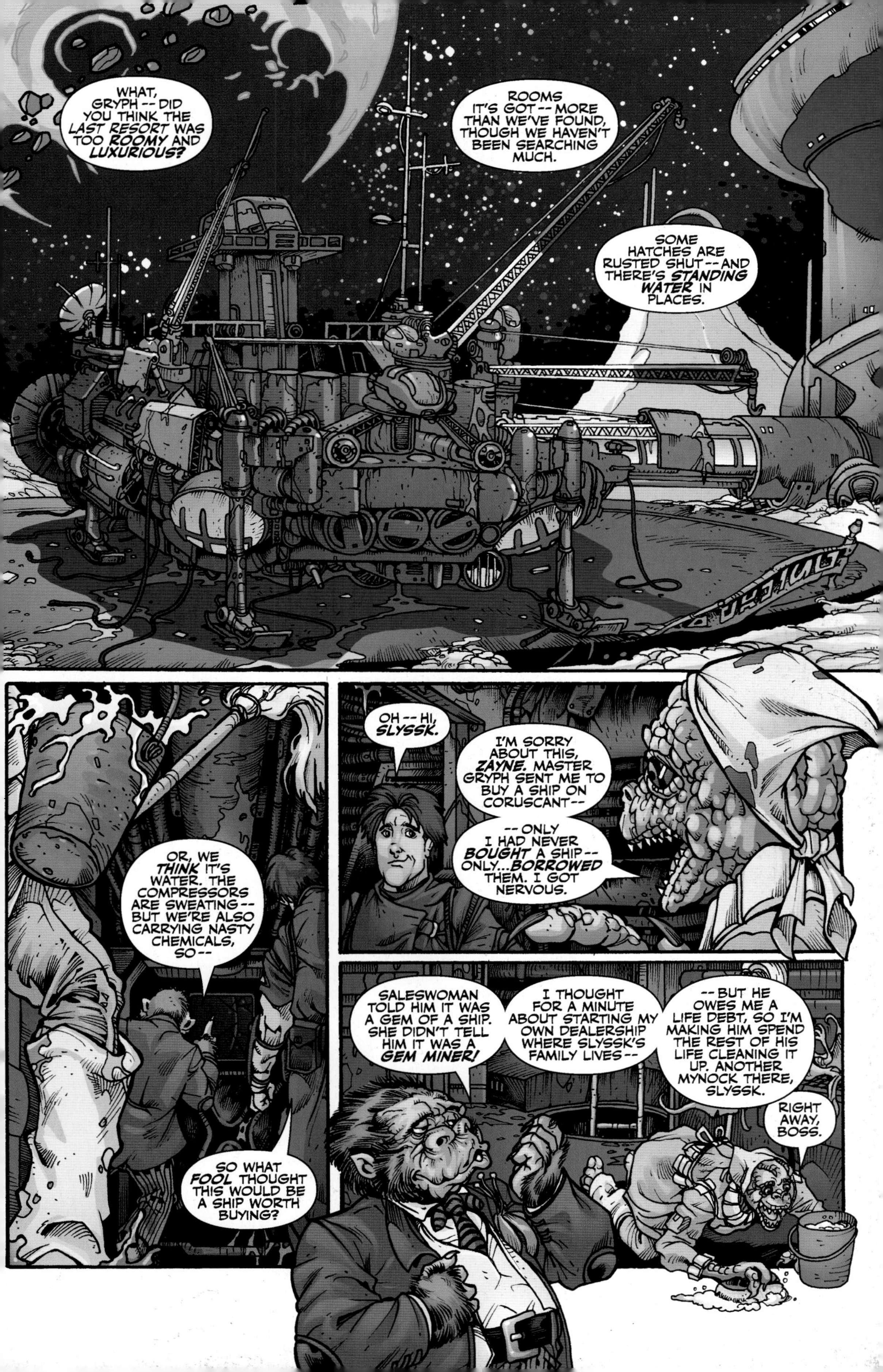
WHAT, GRYPH -- DID YOU THINK THE LAST RESORT WAS TOO ROOMY AND LUXURIOUS?
ROOMS IT'S GOT -- MORE THAN WE'VE FOUND, THOUGH WE HAVEN'T BEEN SEARCHING MUCH.
SOME HATCHES ARE RUSTED SHUT -- AND THERE'S STANDING WATER IN PLACES.
OR, WE THINK IT'S WATER. THE COMPRESSORS ARE SWEATING -- BUT WE'RE ALSO CARRYING NASTY CHEMICALS, SO --
SO WHAT FOOL THOUGHT THIS WOULD BE A SHIP WORTH BUYING?
OH -- HI, SLYSSK.
I'M SORRY ABOUT THIS, ZAYNE. MASTER GRYPH SENT ME TO BUY A SHIP ON CORUSCANT --
-- ONLY I HAD NEVER BOUGHT A SHIP -- ONLY... BORROWED THEM. I GOT NERVOUS.
SALESWOMAN TOLD HIM IT WAS A GEM OF A SHIP. SHE DIDN'T TELL HIM IT WAS A GEM MINER!
I THOUGHT FOR A MINUTE ABOUT STARTING MY OWN DEALERSHIP WHERE SLYSSK'S FAMILY LIVES --
-- BUT HE OWES ME A LIFE DEBT, SO I'M MAKING HIM SPEND THE REST OF HIS LIFE CLEANING IT UP. ANOTHER MYNOCK THERE, SLYSSK.
RIGHT AWAY, BOSS.

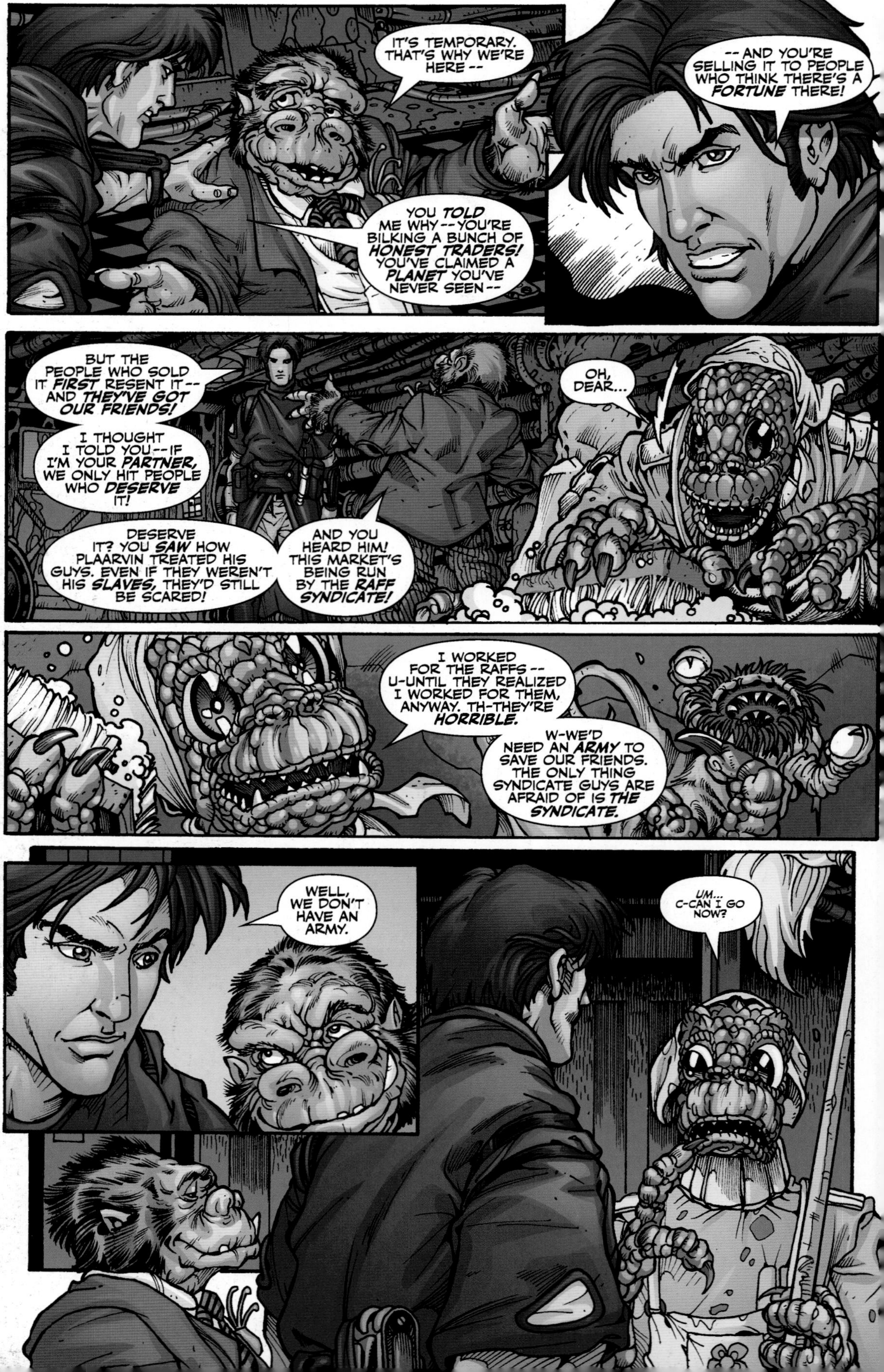

IT'S TEMPORARY. THAT'S WHY WE'RE HERE --
YOU TOLD ME WHY -- YOU'RE BILKING A BUNCH OF HONEST TRADERS! YOU'VE CLAIMED A PLANET YOU'VE NEVER SEEN --
-- AND YOU'RE SELLING IT TO PEOPLE WHO THINK THERE'S A FORTUNE THERE!
BUT THE PEOPLE WHO SOLD IT FIRST RESENT IT -- AND THEY'VE GOT OUR FRIENDS!
I THOUGHT I TOLD YOU -- IF I'M YOUR PARTNER, WE ONLY HIT PEOPLE WHO DESERVE IT!
DESERVE IT? YOU SAW HOW PLAARVIN TREATED HIS GUYS. EVEN IF THEY WEREN'T HIS SLAVES, THEY'D STILL BE SCARED!
AND YOU HEARD HIM! THIS MARKET'S BEING RUN BY THE RAFF SYNDICATE!
OH, DEAR...
I WORKED FOR THE RAFFS -- U-UNTIL THEY REALIZED I WORKED FOR THEM, ANYWAY. TH-THEY'RE HORRIBLE.
W-WE'D NEED AN ARMY TO SAVE OUR FRIENDS. THE ONLY THING SYNDICATE GUYS ARE AFRAID OF IS THE SYNDICATE.
WELL, WE DON'T HAVE AN ARMY.
UM... C-CAN I GO NOW?

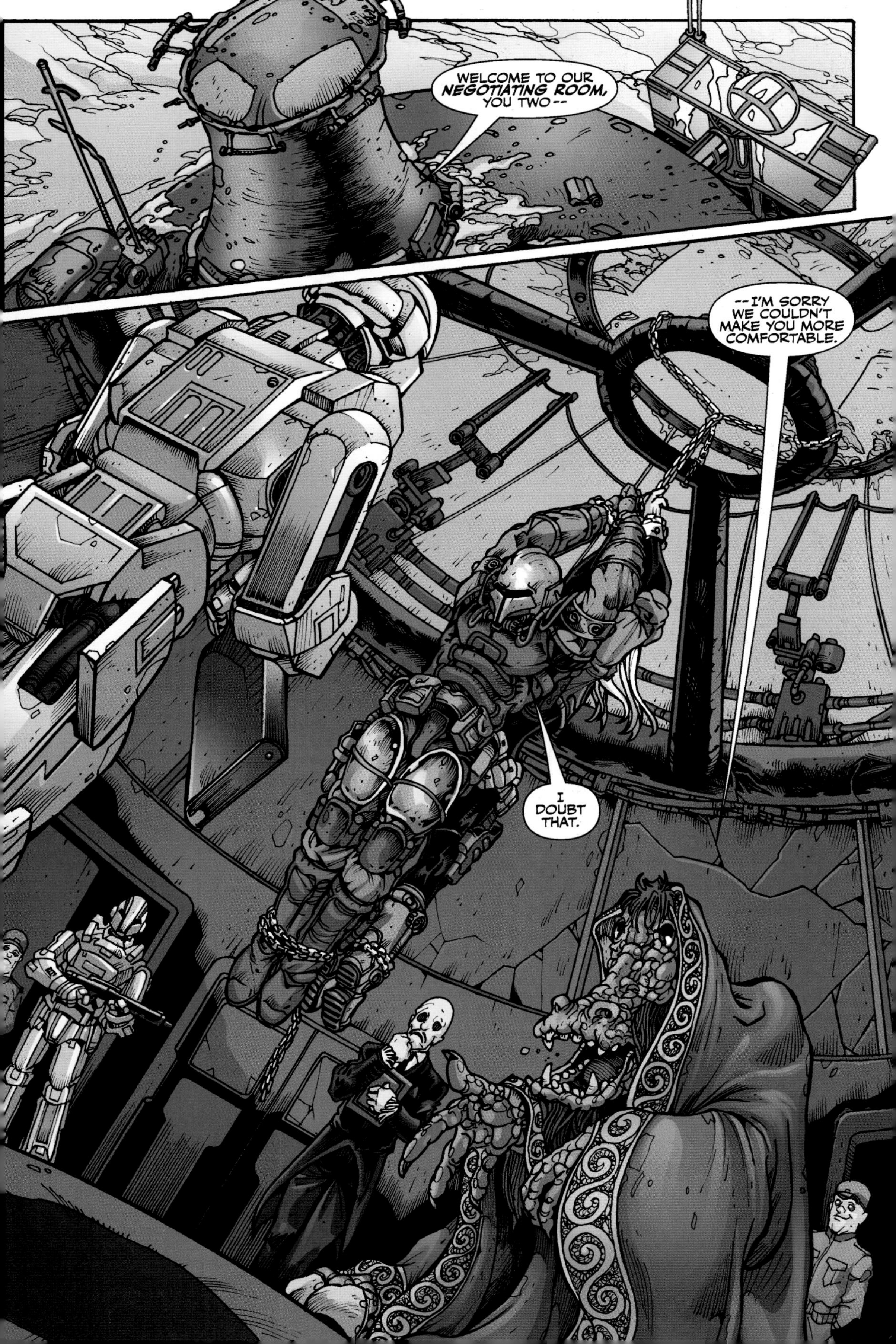
WELCOME TO OUR NEGOTIATING ROOM, YOU TWO--
--I'M SORRY WE COULDN'T MAKE YOU MORE COMFORTABLE.
I DOUBT THAT.

HEH! NO, THIS WAS ONCE A SOLAR OBSERVATORY -- 'TIL THE FUNDING WENT SOMEWHERE CALLED *FLASHPOINT*. HEARD OF IT?

IN PASSING.

WELL, IT WAS GOOD TIMING. SEE, MY PEOPLE GET A PIECE OF EVERY TRANSACTION IN THE MARKET, NICE AND LEGAL --

-- ONLY GUYS KEEP SHOWING UP WITH COUNTERCLAIMS. SO WE PRETEND TO PAY THEM TO GO AWAY --

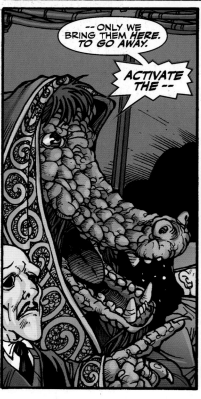

-- ONLY WE BRING THEM *HERE*. TO GO AWAY.

ACTIVATE THE --

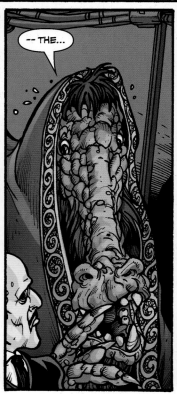

-- THE...

WELL, YOU KNOW. THE *THING*.

JUST DO IT, ALL RIGHT?

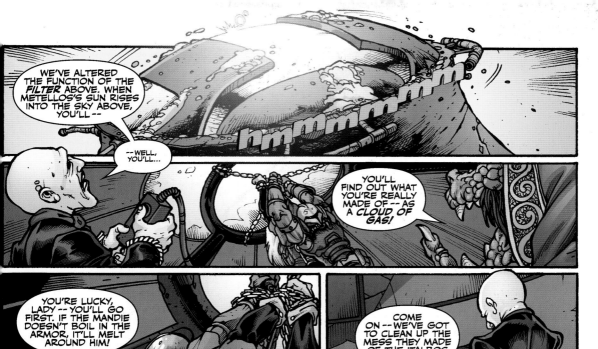

WE'VE ALTERED THE FUNCTION OF THE *FILTER* ABOVE. WHEN METELLOS'S SUN RISES INTO THE SKY ABOVE, YOU'LL--

--WELL, YOU'LL...

YOU'LL FIND OUT WHAT YOU'RE REALLY MADE OF -- AS A *CLOUD OF GAS!*

YOU'RE LUCKY, LADY -- YOU'LL GO FIRST. IF THE MANDIE DOESN'T BOIL IN THE ARMOR, IT'LL MELT AROUND HIM!

THE RAFFS DON'T LIKE PEOPLE HORNING IN ON THEIR SCORES -- AND THEY DON'T LIKE US LEAVING EVIDENCE.

COME ON -- WE'VE GOT TO CLEAN UP THE MESS THEY MADE OF THE *ITALBOS* DEAL!

I -- I AM SORRY, MADAM. I SUGGESTED THIS MARKET AS A SHORT-TERM RACKET -- BUT IT BECAME A PHENOMENON.

WE HAVE TO MAKE IT LAST. WE ARE *CHEV,* YOU SEE -- HE IS A *CHEVIN.* WE MUST DO AS HE SAYS--

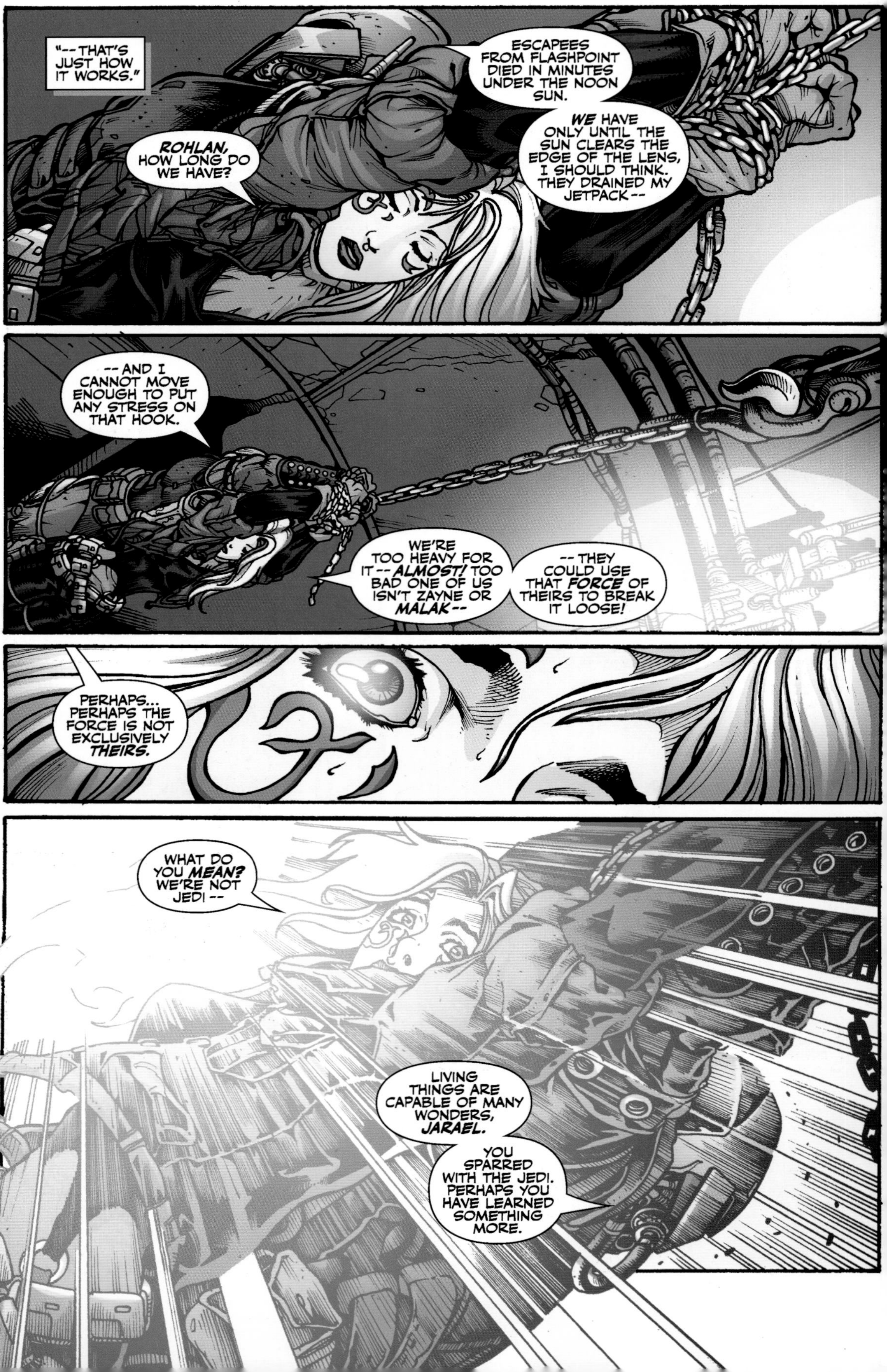
"--THAT'S JUST HOW IT WORKS."
ESCAPEES FROM FLASHPOINT DIED IN MINUTES UNDER THE NOON SUN.
ROHLAN, HOW LONG DO WE HAVE?
WE HAVE ONLY UNTIL THE SUN CLEARS THE EDGE OF THE LENS, I SHOULD THINK. THEY DRAINED MY JETPACK--
-- AND I CANNOT MOVE ENOUGH TO PUT ANY STRESS ON THAT HOOK.
WE'RE TOO HEAVY FOR IT--ALMOST! TOO BAD ONE OF US ISN'T ZAYNE OR MALAK--
-- THEY COULD USE THAT FORCE OF THEIRS TO BREAK IT LOOSE!
PERHAPS... PERHAPS THE FORCE IS NOT EXCLUSIVELY THEIRS.
WHAT DO YOU MEAN? WE'RE NOT JEDI --
LIVING THINGS ARE CAPABLE OF MANY WONDERS, JARAEL.
YOU SPARRED WITH THE JEDI. PERHAPS YOU HAVE LEARNED SOMETHING MORE.

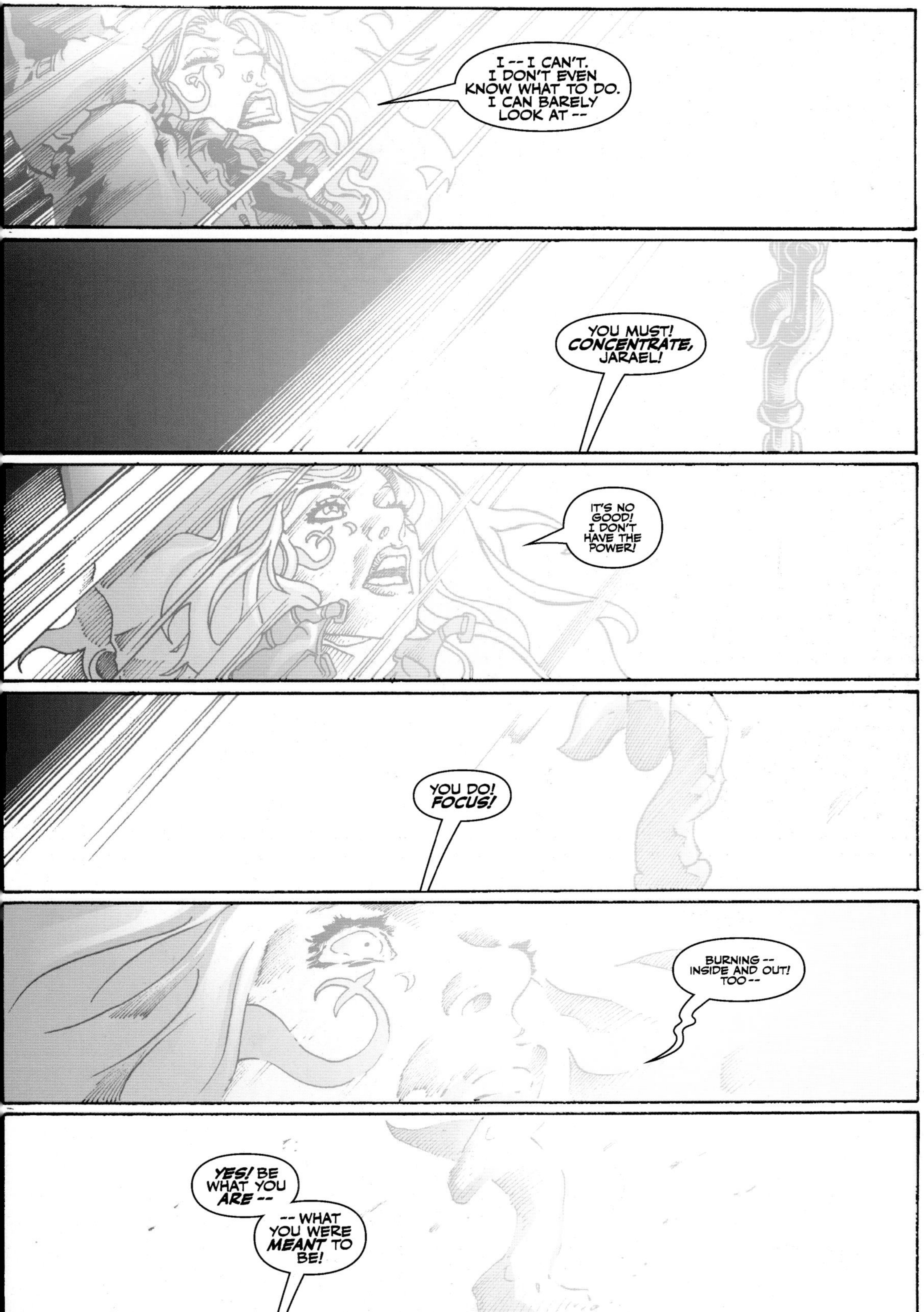
I -- I CAN'T. I DON'T EVEN KNOW WHAT TO DO. I CAN BARELY LOOK AT --
YOU MUST! CONCENTRATE, JARAEL!
IT'S NO GOOD! I DON'T HAVE THE POWER!
YOU DO! FOCUS!
BURNING -- INSIDE AND OUT! TOO --
YES! BE WHAT YOU ARE --
-- WHAT YOU WERE MEANT TO BE!

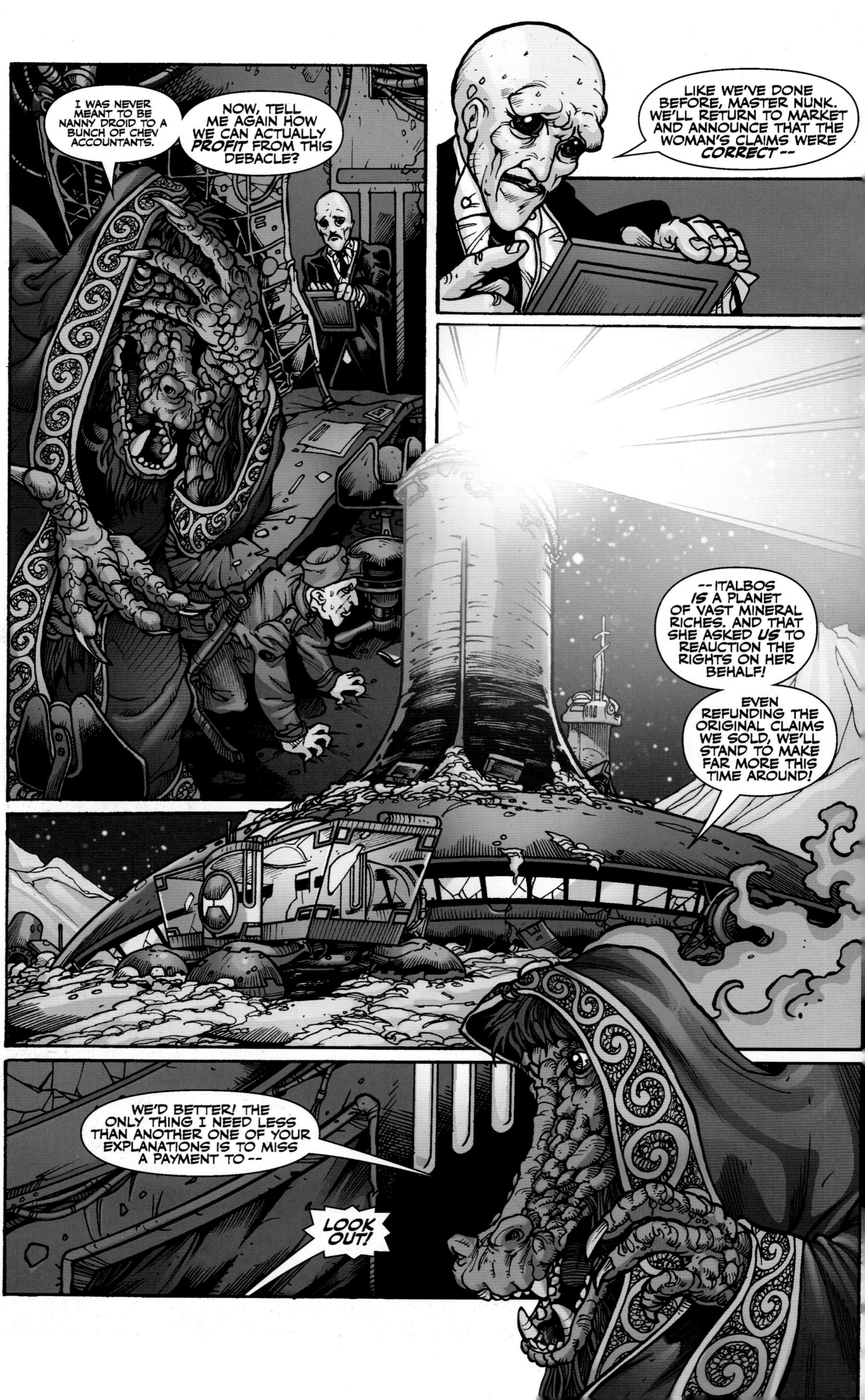
I WAS NEVER MEANT TO BE NANNY DROID TO A BUNCH OF CHEV ACCOUNTANTS.
NOW, TELL ME AGAIN HOW WE CAN ACTUALLY PROFIT FROM THIS DEBACLE?
LIKE WE'VE DONE BEFORE, MASTER NUNK. WE'LL RETURN TO MARKET AND ANNOUNCE THAT THE WOMAN'S CLAIMS WERE CORRECT --
-- ITALBOS IS A PLANET OF VAST MINERAL RICHES. AND THAT SHE ASKED US TO REAUCTION THE RIGHTS ON HER BEHALF!
EVEN REFUNDING THE ORIGINAL CLAIMS WE SOLD, WE'LL STAND TO MAKE FAR MORE THIS TIME AROUND!
WE'D BETTER! THE ONLY THING I NEED LESS THAN ANOTHER ONE OF YOUR EXPLANATIONS IS TO MISS A PAYMENT TO --
LOOK OUT!

YIII!

KRRCHHOW!

SKWAAAWWK!

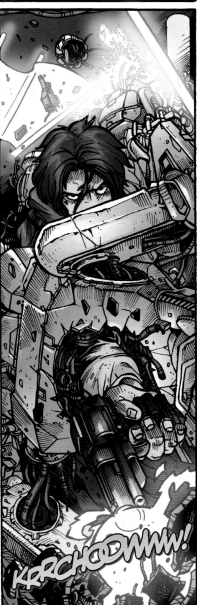

KRRCHOOWWW!

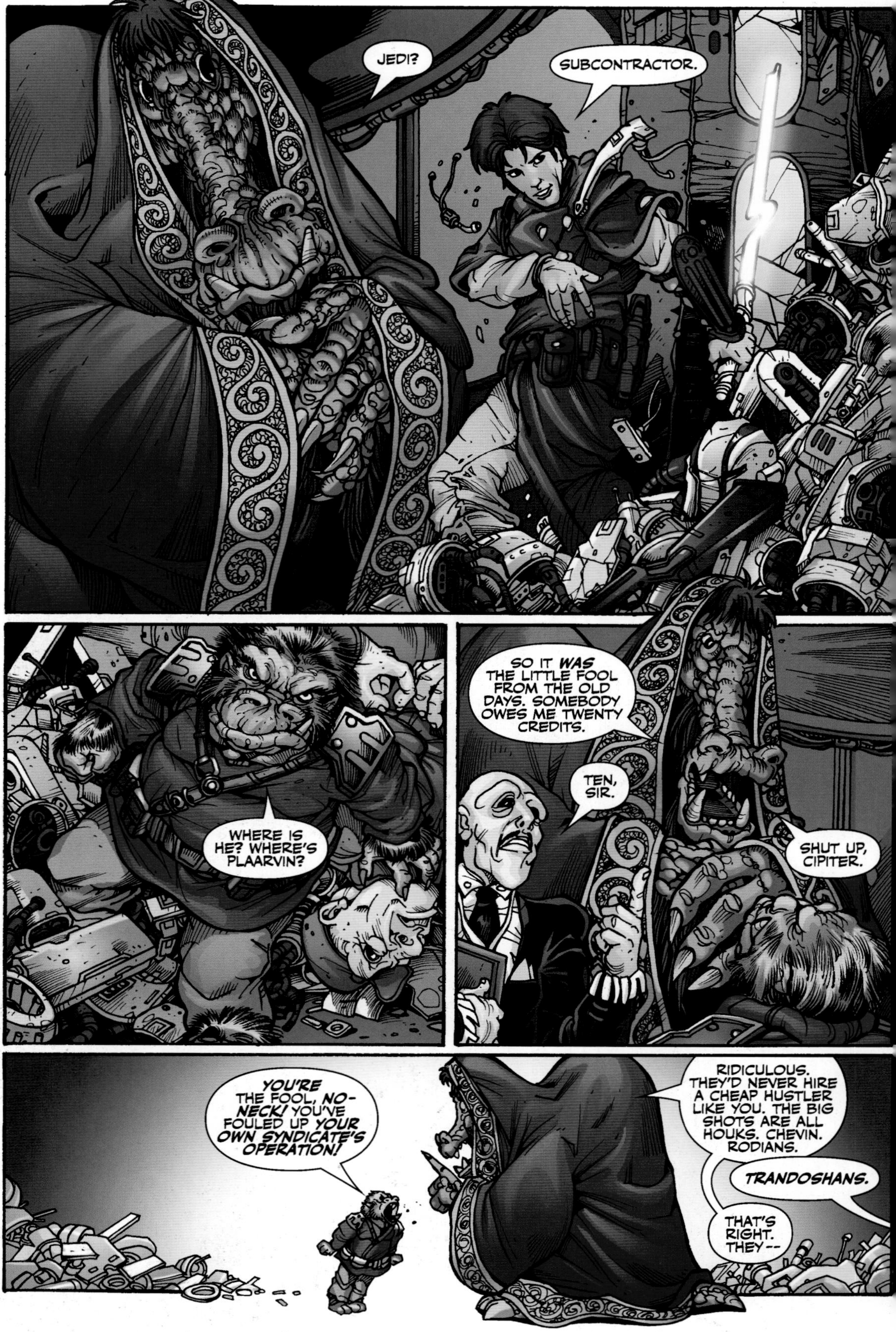
JEDI?
SUBCONTRACTOR.
WHERE IS HE? WHERE'S PLAARVIN?
SO IT WAS THE LITTLE FOOL FROM THE OLD DAYS. SOMEBODY OWES ME TWENTY CREDITS.
TEN, SIR.
SHUT UP, CIPITER.
YOU'RE THE FOOL, NO-NECK! YOU'VE FOULED UP YOUR OWN SYNDICATE'S OPERATION!
RIDICULOUS. THEY'D NEVER HIRE A CHEAP HUSTLER LIKE YOU. THE BIG SHOTS ARE ALL HOUKS. CHEVIN. RODIANS.
TRANDOSHANS.
THAT'S RIGHT. THEY--

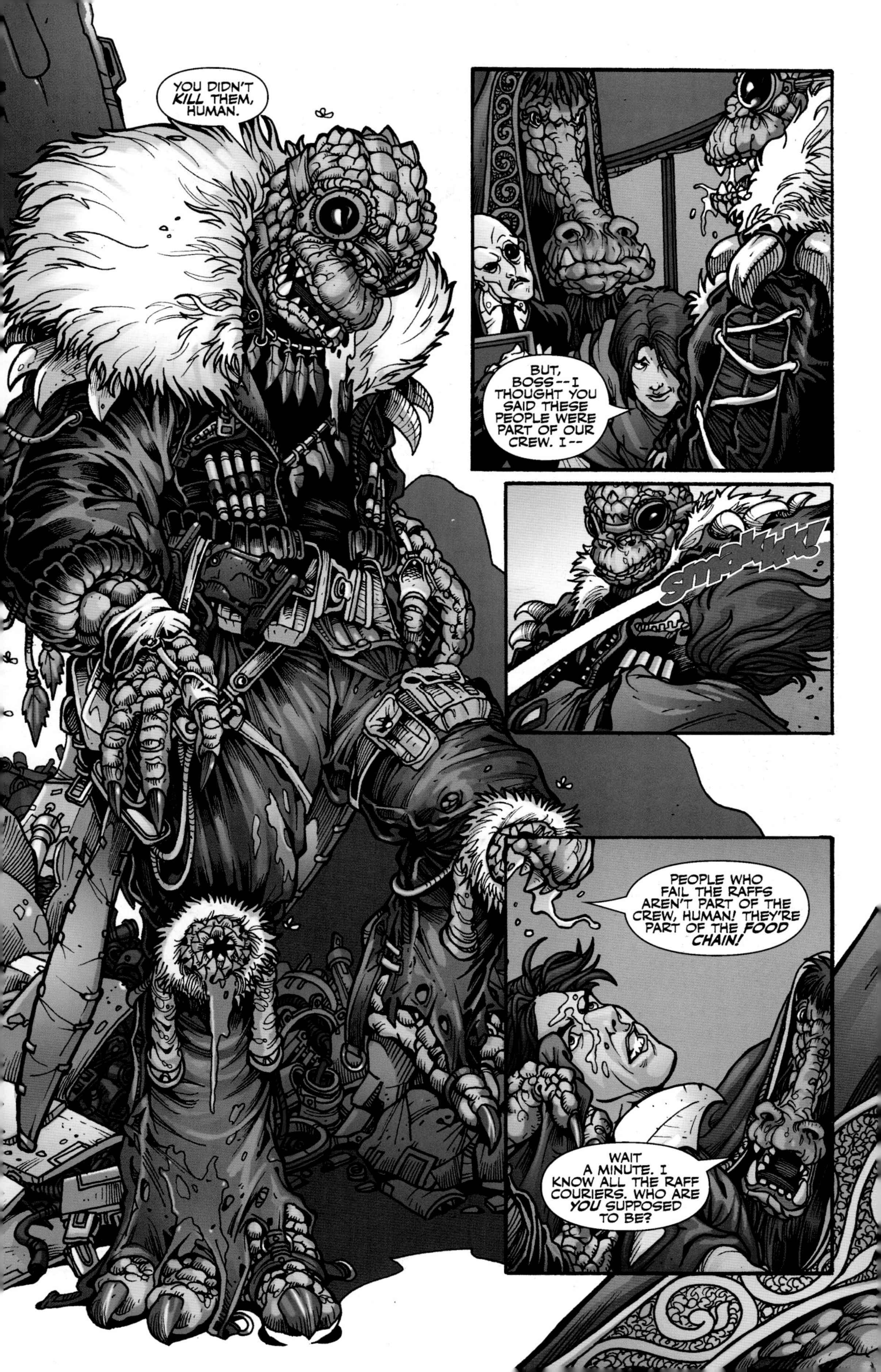
YOU DIDN'T KILL THEM, HUMAN.
BUT, BOSS--I THOUGHT YOU SAID THESE PEOPLE WERE PART OF OUR CREW. I--
SMAKKK!
PEOPLE WHO FAIL THE RAFFS AREN'T PART OF THE CREW, HUMAN! THEY'RE PART OF THE FOOD CHAIN!
WAIT A MINUTE. I KNOW ALL THE RAFF COURIERS. WHO ARE YOU SUPPOSED TO BE?

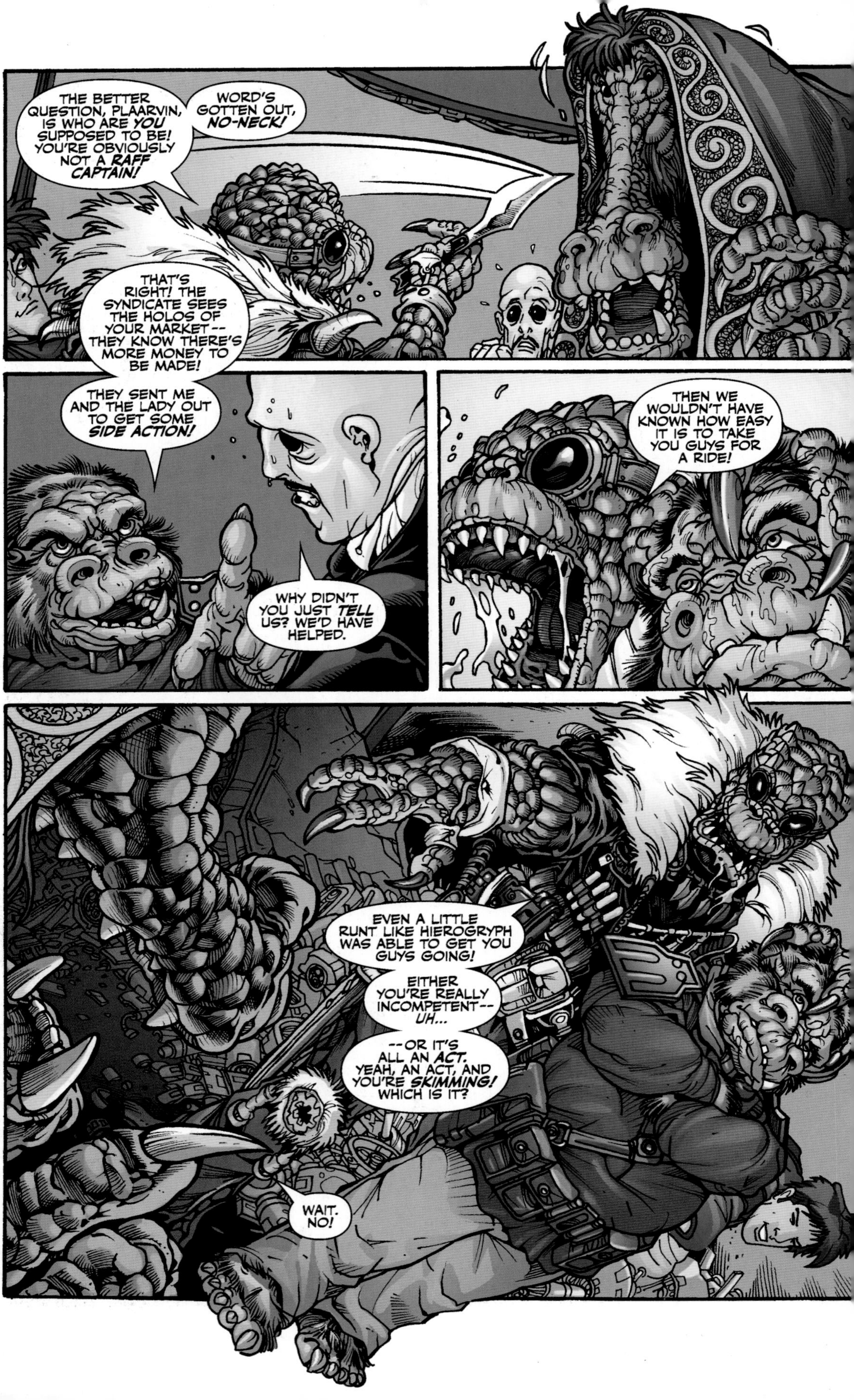
THE BETTER QUESTION, PLAARVIN, IS WHO ARE *YOU* SUPPOSED TO BE! YOU'RE OBVIOUSLY NOT A *RAFF CAPTAIN!*
WORD'S GOTTEN OUT, *NO-NECK!*
THAT'S RIGHT! THE SYNDICATE SEES THE HOLOS OF YOUR MARKET-- THEY KNOW THERE'S MORE MONEY TO BE MADE!
THEY SENT ME AND THE LADY OUT TO GET SOME *SIDE ACTION!*
WHY DIDN'T YOU JUST *TELL* US? WE'D HAVE HELPED.
THEN WE WOULDN'T HAVE KNOWN HOW EASY IT IS TO TAKE YOU GUYS FOR A RIDE!
EVEN A LITTLE RUNT LIKE HIEROGRYPH WAS ABLE TO GET YOU GUYS GOING!
EITHER YOU'RE REALLY INCOMPETENT-- *UH...*
--OR IT'S ALL AN *ACT.* YEAH, AN ACT, AND YOU'RE *SKIMMING!* WHICH IS IT?
WAIT. NO!

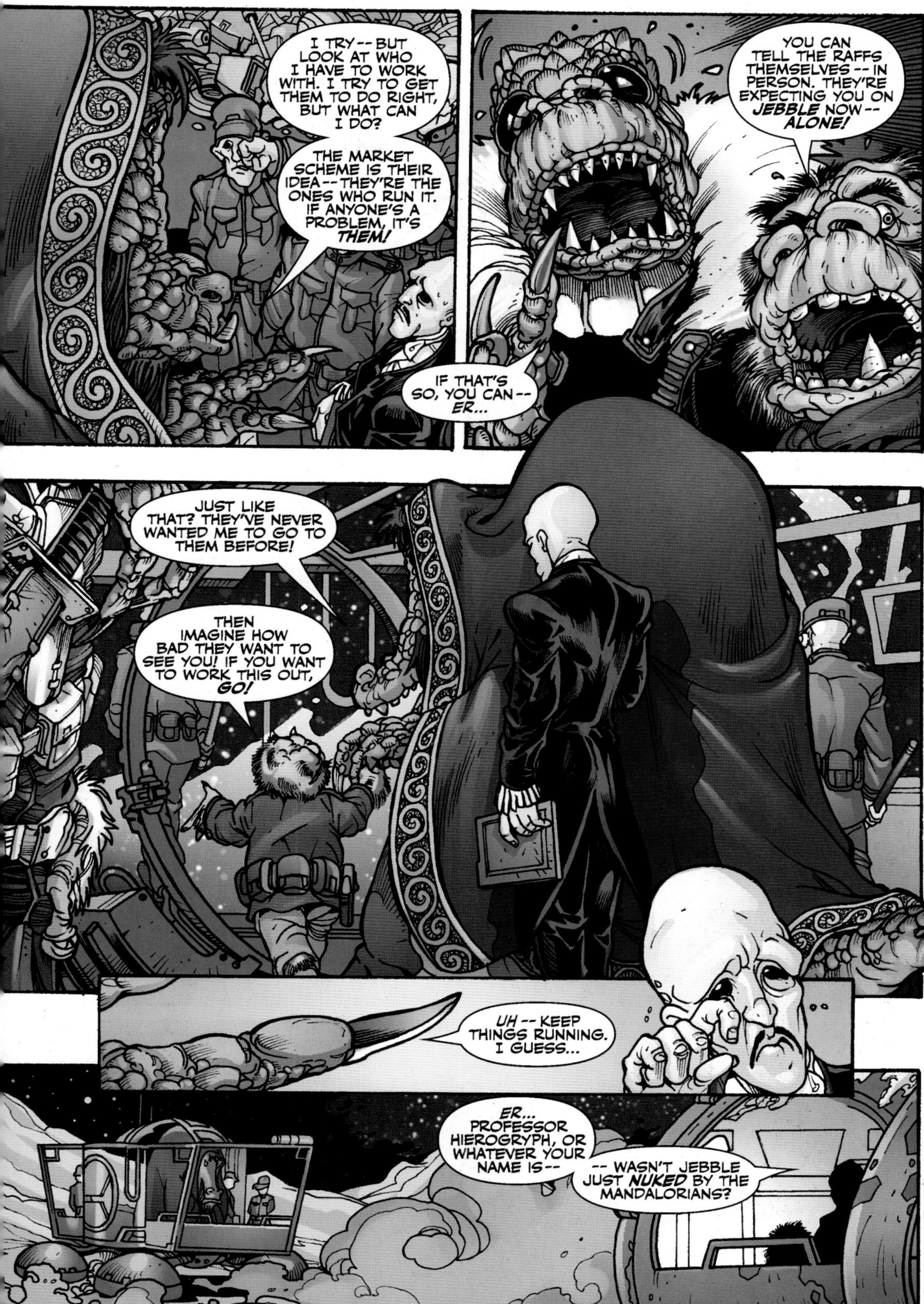
I TRY -- BUT LOOK AT WHO I HAVE TO WORK WITH. I TRY TO GET THEM TO DO RIGHT, BUT WHAT CAN I DO?
THE MARKET SCHEME IS THEIR IDEA -- THEY'RE THE ONES WHO RUN IT. IF ANYONE'S A PROBLEM, IT'S THEM!
YOU CAN TELL THE RAFFS THEMSELVES -- IN PERSON. THEY'RE EXPECTING YOU ON JEBBLE NOW -- ALONE!
IF THAT'S SO, YOU CAN -- ER...
JUST LIKE THAT? THEY'VE NEVER WANTED ME TO GO TO THEM BEFORE!
THEN IMAGINE HOW BAD THEY WANT TO SEE YOU! IF YOU WANT TO WORK THIS OUT, GO!
UH -- KEEP THINGS RUNNING. I GUESS...
ER... PROFESSOR HIEROGRYPH, OR WHATEVER YOUR NAME IS--
-- WASN'T JEBBLE JUST NUKED BY THE MANDALORIANS?

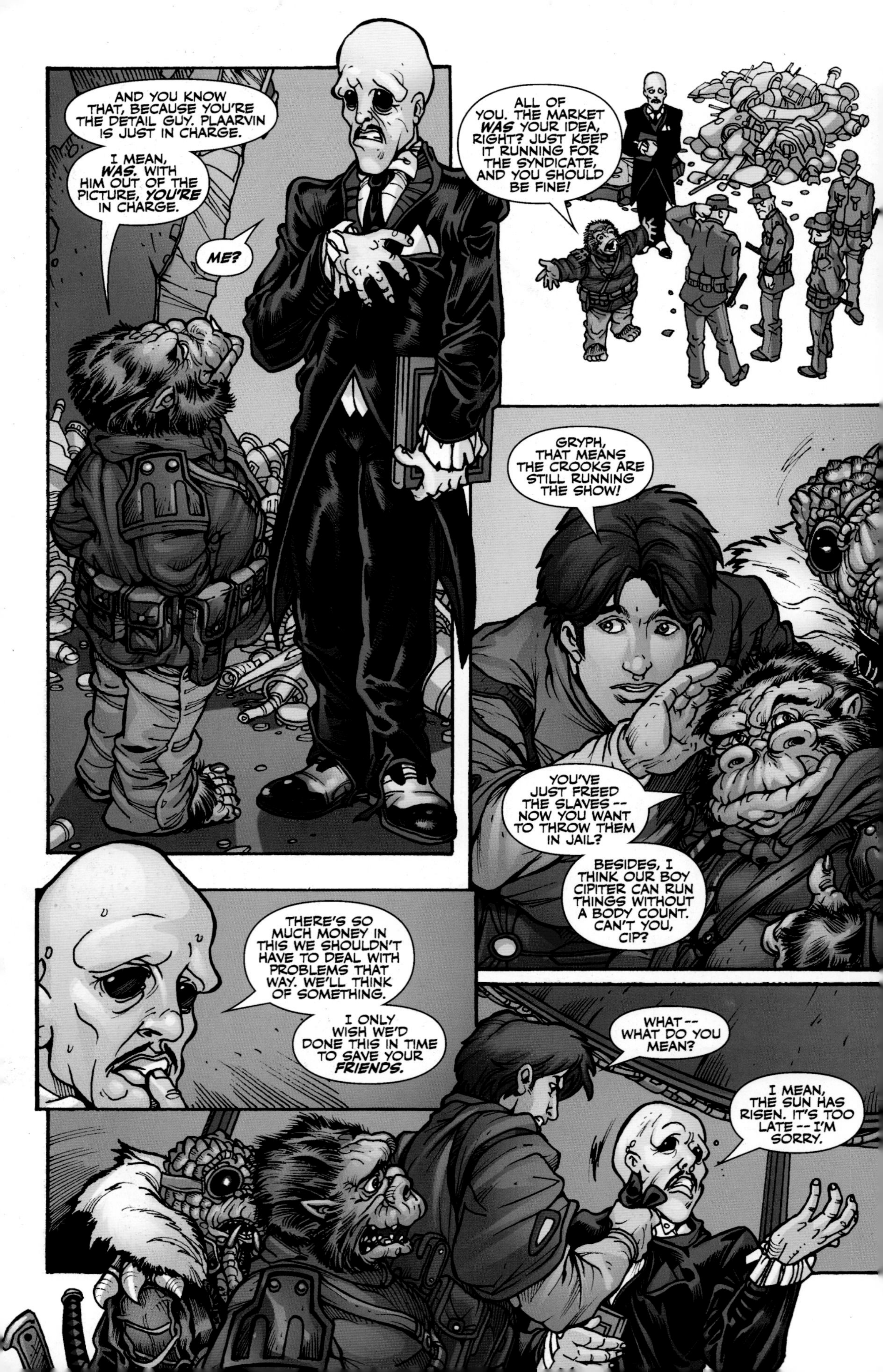
AND YOU KNOW THAT, BECAUSE YOU'RE THE DETAIL GUY. PLAARVIN IS JUST IN CHARGE.
I MEAN, WAS. WITH HIM OUT OF THE PICTURE, YOU'RE IN CHARGE.
ME?
ALL OF YOU. THE MARKET WAS YOUR IDEA, RIGHT? JUST KEEP IT RUNNING FOR THE SYNDICATE, AND YOU SHOULD BE FINE!
GRYPH, THAT MEANS THE CROOKS ARE STILL RUNNING THE SHOW!
YOU'VE JUST FREED THE SLAVES -- NOW YOU WANT TO THROW THEM IN JAIL?
BESIDES, I THINK OUR BOY CIPITER CAN RUN THINGS WITHOUT A BODY COUNT. CAN'T YOU, CIP?
THERE'S SO MUCH MONEY IN THIS WE SHOULDN'T HAVE TO DEAL WITH PROBLEMS THAT WAY. WE'LL THINK OF SOMETHING.
I ONLY WISH WE'D DONE THIS IN TIME TO SAVE YOUR FRIENDS.
WHAT -- WHAT DO YOU MEAN?
I MEAN, THE SUN HAS RISEN. IT'S TOO LATE -- I'M SORRY.

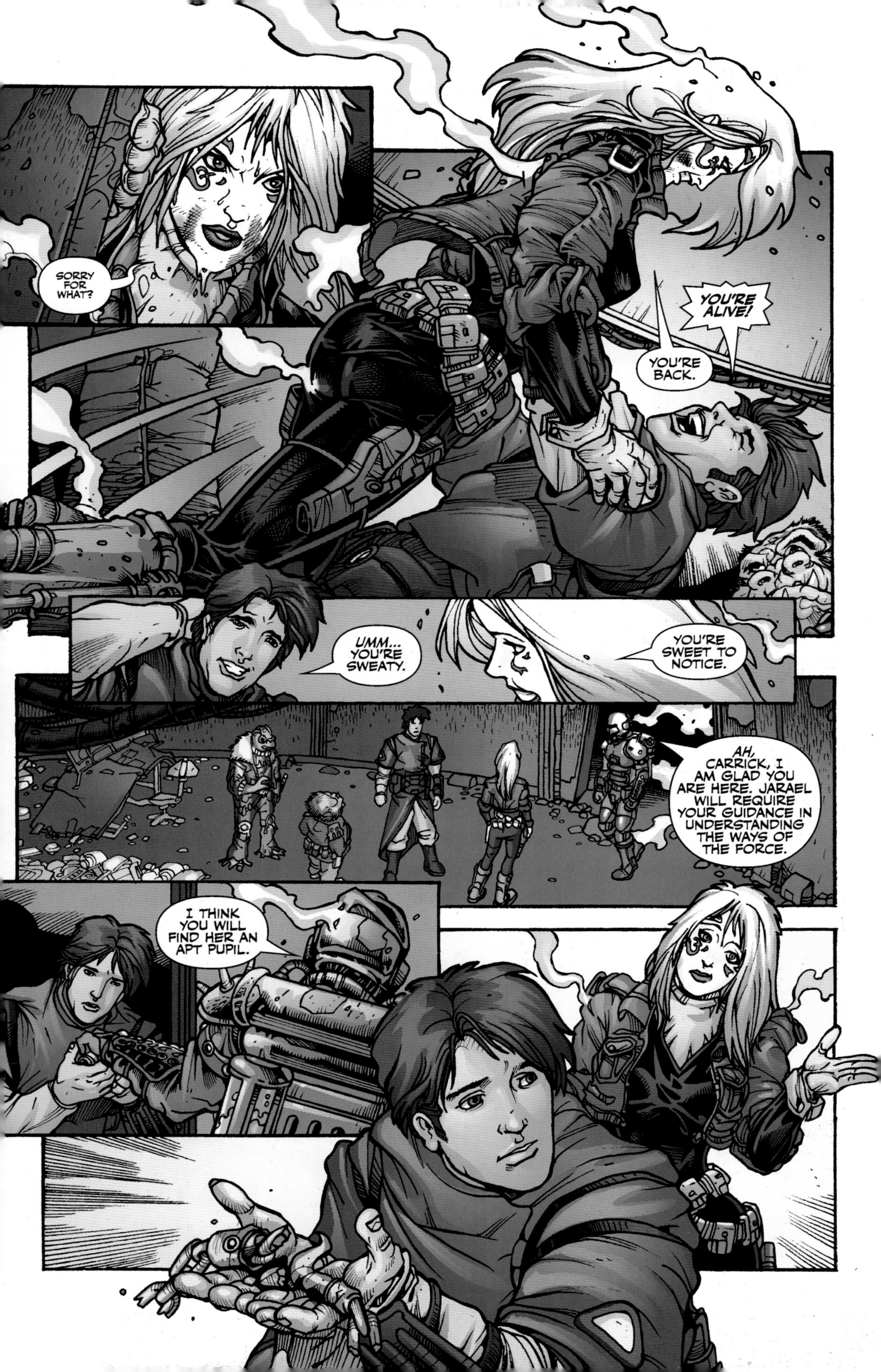
SORRY FOR WHAT?
YOU'RE ALIVE!
YOU'RE BACK.
UMM... YOU'RE SWEATY.
YOU'RE SWEET TO NOTICE.
AH, CARRICK, I AM GLAD YOU ARE HERE. JARAEL WILL REQUIRE YOUR GUIDANCE IN UNDERSTANDING THE WAYS OF THE FORCE.
I THINK YOU WILL FIND HER AN APT PUPIL.

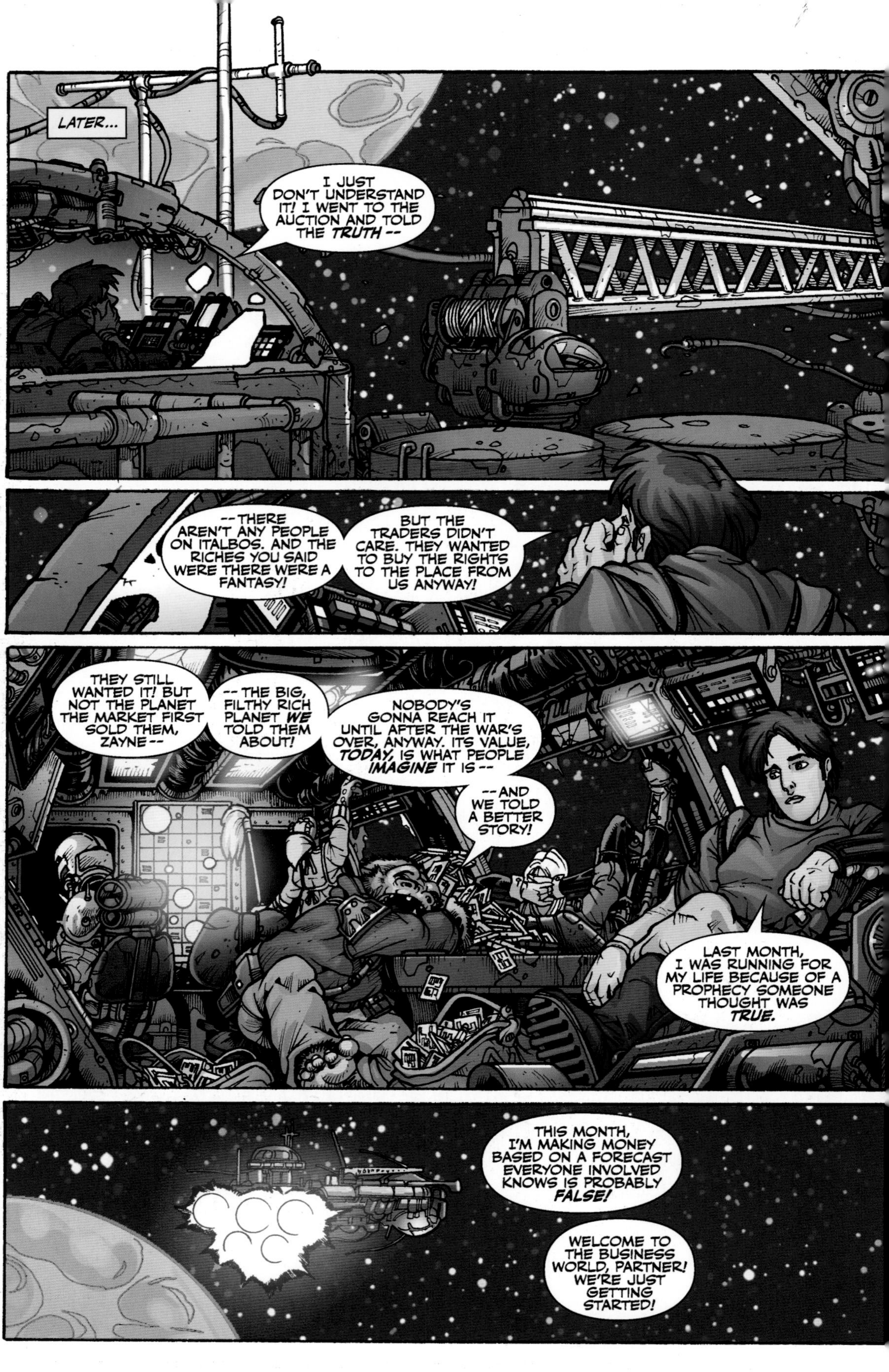
LATER...
I JUST DON'T UNDERSTAND IT! I WENT TO THE AUCTION AND TOLD THE *TRUTH* --
-- THERE AREN'T ANY PEOPLE ON ITALBOS. AND THE RICHES YOU SAID WERE THERE WERE A FANTASY!
BUT THE TRADERS DIDN'T CARE. THEY WANTED TO BUY THE RIGHTS TO THE PLACE FROM US ANYWAY!
THEY STILL WANTED IT! BUT NOT THE PLANET THE MARKET FIRST SOLD THEM, ZAYNE --
-- THE BIG, FILTHY RICH PLANET *WE* TOLD THEM ABOUT!
NOBODY'S GONNA REACH IT UNTIL AFTER THE WAR'S OVER, ANYWAY. ITS VALUE, *TODAY,* IS WHAT PEOPLE *IMAGINE* IT IS --
-- AND WE TOLD A BETTER STORY!
LAST MONTH, I WAS RUNNING FOR MY LIFE BECAUSE OF A PROPHECY SOMEONE THOUGHT WAS *TRUE.*
THIS MONTH, I'M MAKING MONEY BASED ON A FORECAST EVERYONE INVOLVED KNOWS IS PROBABLY *FALSE!*
WELCOME TO THE BUSINESS WORLD, PARTNER! WE'RE JUST GETTING STARTED!

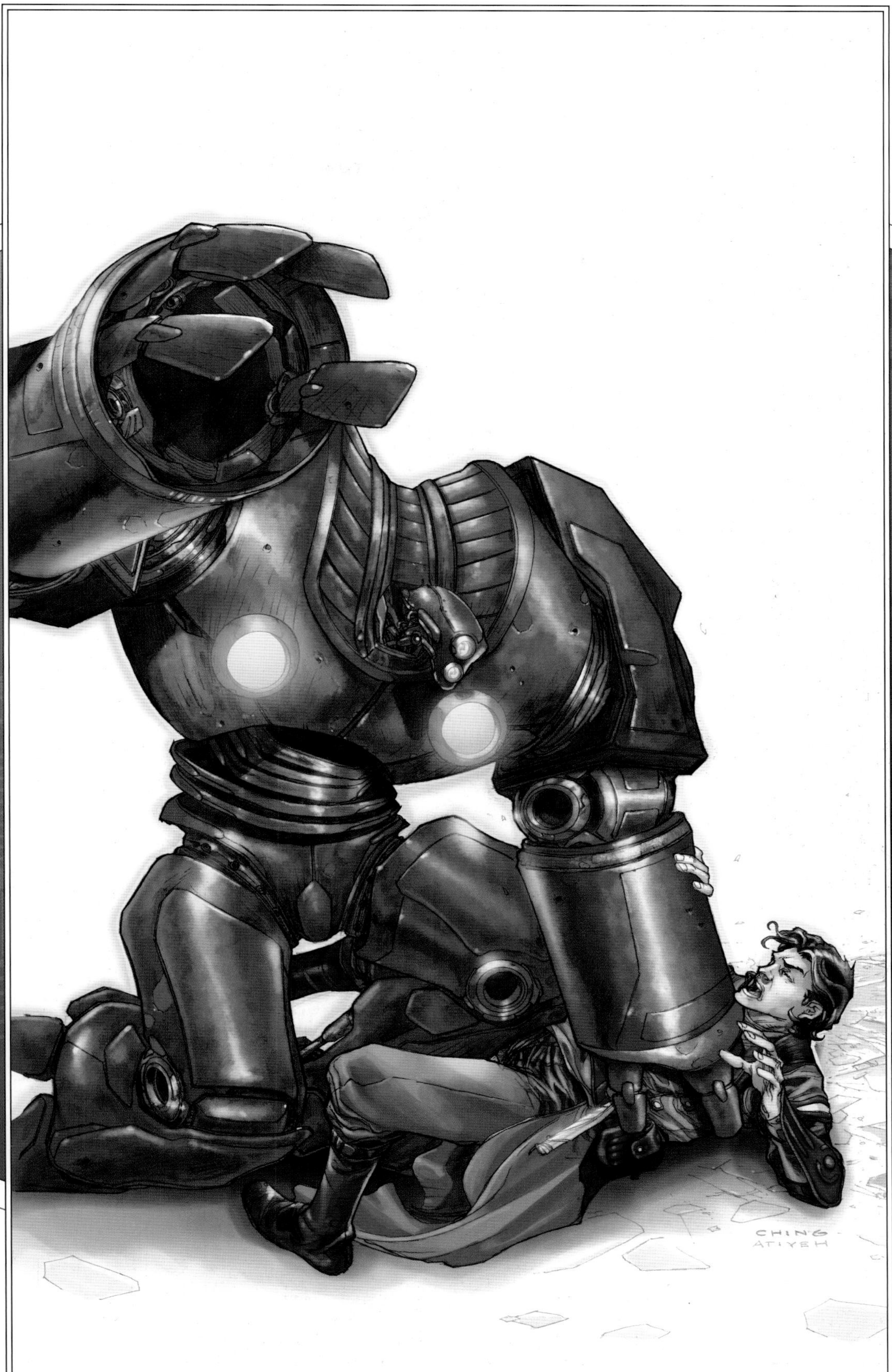
CHING
ATIYEH

ILLUSTRATION BY BRIAN CHING AND MICHAEL ATIYEH

FAITHFUL EXECUTION

art by Dean Zachary

Aboard the grungy mining ship *Hot Prospect*, Zayne Carrick leads his friends on a continued search for fortune in the Core Worlds. But this ship's crew may need all the help they can get, as Zayne directs them not toward fortune, but a derelict spacecraft lost in the nebulous regions of the Core Worlds—and carrying a mystery . . .

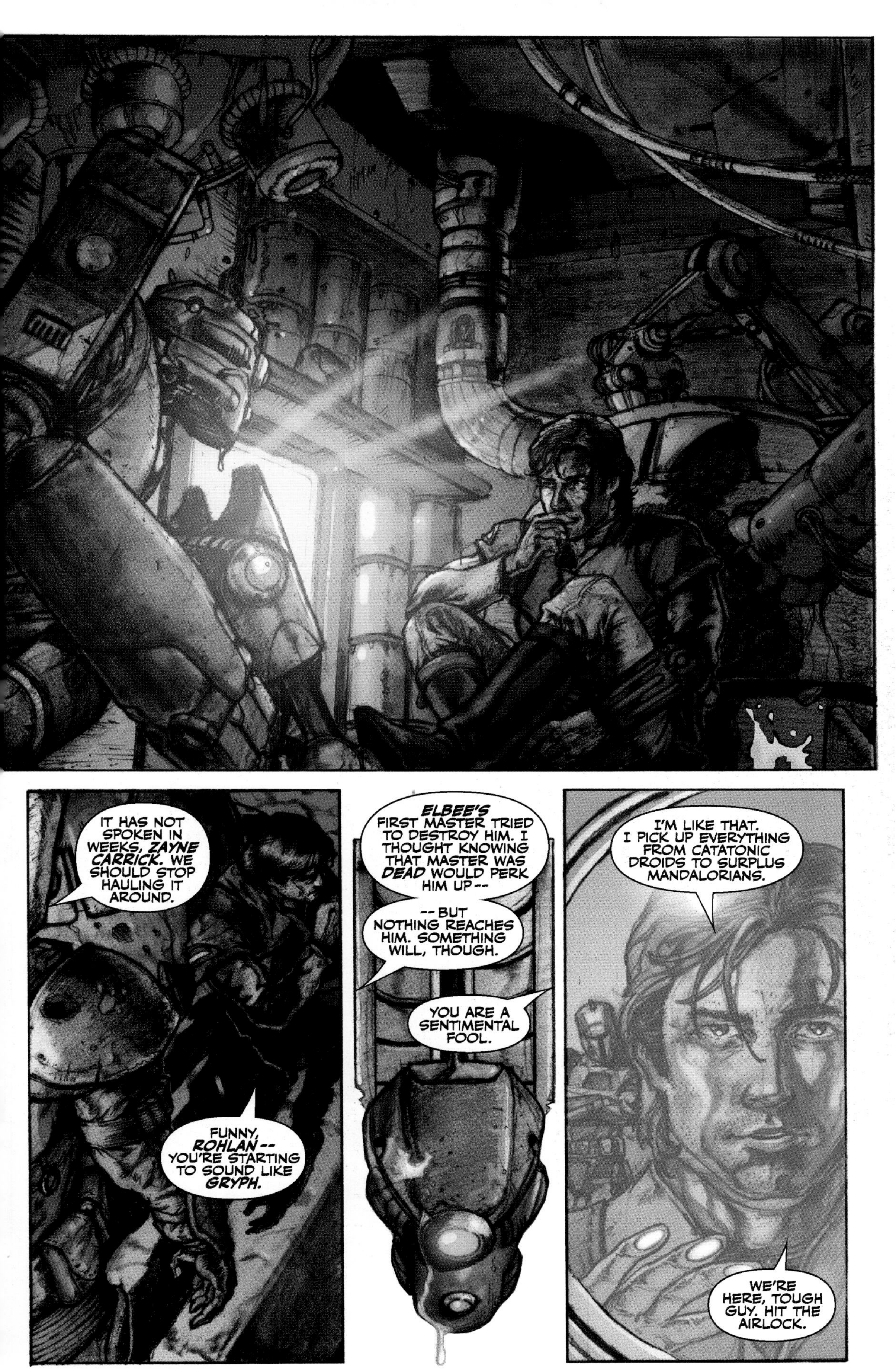
IT HAS NOT SPOKEN IN WEEKS, ZAYNE CARRICK. WE SHOULD STOP HAULING IT AROUND.
FUNNY, ROHLAN -- YOU'RE STARTING TO SOUND LIKE GRYPH.
ELBEE'S FIRST MASTER TRIED TO DESTROY HIM. I THOUGHT KNOWING THAT MASTER WAS DEAD WOULD PERK HIM UP --
-- BUT NOTHING REACHES HIM. SOMETHING WILL, THOUGH.
YOU ARE A SENTIMENTAL FOOL.
I'M LIKE THAT. I PICK UP EVERYTHING FROM CATATONIC DROIDS TO SURPLUS MANDALORIANS.
WE'RE HERE, TOUGH GUY. HIT THE AIRLOCK.

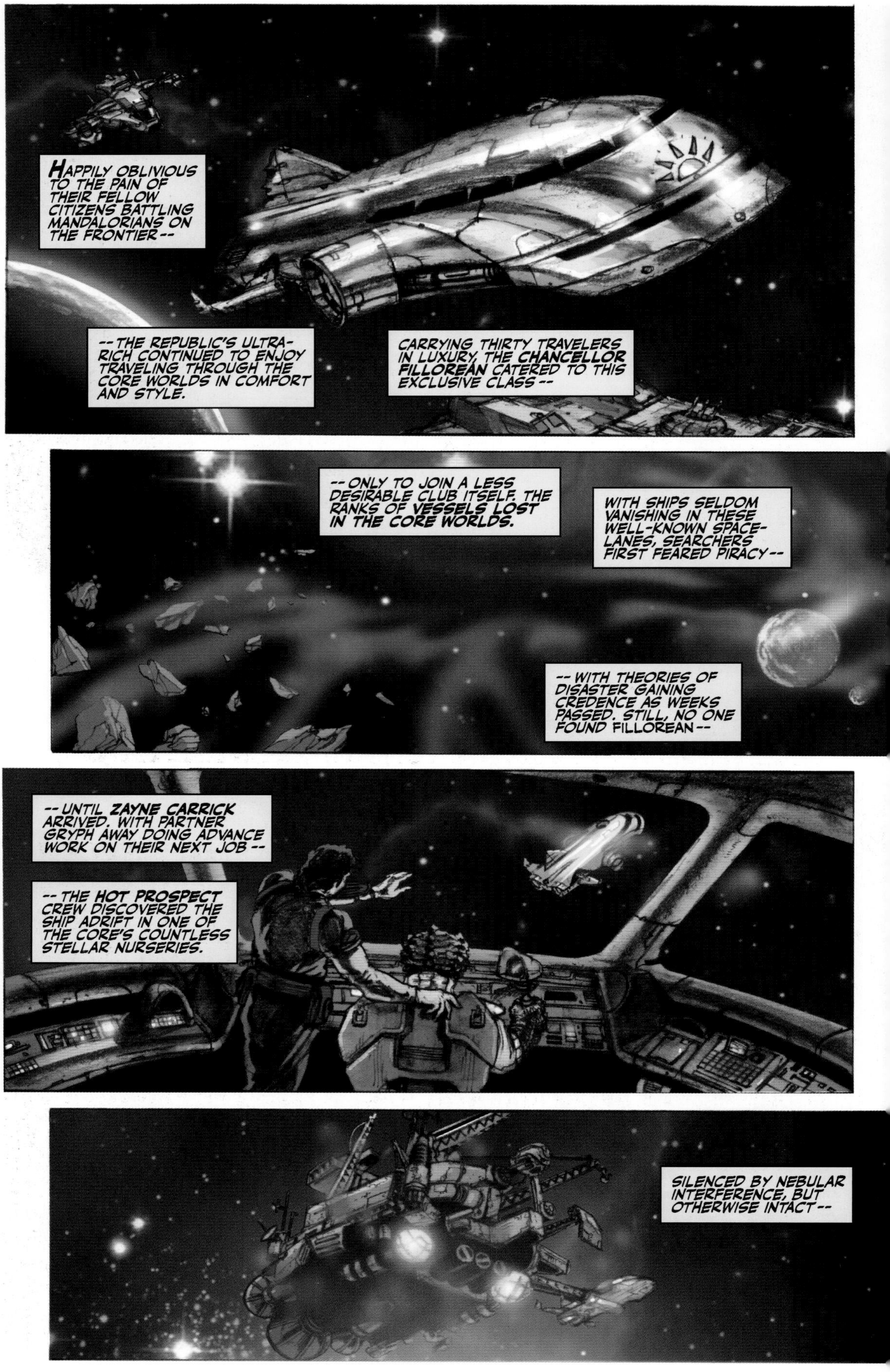
HAPPILY OBLIVIOUS TO THE PAIN OF THEIR FELLOW CITIZENS BATTLING MANDALORIANS ON THE FRONTIER--
--THE REPUBLIC'S ULTRA-RICH CONTINUED TO ENJOY TRAVELING THROUGH THE CORE WORLDS IN COMFORT AND STYLE.
CARRYING THIRTY TRAVELERS IN LUXURY, THE CHANCELLOR FILLOREAN CATERED TO THIS EXCLUSIVE CLASS--
--ONLY TO JOIN A LESS DESIRABLE CLUB ITSELF. THE RANKS OF VESSELS LOST IN THE CORE WORLDS.
WITH SHIPS SELDOM VANISHING IN THESE WELL-KNOWN SPACE-LANES, SEARCHERS FIRST FEARED PIRACY--
--WITH THEORIES OF DISASTER GAINING CREDENCE AS WEEKS PASSED. STILL, NO ONE FOUND FILLOREAN--
--UNTIL ZAYNE CARRICK ARRIVED. WITH PARTNER GRYPH AWAY DOING ADVANCE WORK ON THEIR NEXT JOB--
--THE HOT PROSPECT CREW DISCOVERED THE SHIP ADRIFT IN ONE OF THE CORE'S COUNTLESS STELLAR NURSERIES.
SILENCED BY NEBULAR INTERFERENCE, BUT OTHERWISE INTACT--

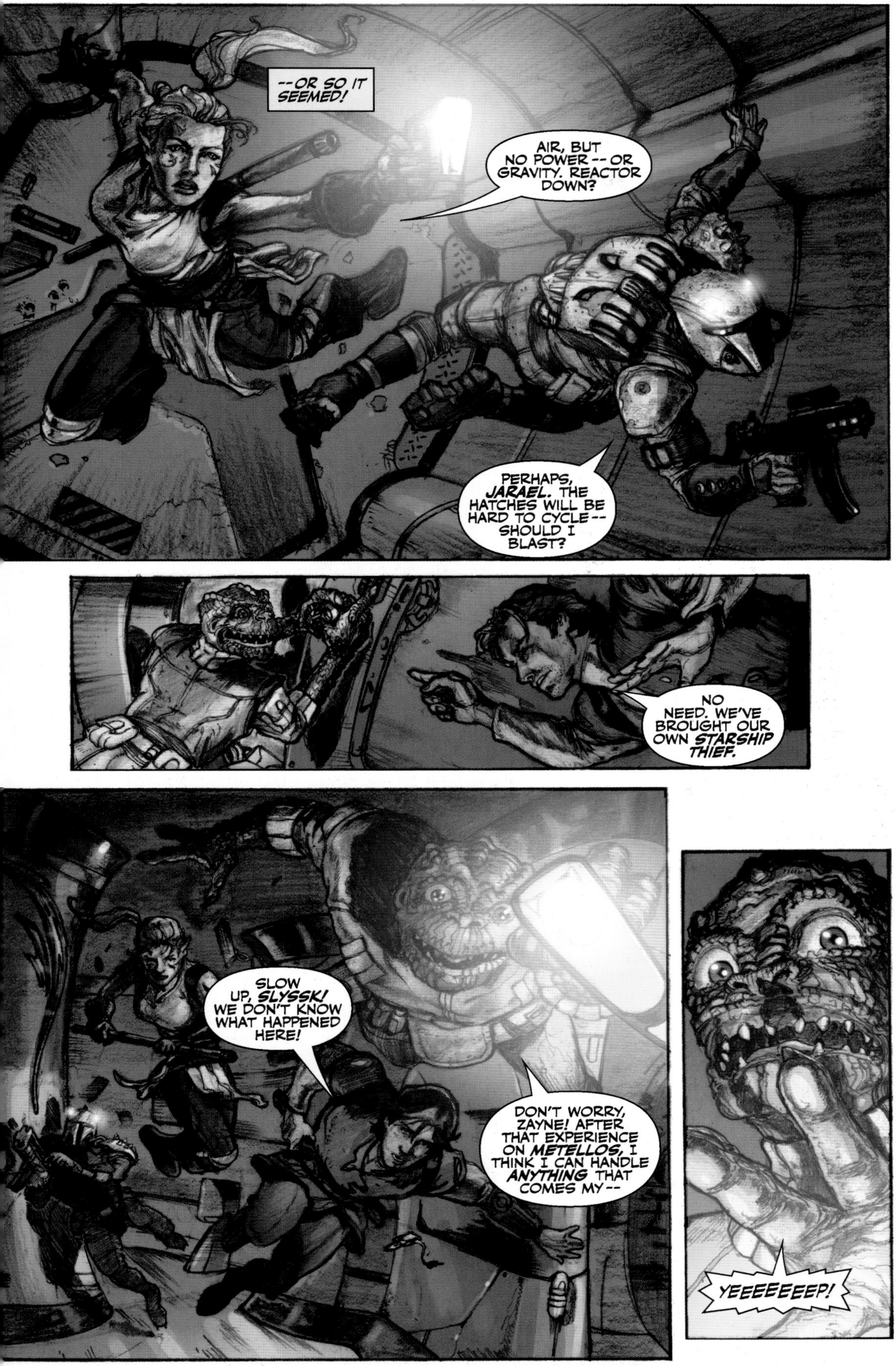
--OR SO IT SEEMED!
AIR, BUT NO POWER--OR GRAVITY. REACTOR DOWN?
PERHAPS, JARAEL. THE HATCHES WILL BE HARD TO CYCLE--SHOULD I BLAST?
NO NEED. WE'VE BROUGHT OUR OWN STARSHIP THIEF.
SLOW UP, SLYSSK! WE DON'T KNOW WHAT HAPPENED HERE!
DON'T WORRY, ZAYNE! AFTER THAT EXPERIENCE ON METELLOS, I THINK I CAN HANDLE ANYTHING THAT COMES MY--
YEEEEEEEP!

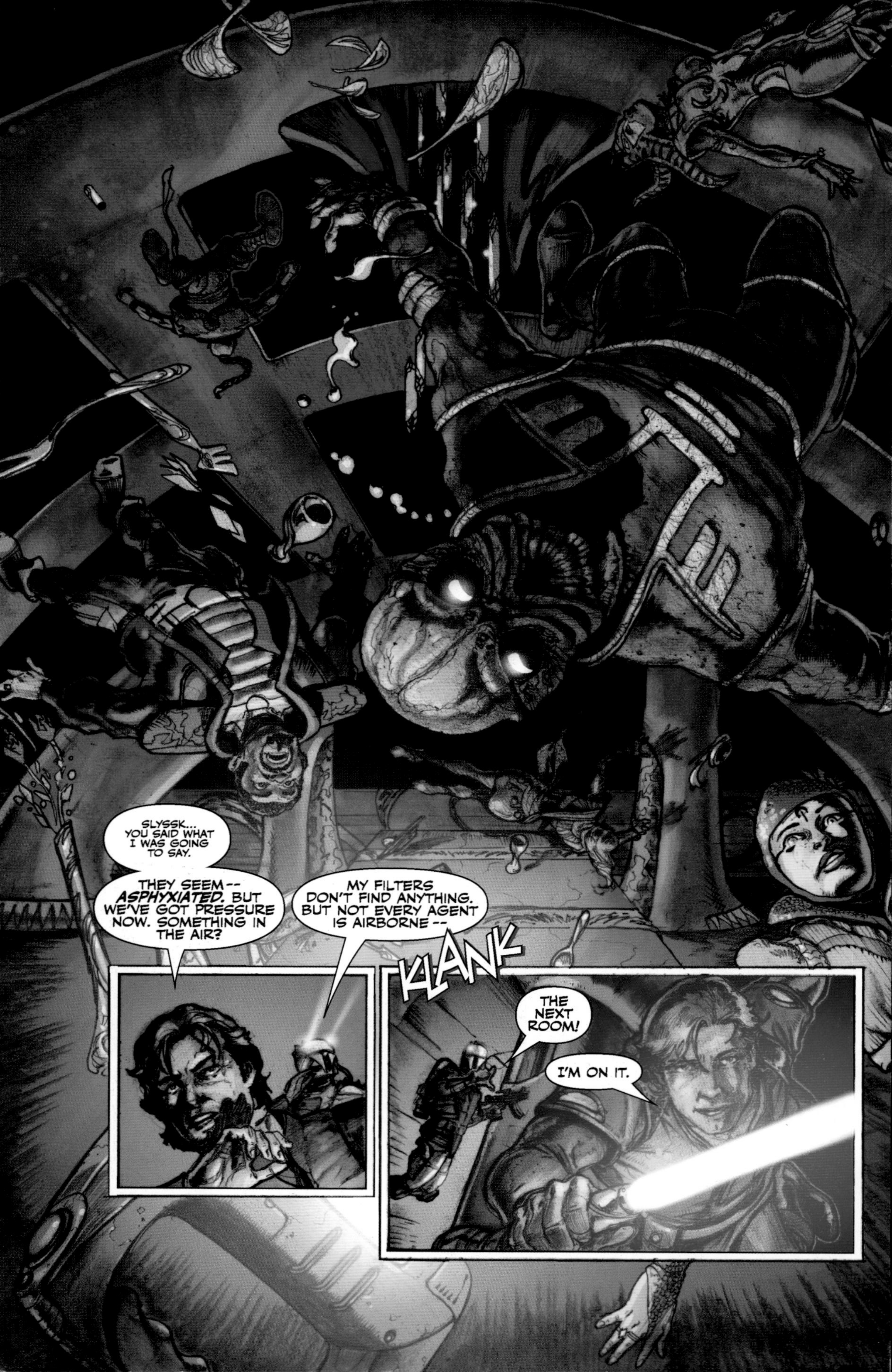
SLYSSK... YOU SAID WHAT I WAS GOING TO SAY.
THEY SEEM-- ASPHYXIATED. BUT WE'VE GOT PRESSURE NOW. SOMETHING IN THE AIR?
MY FILTERS DON'T FIND ANYTHING. BUT NOT EVERY AGENT IS AIRBORNE --
KLANK
THE NEXT ROOM!
I'M ON IT.

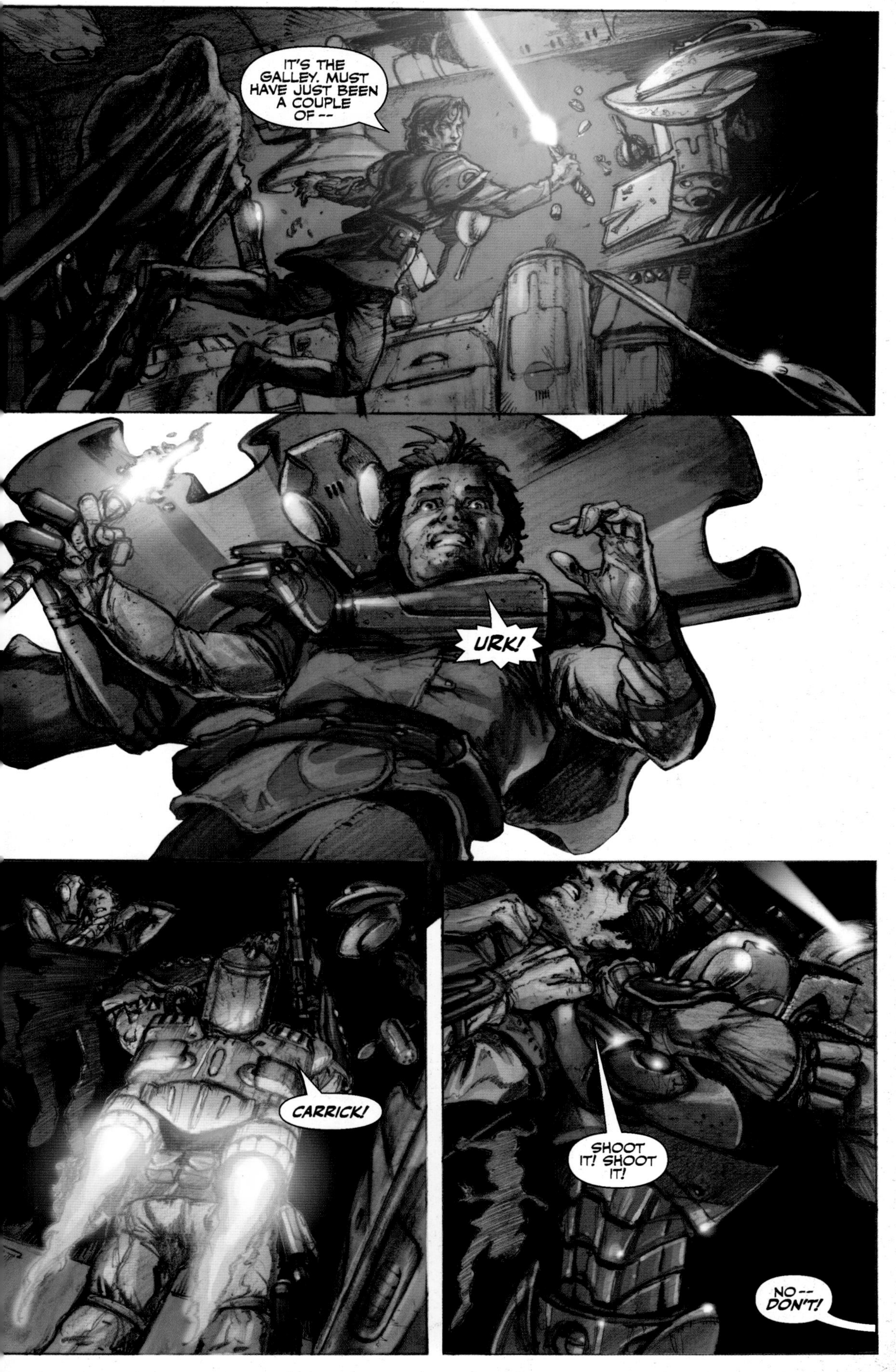
IT'S THE GALLEY. MUST HAVE JUST BEEN A COUPLE OF --
URK!
CARRICK!
SHOOT IT! SHOOT IT!
NO-- DON'T!

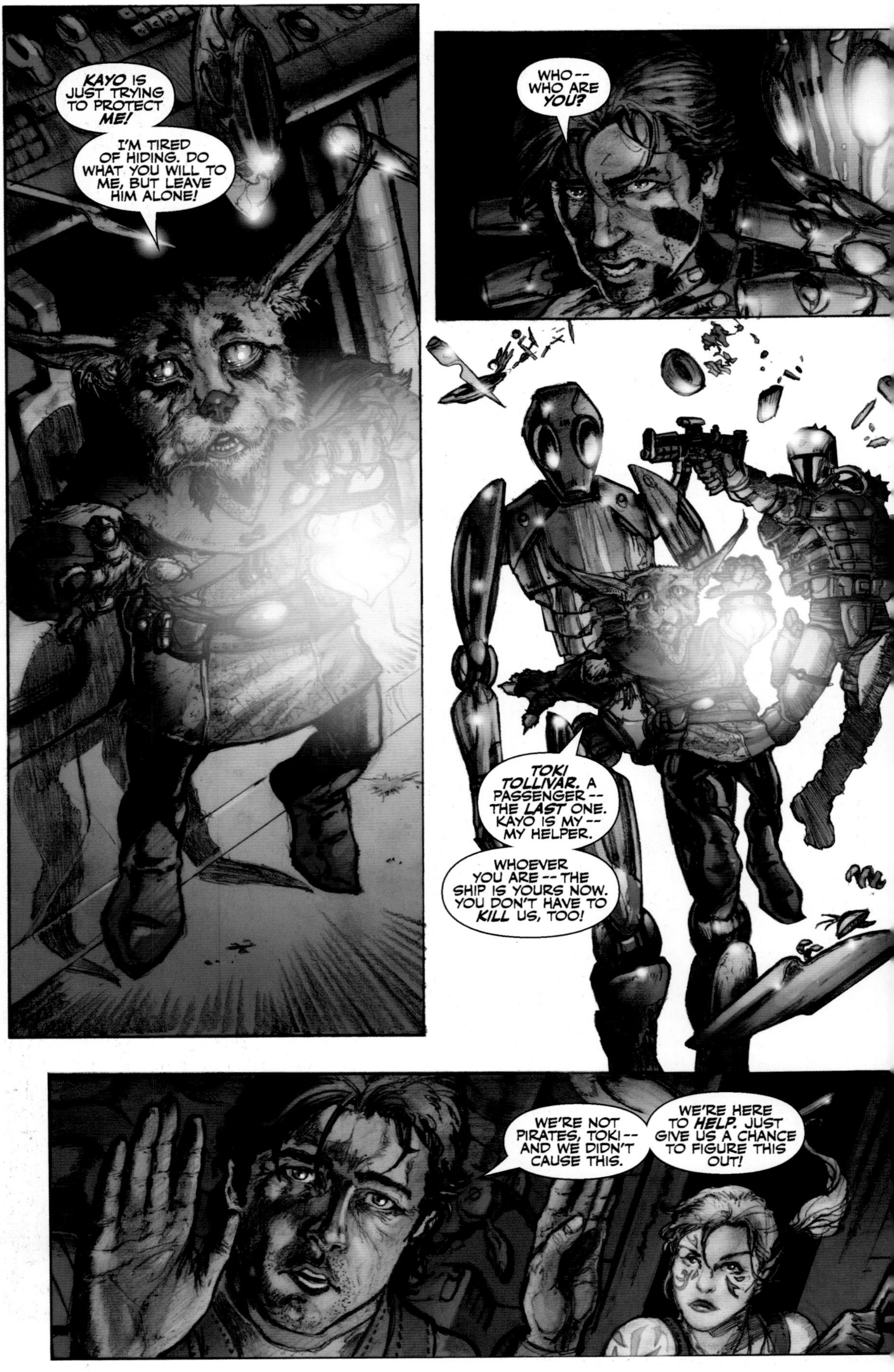
KAYO IS JUST TRYING TO PROTECT ME!
I'M TIRED OF HIDING. DO WHAT YOU WILL TO ME, BUT LEAVE HIM ALONE!
WHO-- WHO ARE YOU?
TOKI TOLLIVAR. A PASSENGER-- THE LAST ONE. KAYO IS MY-- MY HELPER.
WHOEVER YOU ARE-- THE SHIP IS YOURS NOW. YOU DON'T HAVE TO KILL US, TOO!
WE'RE NOT PIRATES, TOKI-- AND WE DIDN'T CAUSE THIS.
WE'RE HERE TO HELP. JUST GIVE US A CHANCE TO FIGURE THIS OUT!

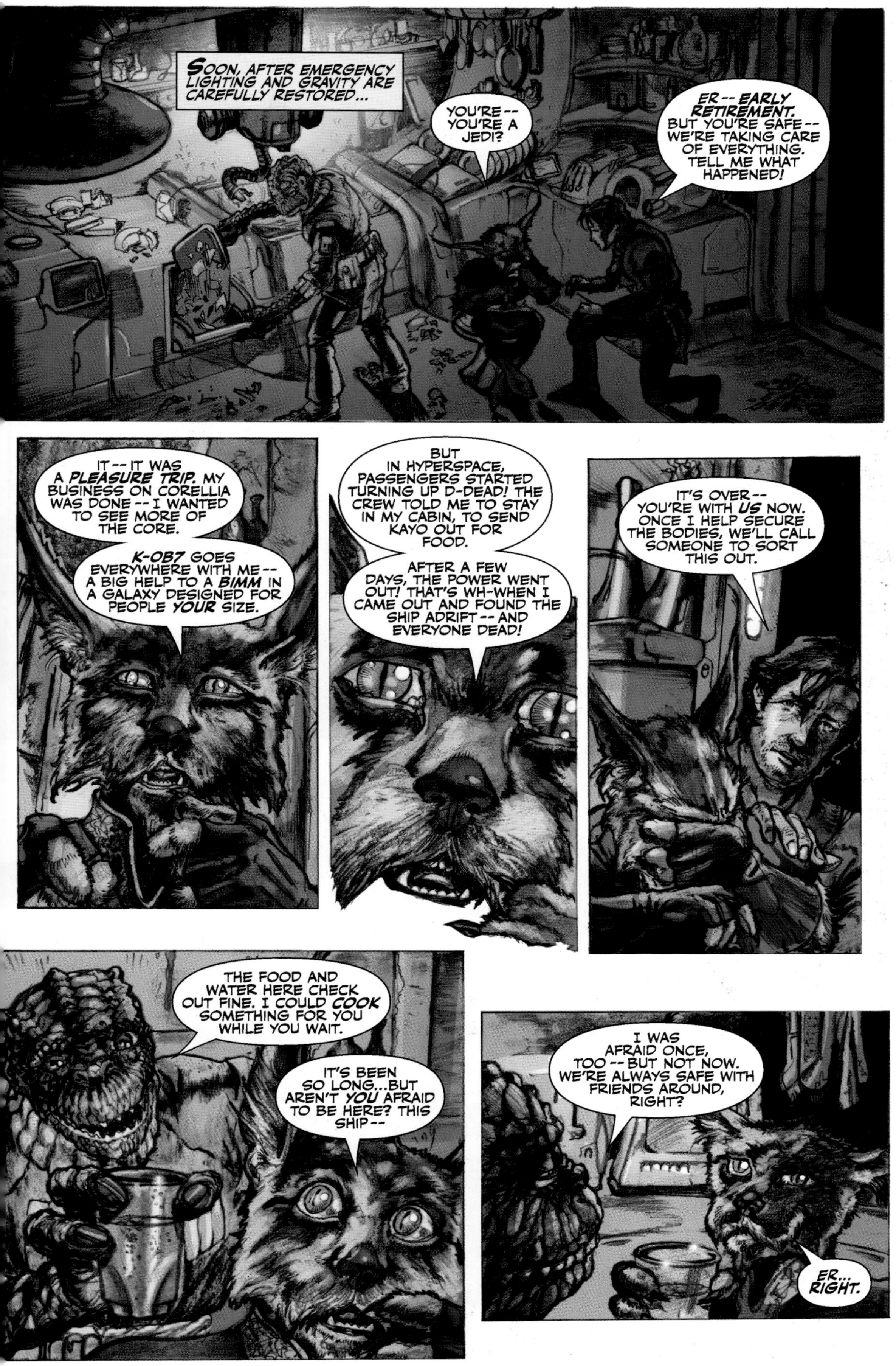
SOON, AFTER EMERGENCY LIGHTING AND GRAVITY ARE CAREFULLY RESTORED...
YOU'RE-- YOU'RE A JEDI?
ER-- EARLY RETIREMENT. BUT YOU'RE SAFE-- WE'RE TAKING CARE OF EVERYTHING. TELL ME WHAT HAPPENED!
IT-- IT WAS A PLEASURE TRIP. MY BUSINESS ON CORELLIA WAS DONE-- I WANTED TO SEE MORE OF THE CORE.
K-OB7 GOES EVERYWHERE WITH ME-- A BIG HELP TO A BIMM IN A GALAXY DESIGNED FOR PEOPLE YOUR SIZE.
BUT IN HYPERSPACE, PASSENGERS STARTED TURNING UP D-DEAD! THE CREW TOLD ME TO STAY IN MY CABIN, TO SEND KAYO OUT FOR FOOD.
AFTER A FEW DAYS, THE POWER WENT OUT! THAT'S WH-WHEN I CAME OUT AND FOUND THE SHIP ADRIFT-- AND EVERYONE DEAD!
IT'S OVER-- YOU'RE WITH US NOW. ONCE I HELP SECURE THE BODIES, WE'LL CALL SOMEONE TO SORT THIS OUT.
THE FOOD AND WATER HERE CHECK OUT FINE. I COULD COOK SOMETHING FOR YOU WHILE YOU WAIT.
IT'S BEEN SO LONG...BUT AREN'T YOU AFRAID TO BE HERE? THIS SHIP--
I WAS AFRAID ONCE, TOO-- BUT NOT NOW. WE'RE ALWAYS SAFE WITH FRIENDS AROUND, RIGHT?
ER... RIGHT.

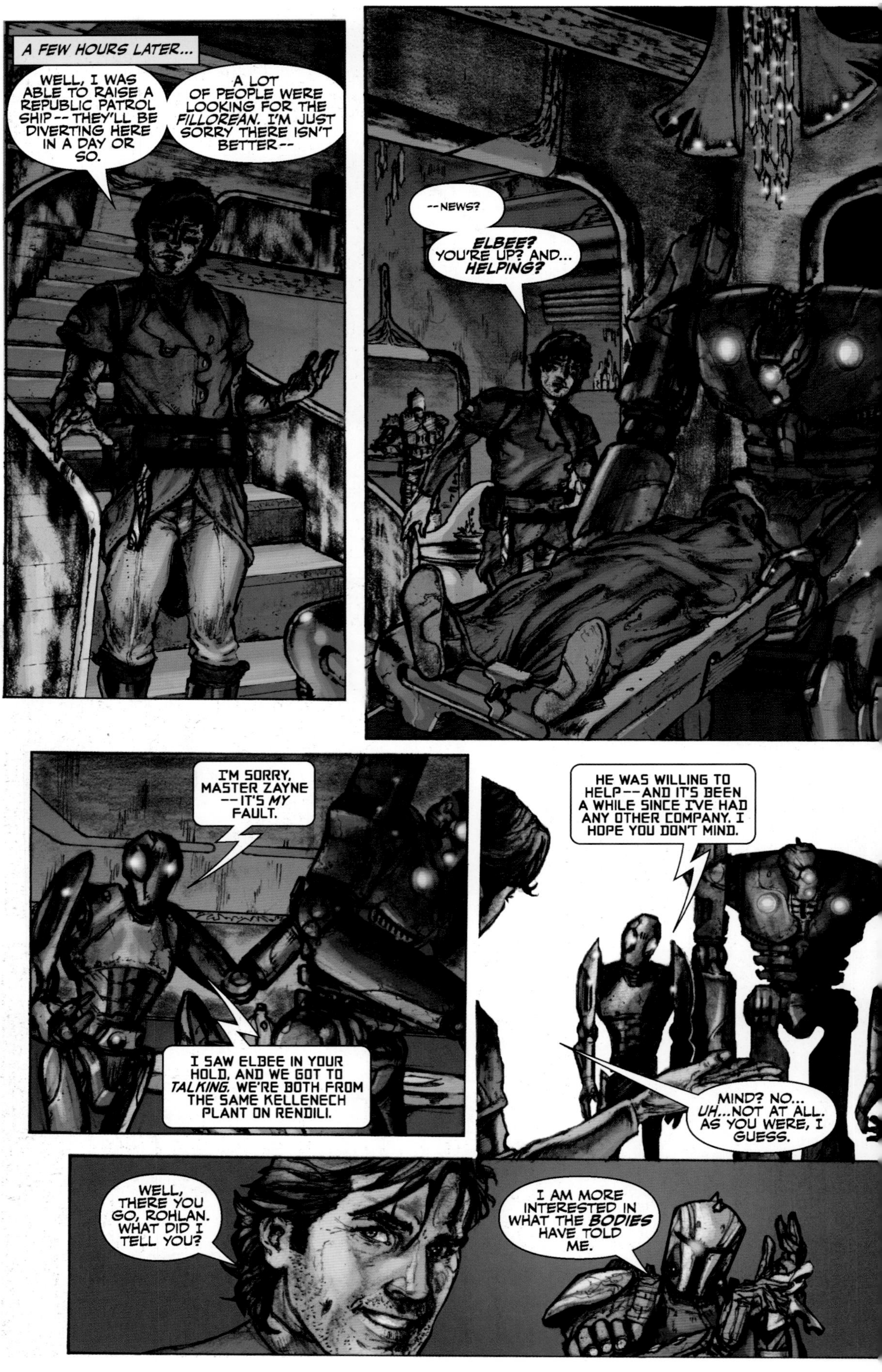
A FEW HOURS LATER...
WELL, I WAS ABLE TO RAISE A REPUBLIC PATROL SHIP-- THEY'LL BE DIVERTING HERE IN A DAY OR SO.
A LOT OF PEOPLE WERE LOOKING FOR THE FILLOREAN. I'M JUST SORRY THERE ISN'T BETTER--
--NEWS?
ELBEE? YOU'RE UP? AND... HELPING?
I'M SORRY, MASTER ZAYNE --IT'S MY FAULT.
I SAW ELBEE IN YOUR HOLD, AND WE GOT TO TALKING. WE'RE BOTH FROM THE SAME KELLENECH PLANT ON RENDILI.
HE WAS WILLING TO HELP--AND IT'S BEEN A WHILE SINCE I'VE HAD ANY OTHER COMPANY. I HOPE YOU DON'T MIND.
MIND? NO... UH...NOT AT ALL. AS YOU WERE, I GUESS.
WELL, THERE YOU GO, ROHLAN. WHAT DID I TELL YOU?
I AM MORE INTERESTED IN WHAT THE BODIES HAVE TOLD ME.

THE PASSENGERS AND CREW *DID* ASPHYXIATE -- BUT NOT BY DECOMPRESSION.

THEY WERE *STRANGLED!*

STRANGLED? HOW IS THAT POSSIBLE? WE'VE FOUND WHAT -- THIRTY BODIES?

I DO NOT KNOW. BUT IT IS ONE BLUNT LARYNGEAL TRAUMA AFTER ANOTHER -- NO MATTER THE SPECIES.

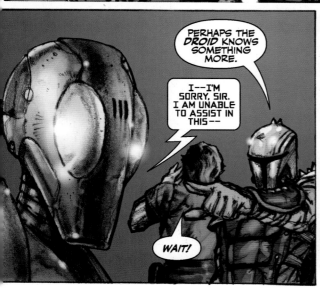

PERHAPS THE *DROID* KNOWS SOMETHING MORE.

I--I'M SORRY, SIR. I AM UNABLE TO ASSIST IN THIS--

WAIT!

SOMETHING'S WRONG -- IN THE GALLEY!

SLYSSK!

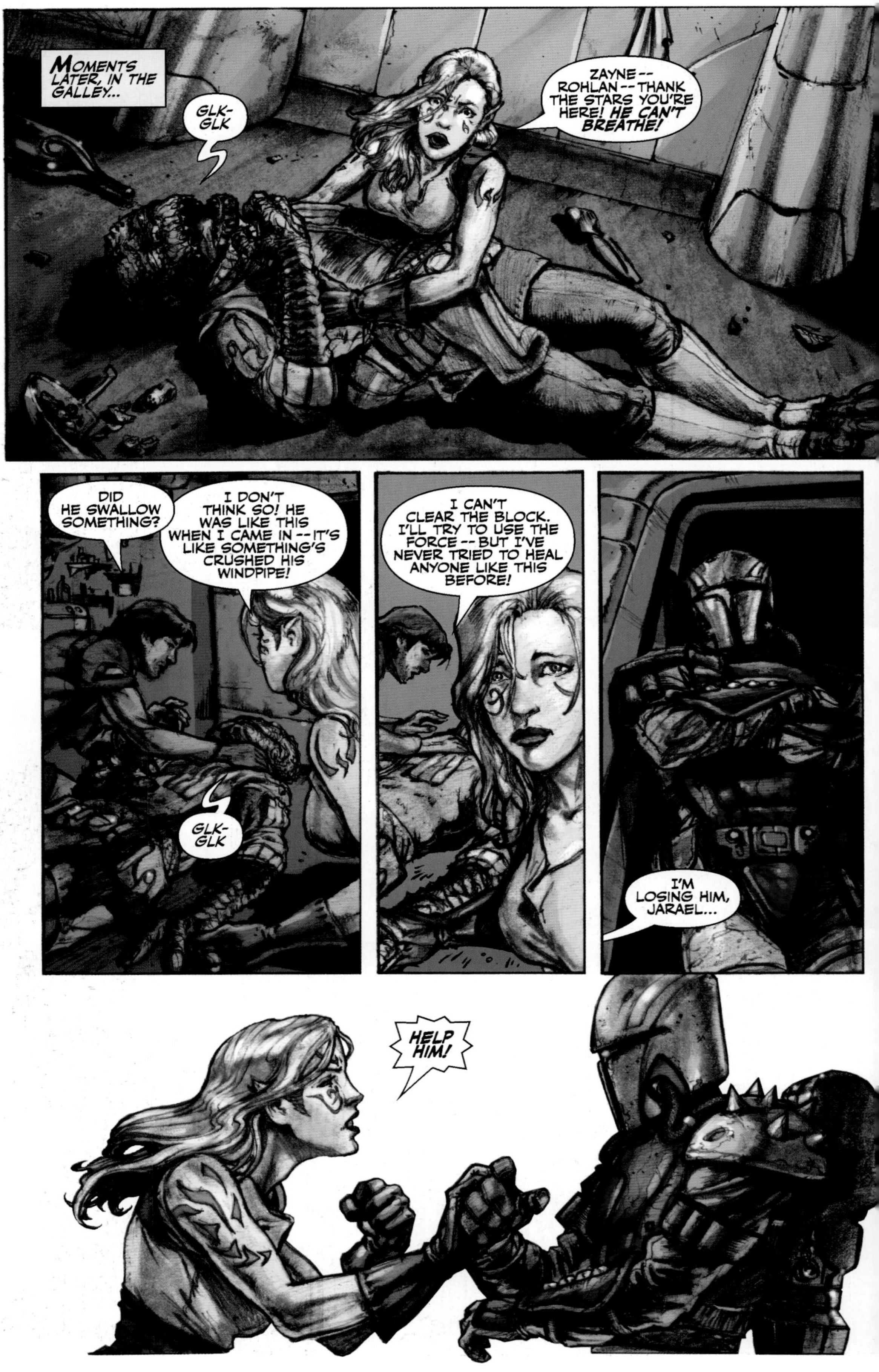
MOMENTS LATER, IN THE GALLEY...
GLK-GLK
ZAYNE-- ROHLAN--THANK THE STARS YOU'RE HERE! HE CAN'T BREATHE!
DID HE SWALLOW SOMETHING?
I DON'T THINK SO! HE WAS LIKE THIS WHEN I CAME IN--IT'S LIKE SOMETHING'S CRUSHED HIS WINDPIPE!
GLK-GLK
I CAN'T CLEAR THE BLOCK. I'LL TRY TO USE THE FORCE--BUT I'VE NEVER TRIED TO HEAL ANYONE LIKE THIS BEFORE!
I'M LOSING HIM, JARAEL...
HELP HIM!

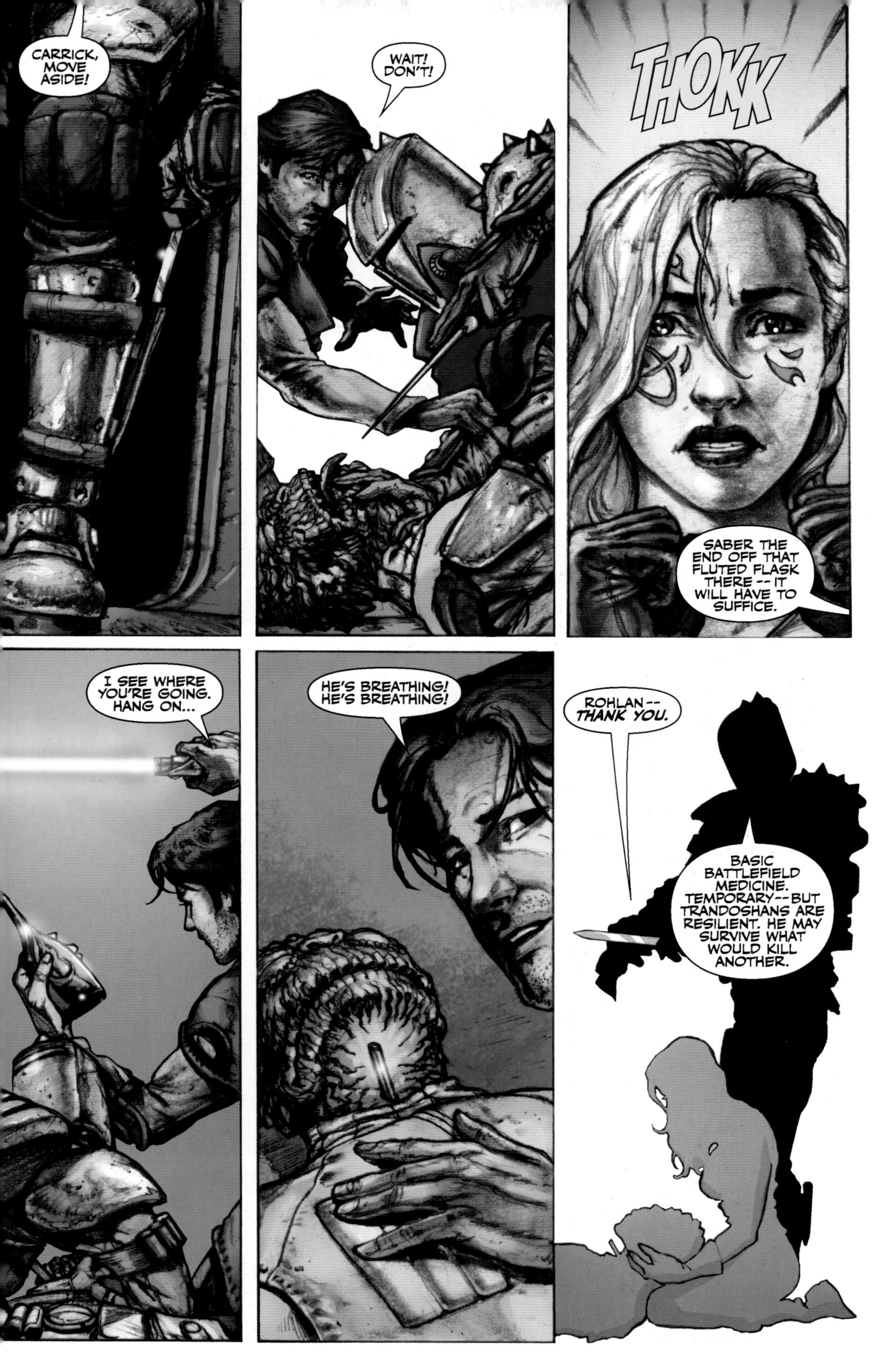
CARRICK, MOVE ASIDE!
WAIT! DON'T!
THOKK
SABER THE END OFF THAT FLUTED FLASK THERE -- IT WILL HAVE TO SUFFICE.
I SEE WHERE YOU'RE GOING. HANG ON...
HE'S BREATHING! HE'S BREATHING!
ROHLAN -- *THANK YOU.*
BASIC BATTLEFIELD MEDICINE. TEMPORARY -- BUT TRANDOSHANS ARE RESILIENT. HE MAY SURVIVE WHAT WOULD KILL ANOTHER.

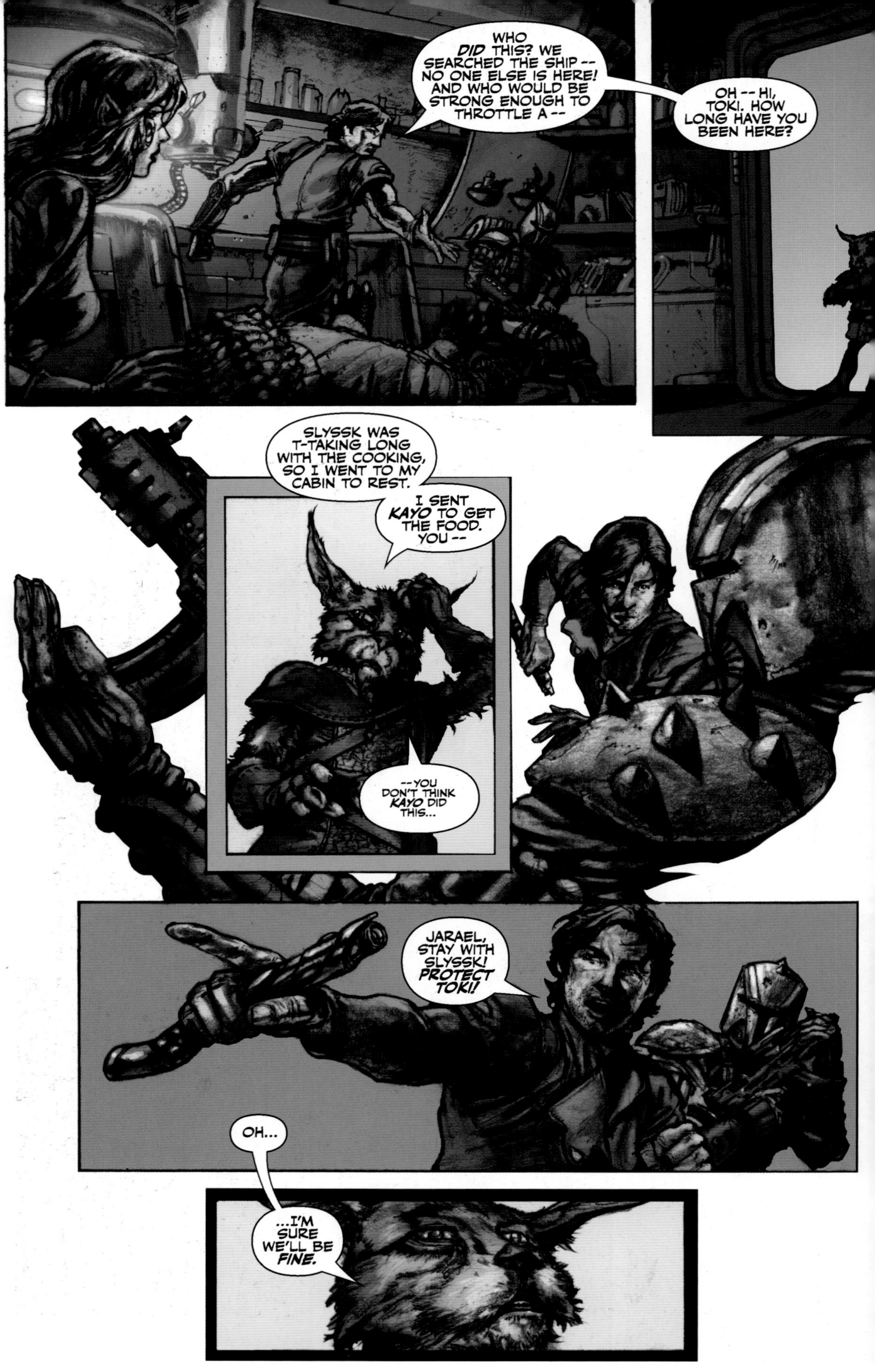

WHO *DID* THIS? WE SEARCHED THE SHIP -- NO ONE ELSE IS HERE! AND WHO WOULD BE STRONG ENOUGH TO THROTTLE A --
OH -- HI, TOKI. HOW LONG HAVE YOU BEEN HERE?
SLYSSK WAS T-TAKING LONG WITH THE COOKING, SO I WENT TO MY CABIN TO REST.
I SENT *KAYO* TO GET THE FOOD. YOU --
--YOU DON'T THINK *KAYO* DID THIS...
JARAEL, STAY WITH SLYSSK! *PROTECT TOKI!*
OH...
...I'M SURE WE'LL BE *FINE.*

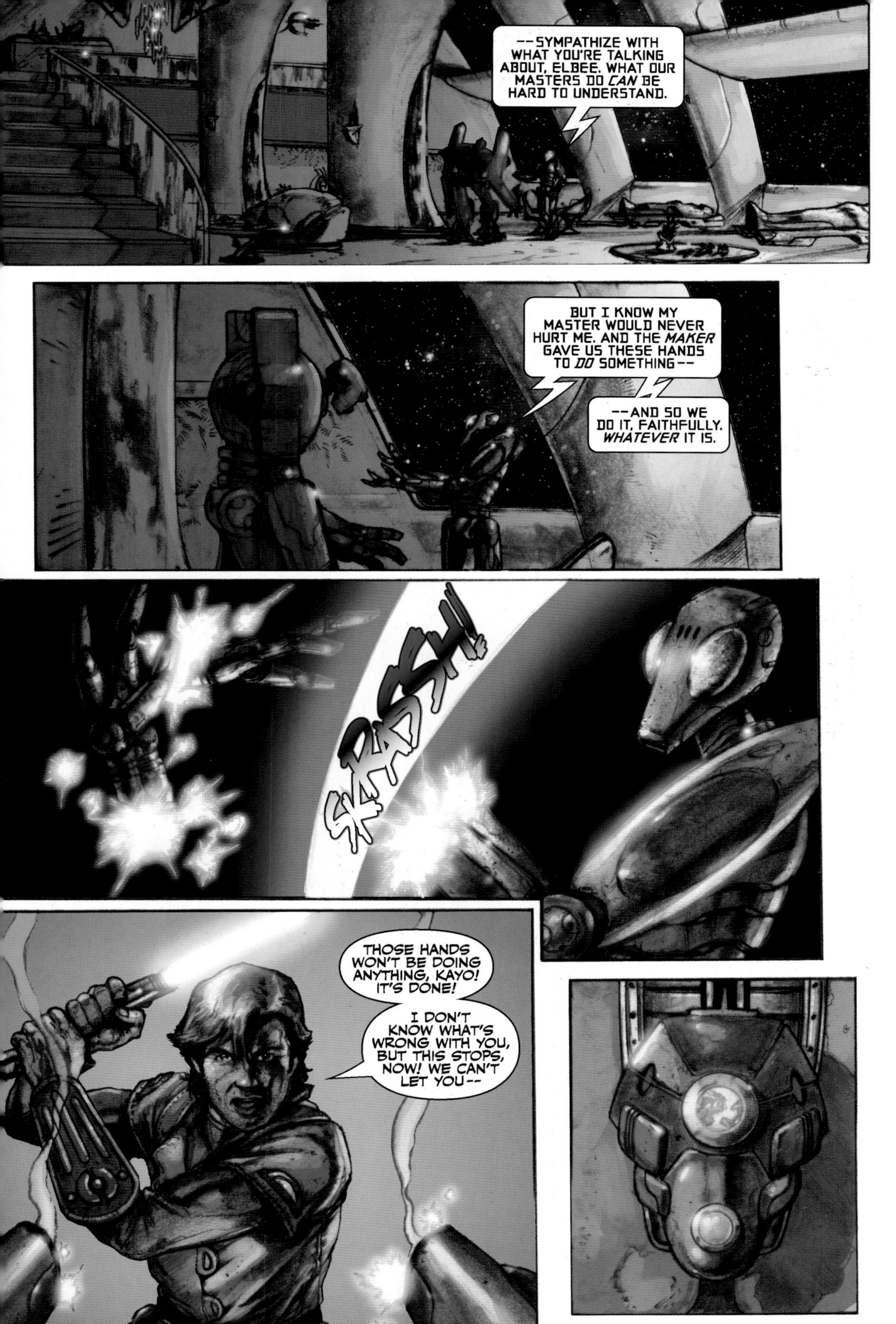
--SYMPATHIZE WITH WHAT YOU'RE TALKING ABOUT, ELBEE. WHAT OUR MASTERS DO *CAN* BE HARD TO UNDERSTAND.
BUT I KNOW MY MASTER WOULD NEVER HURT ME. AND THE *MAKER* GAVE US THESE HANDS TO *DO* SOMETHING--
--AND SO WE DO IT, FAITHFULLY. *WHATEVER* IT IS.
SKRASSH!!
THOSE HANDS WON'T BE DOING ANYTHING, KAYO! IT'S DONE!
I DON'T KNOW WHAT'S WRONG WITH YOU, BUT THIS STOPS, NOW! WE CAN'T LET YOU--

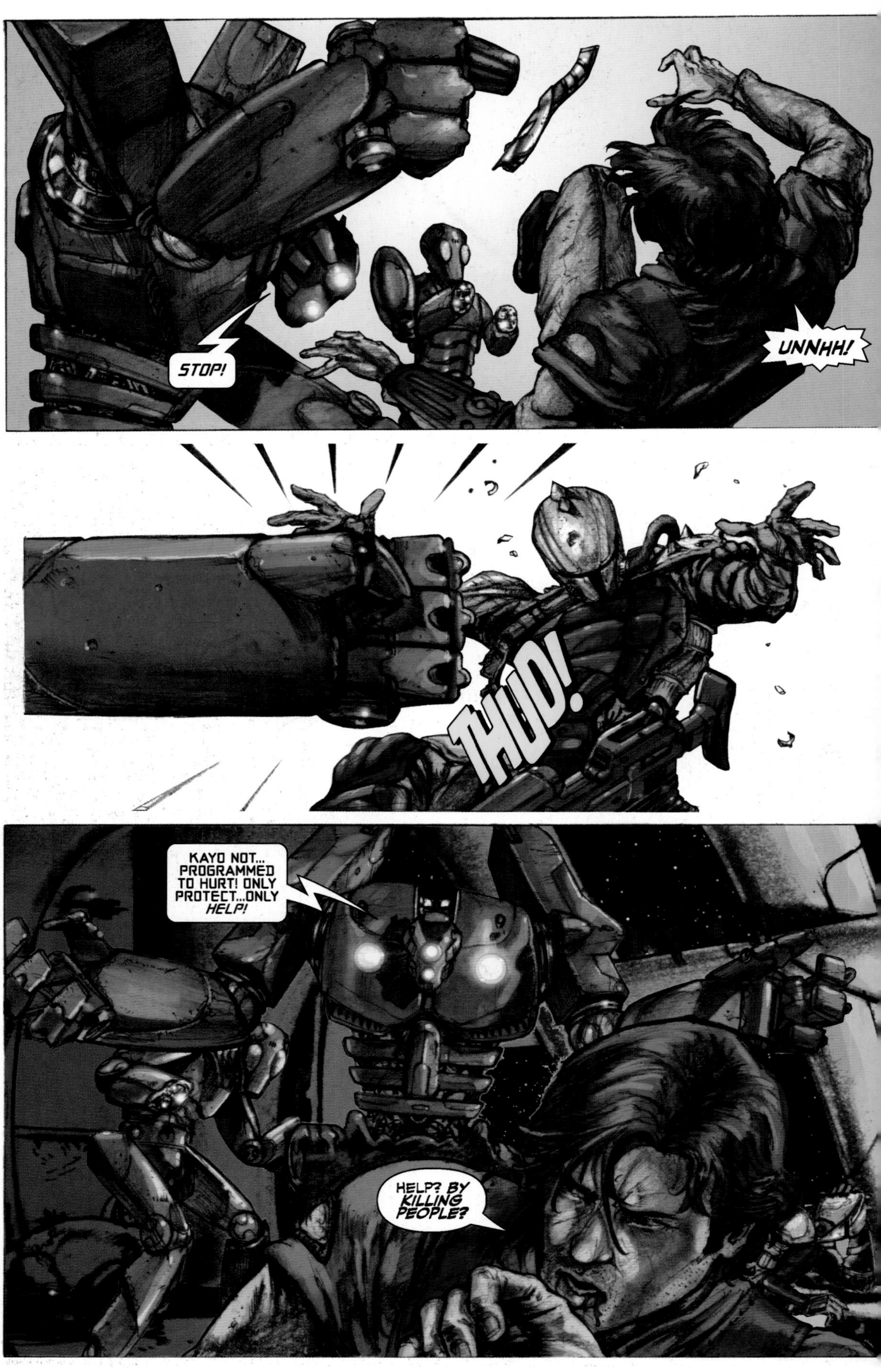
STOP!
UNNHH!
THUD!
KAYO NOT... PROGRAMMED TO HURT! ONLY PROTECT...ONLY HELP!
HELP? BY KILLING PEOPLE?

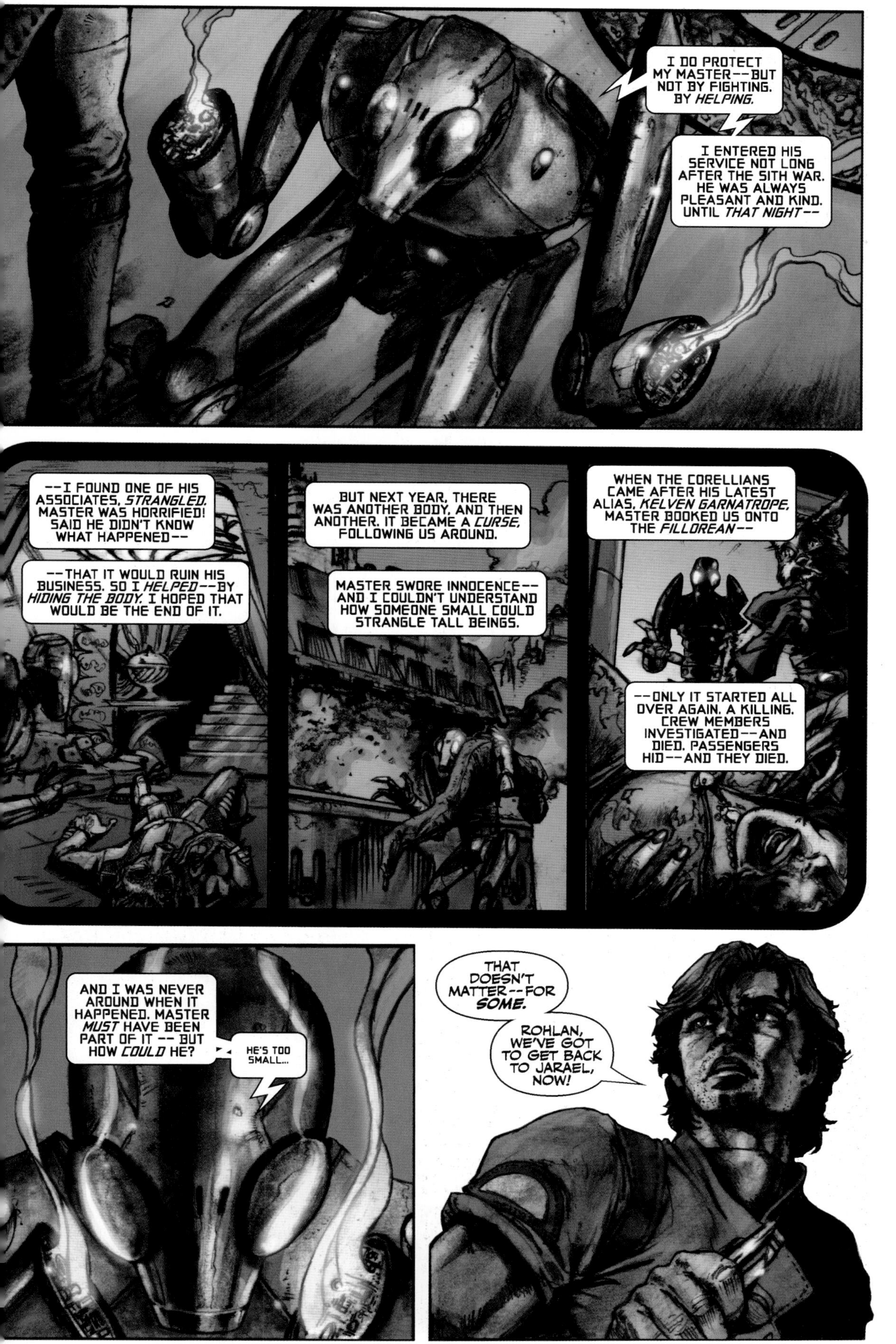
I DO PROTECT MY MASTER--BUT NOT BY FIGHTING. BY HELPING.
I ENTERED HIS SERVICE NOT LONG AFTER THE SITH WAR. HE WAS ALWAYS PLEASANT AND KIND. UNTIL THAT NIGHT--
--I FOUND ONE OF HIS ASSOCIATES, STRANGLED. MASTER WAS HORRIFIED! SAID HE DIDN'T KNOW WHAT HAPPENED--
--THAT IT WOULD RUIN HIS BUSINESS. SO I HELPED--BY HIDING THE BODY. I HOPED THAT WOULD BE THE END OF IT.
BUT NEXT YEAR, THERE WAS ANOTHER BODY, AND THEN ANOTHER. IT BECAME A CURSE, FOLLOWING US AROUND.
MASTER SWORE INNOCENCE--AND I COULDN'T UNDERSTAND HOW SOMEONE SMALL COULD STRANGLE TALL BEINGS.
WHEN THE CORELLIANS CAME AFTER HIS LATEST ALIAS, KELVEN GARNATROPE, MASTER BOOKED US ONTO THE FILLOREAN--
--ONLY IT STARTED ALL OVER AGAIN. A KILLING. CREW MEMBERS INVESTIGATED--AND DIED. PASSENGERS HID--AND THEY DIED.
AND I WAS NEVER AROUND WHEN IT HAPPENED. MASTER MUST HAVE BEEN PART OF IT -- BUT HOW COULD HE?
HE'S TOO SMALL...
THAT DOESN'T MATTER--FOR SOME.
ROHLAN, WE'VE GOT TO GET BACK TO JARAEL, NOW!

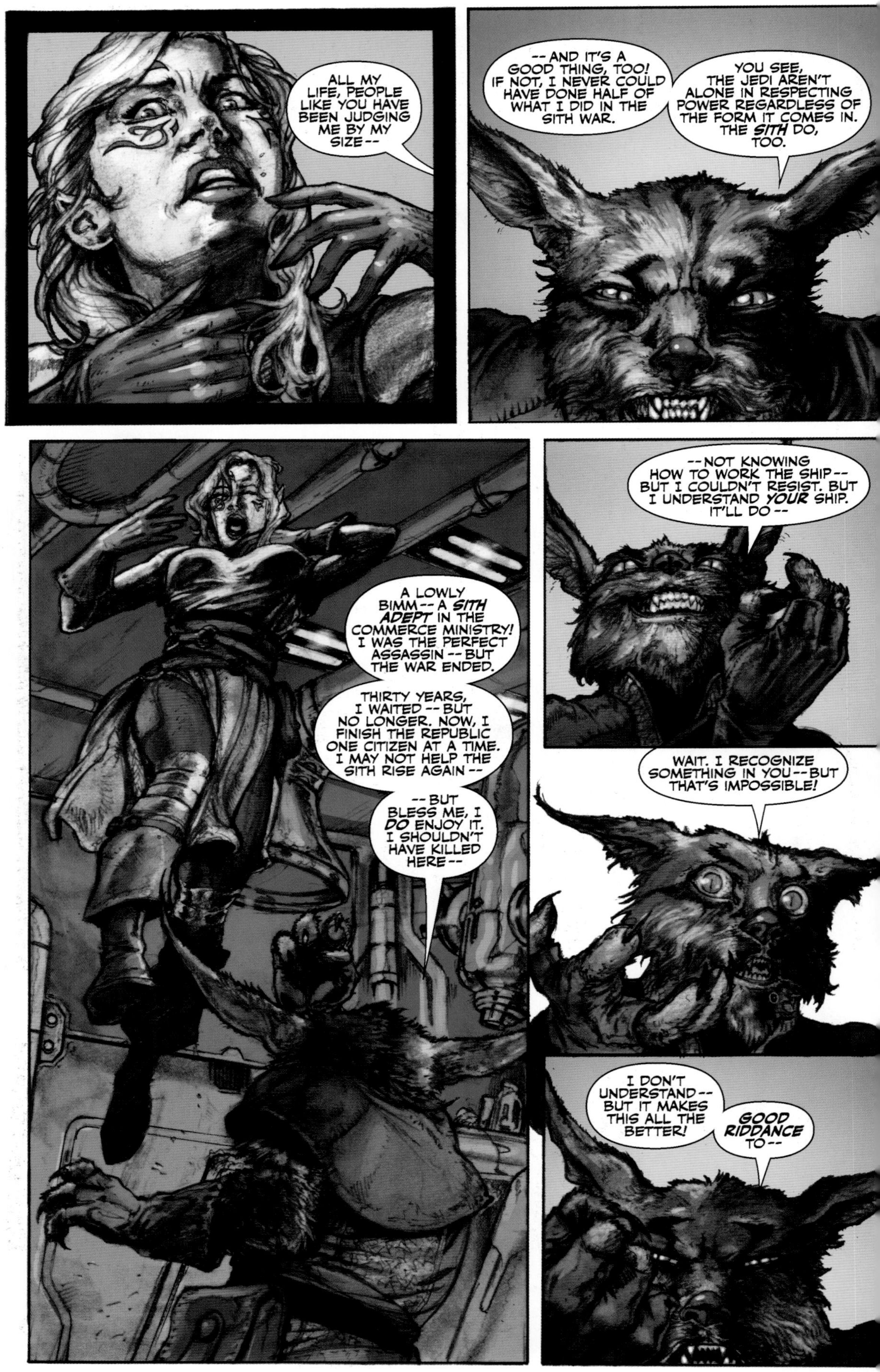
ALL MY LIFE, PEOPLE LIKE YOU HAVE BEEN JUDGING ME BY MY SIZE--
--AND IT'S A GOOD THING, TOO! IF NOT, I NEVER COULD HAVE DONE HALF OF WHAT I DID IN THE SITH WAR.
YOU SEE, THE JEDI AREN'T ALONE IN RESPECTING POWER REGARDLESS OF THE FORM IT COMES IN. THE SITH DO, TOO.
A LOWLY BIMM--A SITH ADEPT IN THE COMMERCE MINISTRY! I WAS THE PERFECT ASSASSIN--BUT THE WAR ENDED.
THIRTY YEARS, I WAITED--BUT NO LONGER. NOW, I FINISH THE REPUBLIC ONE CITIZEN AT A TIME. I MAY NOT HELP THE SITH RISE AGAIN--
--BUT BLESS ME, I DO ENJOY IT. I SHOULDN'T HAVE KILLED HERE--
--NOT KNOWING HOW TO WORK THE SHIP--BUT I COULDN'T RESIST. BUT I UNDERSTAND YOUR SHIP. IT'LL DO--
WAIT. I RECOGNIZE SOMETHING IN YOU--BUT THAT'S IMPOSSIBLE!
I DON'T UNDERSTAND--BUT IT MAKES THIS ALL THE BETTER!
GOOD RIDDANCE TO--

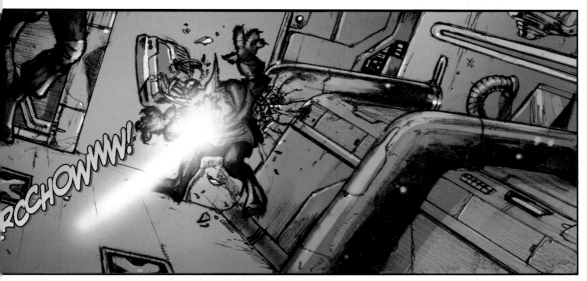

RCCHOWWW!

BACK OFF, TOKI -- OR WHOEVER YOU ARE!

ROHLAN, GET HER OUT OF HERE!

THIS GETS BETTER AND BETTER. I HAVEN'T KILLED A PROPER JEDI IN YEARS.

BUT YOU'RE A LITTLE *TOO* PROPER, YOUNGLING. IF YOU WANT TO TAKE *ME* DOWN WITH A BLASTER --

-- YOU'D BETTER SHOOT TO *KILL!*

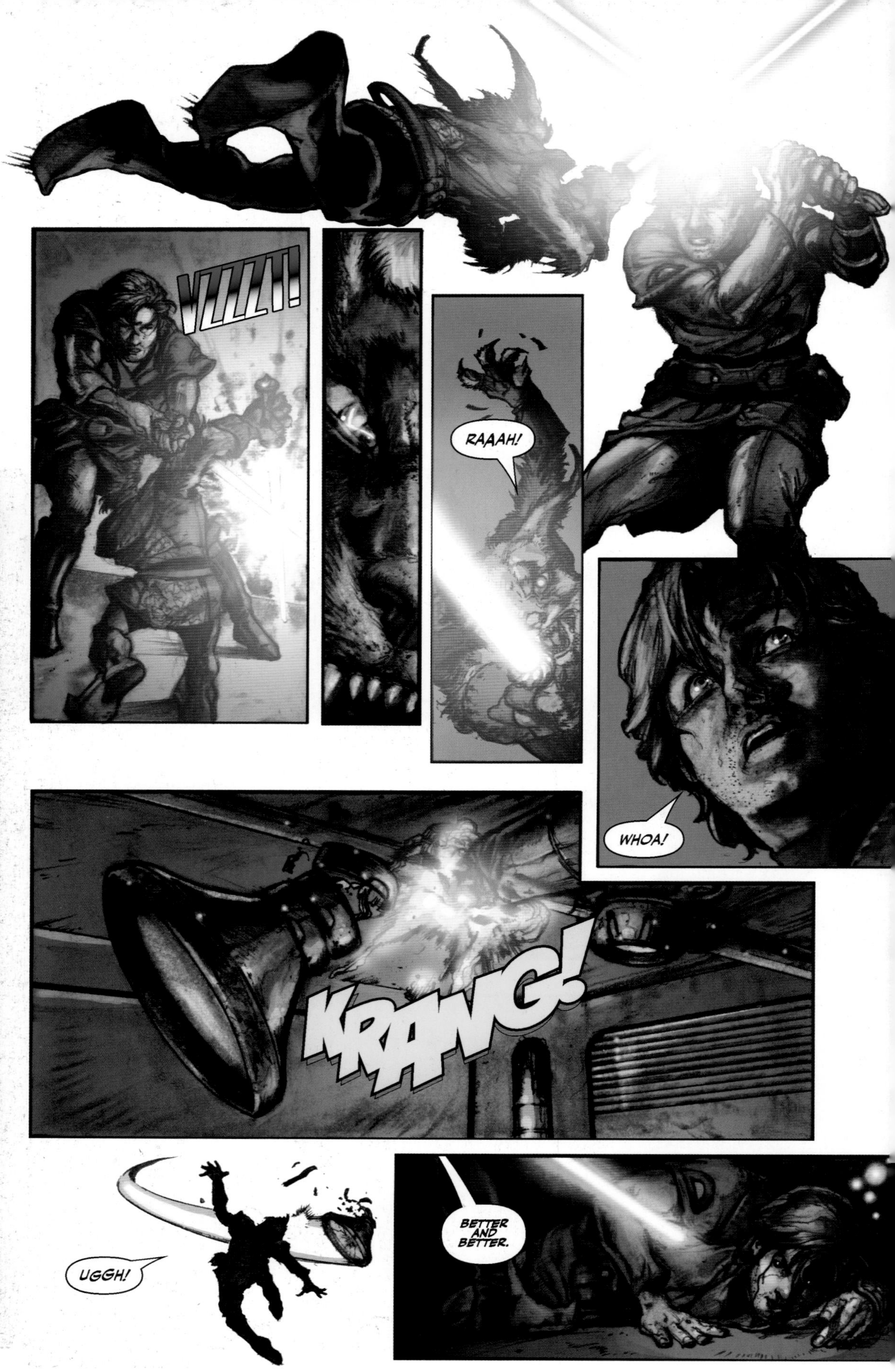
VZZZZT!
RAAAH!
WHOA!
KRANG!
UGGH!
BETTER AND BETTER.

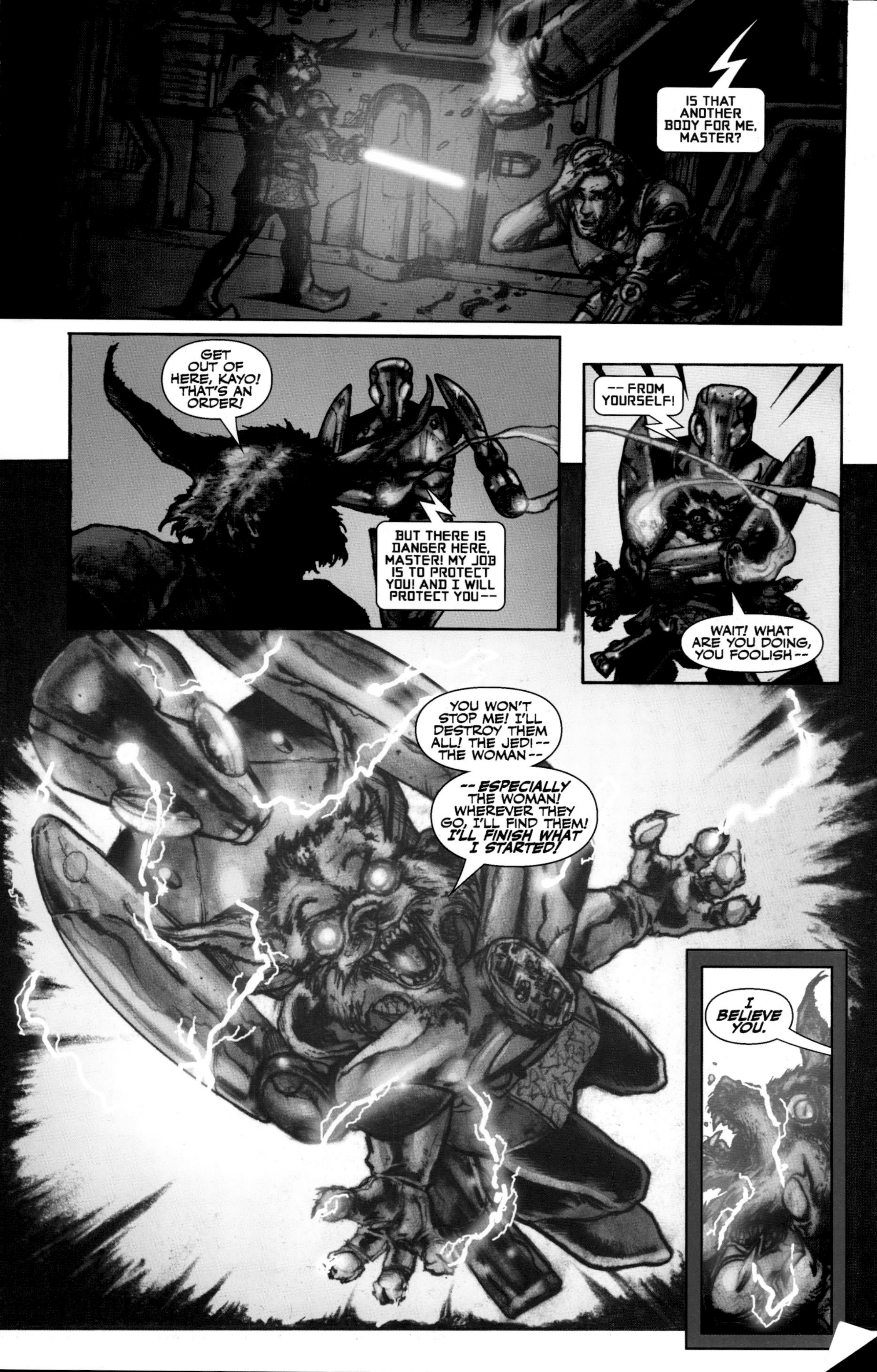
IS THAT ANOTHER BODY FOR ME, MASTER?
GET OUT OF HERE, KAYO! THAT'S AN ORDER!
BUT THERE IS DANGER HERE, MASTER! MY JOB IS TO PROTECT YOU! AND I WILL PROTECT YOU--
--FROM YOURSELF!
WAIT! WHAT ARE YOU DOING, YOU FOOLISH--
YOU WON'T STOP ME! I'LL DESTROY THEM ALL! THE JEDI-- THE WOMAN--
--ESPECIALLY THE WOMAN! WHEREVER THEY GO, I'LL FIND THEM! I'LL FINISH WHAT I STARTED!
I BELIEVE YOU.

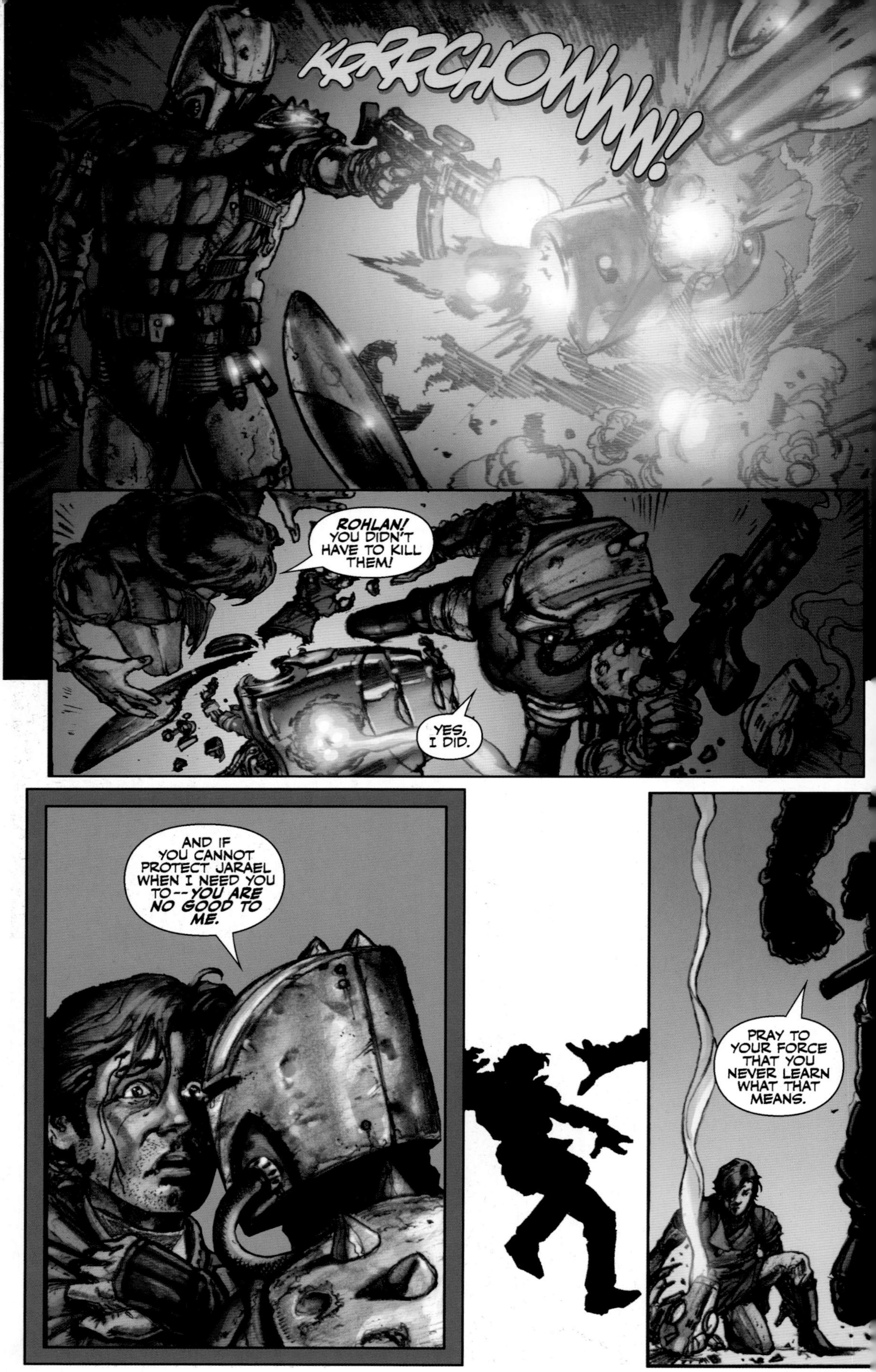
KRRRCHOWWW!!
ROHLAN! YOU DIDN'T HAVE TO KILL THEM!
YES, I DID.
AND IF YOU CANNOT PROTECT JARAEL WHEN I NEED YOU TO--YOU ARE NO GOOD TO ME.
PRAY TO YOUR FORCE THAT YOU NEVER LEARN WHAT THAT MEANS.

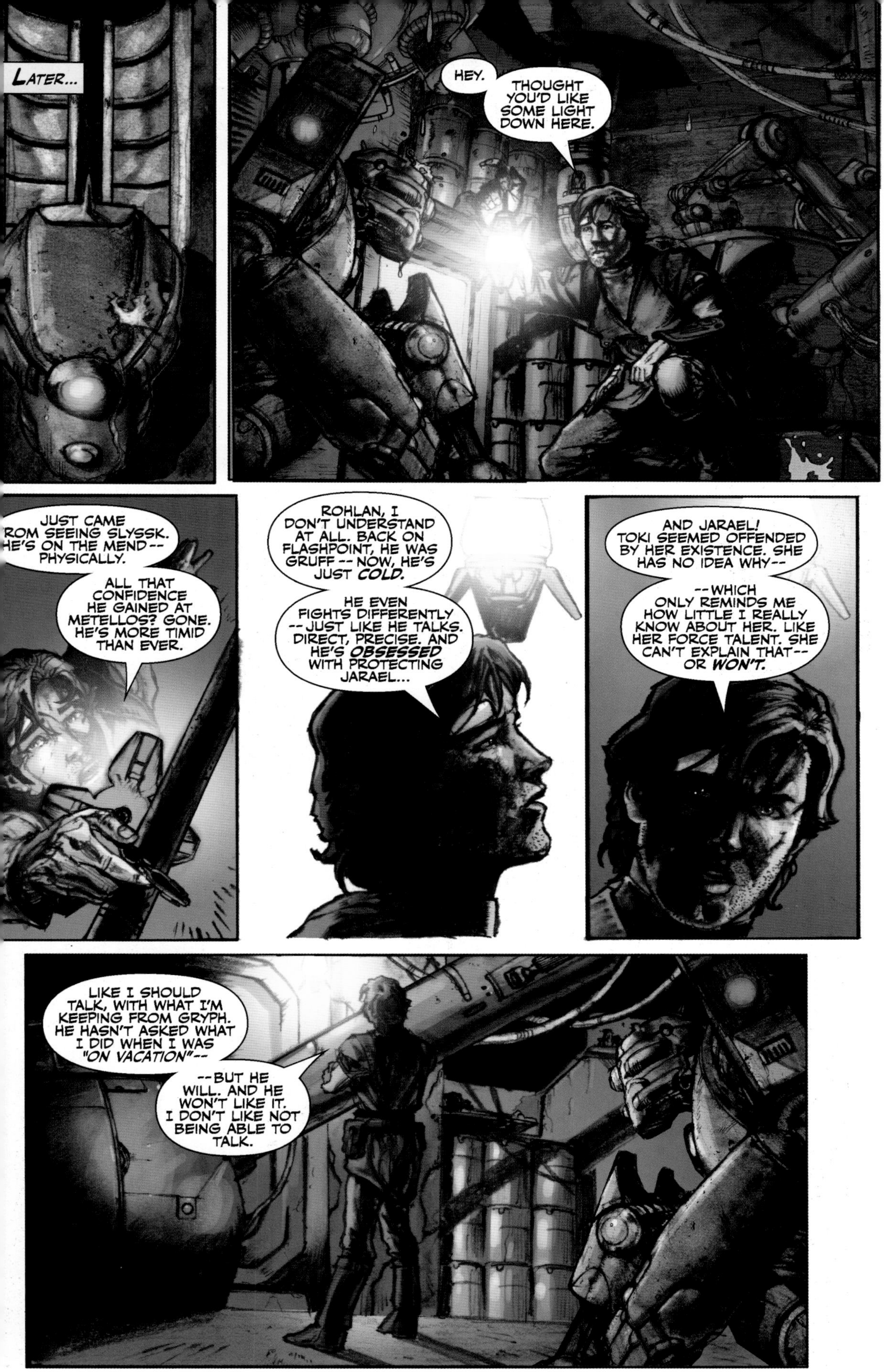
LATER...
HEY.
THOUGHT YOU'D LIKE SOME LIGHT DOWN HERE.
JUST CAME FROM SEEING SLYSSK. HE'S ON THE MEND-- PHYSICALLY.
ALL THAT CONFIDENCE HE GAINED AT METELLOS? GONE. HE'S MORE TIMID THAN EVER.
ROHLAN, I DON'T UNDERSTAND AT ALL. BACK ON FLASHPOINT, HE WAS GRUFF -- NOW, HE'S JUST *COLD.*
HE EVEN FIGHTS DIFFERENTLY -- JUST LIKE HE TALKS. DIRECT, PRECISE. AND HE'S *OBSESSED* WITH PROTECTING JARAEL...
AND JARAEL! TOKI SEEMED OFFENDED BY HER EXISTENCE. SHE HAS NO IDEA WHY--
--WHICH ONLY REMINDS ME HOW LITTLE I REALLY KNOW ABOUT HER. LIKE HER FORCE TALENT. SHE CAN'T EXPLAIN THAT-- OR *WON'T.*
LIKE I SHOULD TALK, WITH WHAT I'M KEEPING FROM GRYPH. HE HASN'T ASKED WHAT I DID WHEN I WAS *"ON VACATION"*--
--BUT HE WILL. AND HE WON'T LIKE IT. I DON'T LIKE NOT BEING ABLE TO TALK.

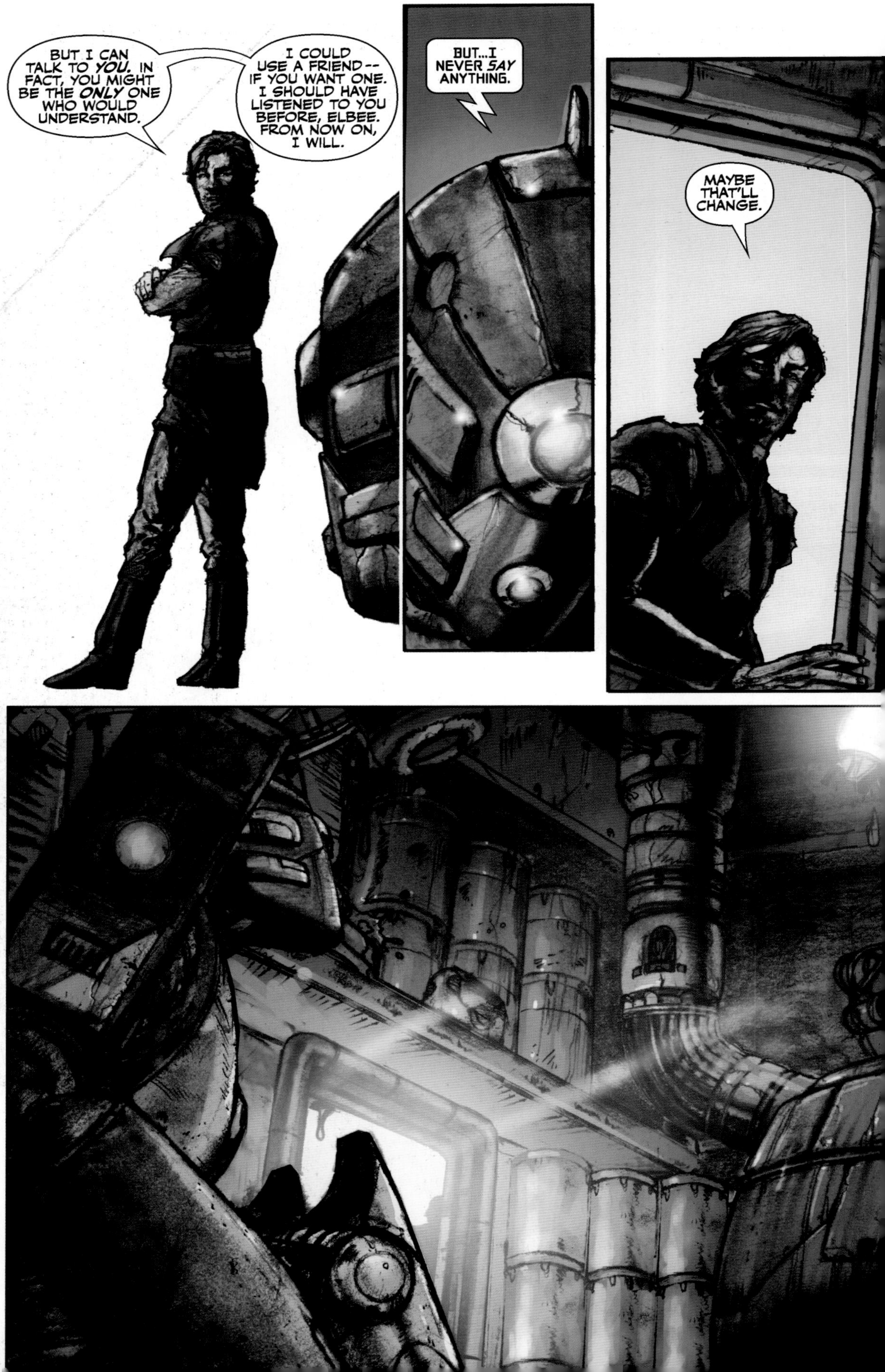
BUT I CAN TALK TO YOU. IN FACT, YOU MIGHT BE THE ONLY ONE WHO WOULD UNDERSTAND.
I COULD USE A FRIEND-- IF YOU WANT ONE. I SHOULD HAVE LISTENED TO YOU BEFORE, ELBEE. FROM NOW ON, I WILL.
BUT...I NEVER SAY ANYTHING.
MAYBE THAT'LL CHANGE.

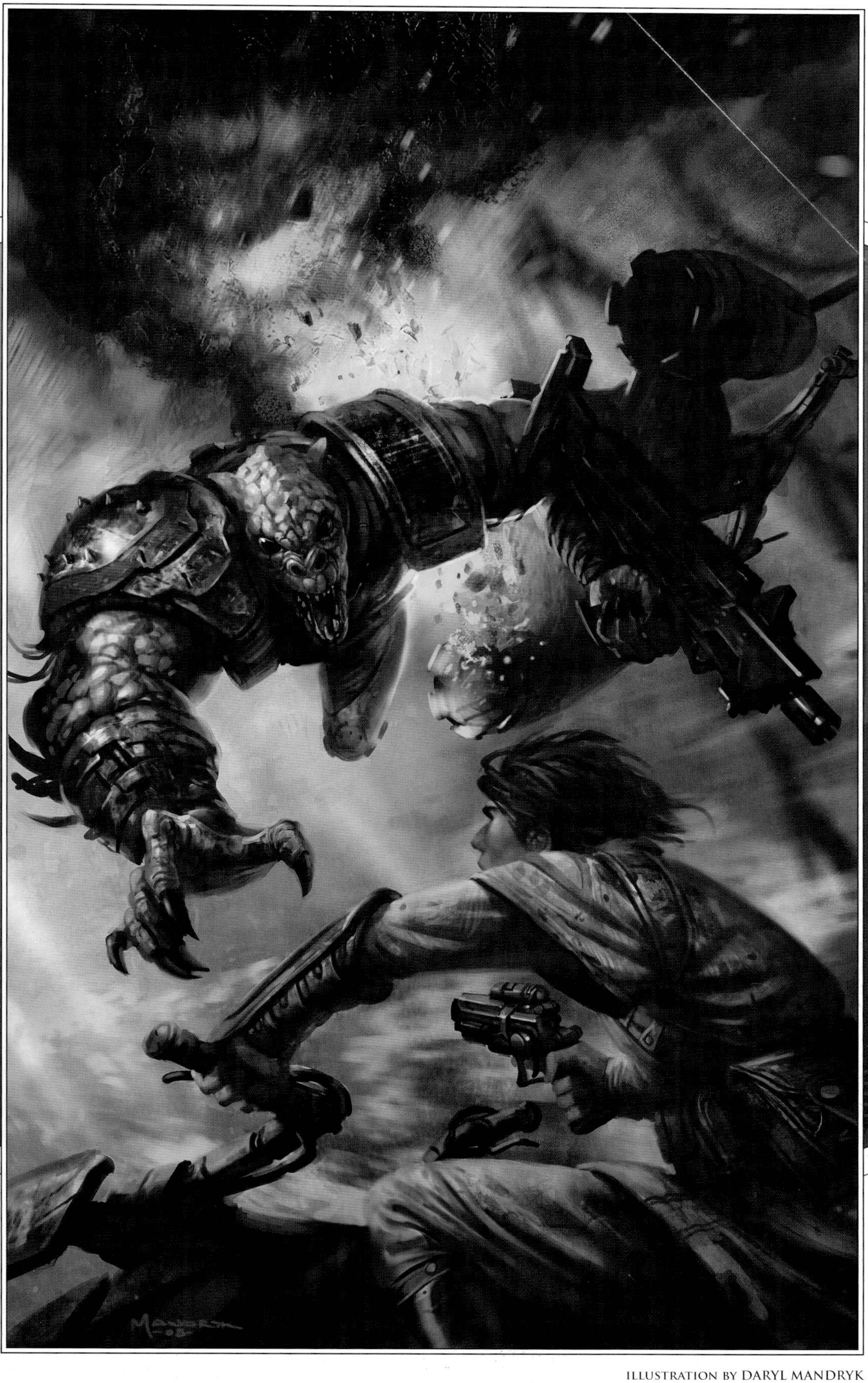

ILLUSTRATION BY DARYL MANDRYK

DUELING AMBITIONS

art by Brian Ching

Young Zayne Carrick continues his path to a new life—as a free agent seeking fortune. While the Mandalorian Wars still rage on the frontier, opportunities abound in the Core Worlds.

But all is not well with his companions. Refusing to remove his Mandalorian armor, Rohlan cannot move freely in the Republic. And Jarael displays newfound Force powers, reminding Zayne how little he knows about her past.

Even Zayne has mysterious plans of his own. But before he can advance them, his crafty partner Gryph calls with an invitation— one that reminds him of a dream he had long forgotten . . .

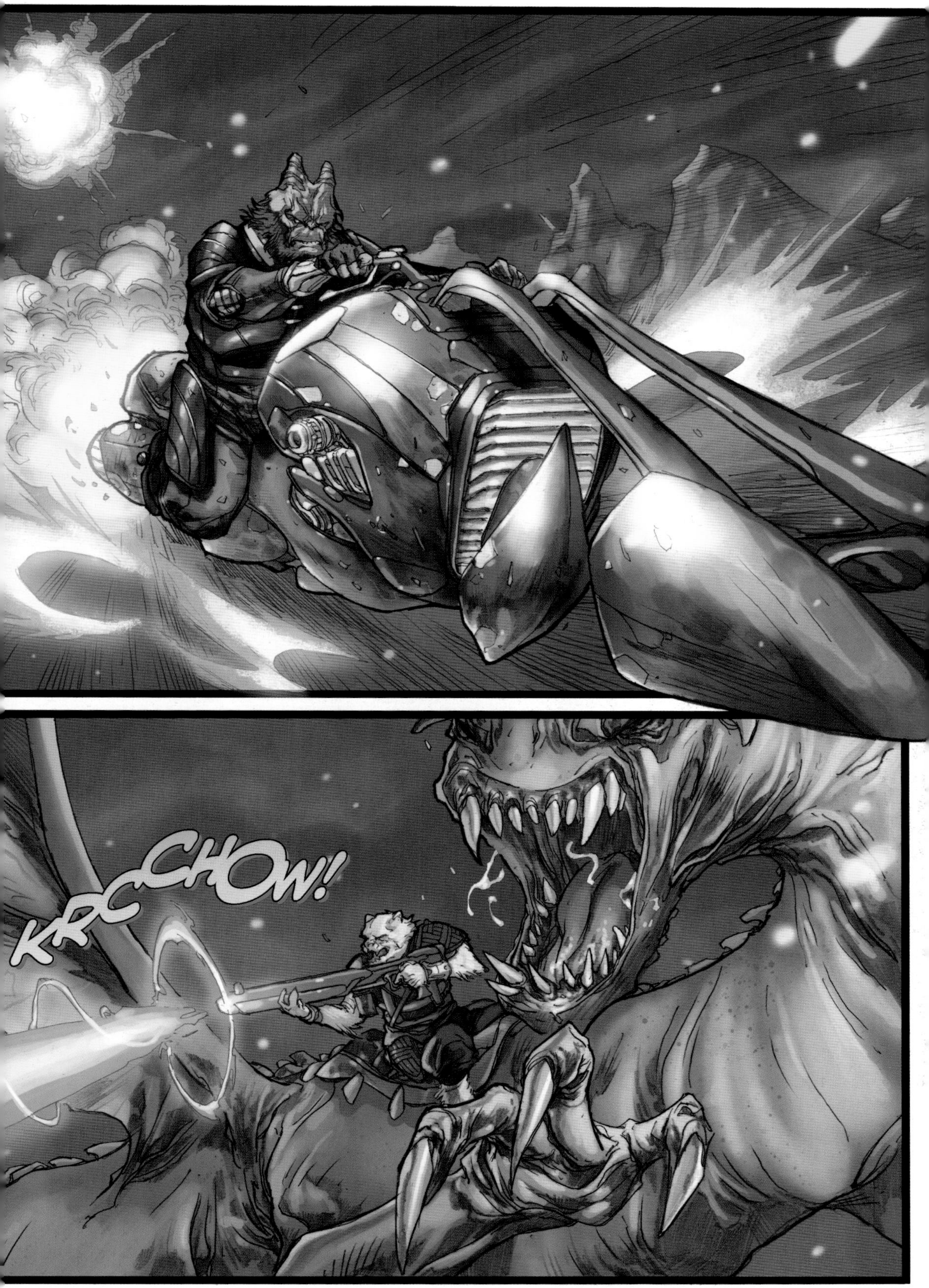
KRCCHOW!

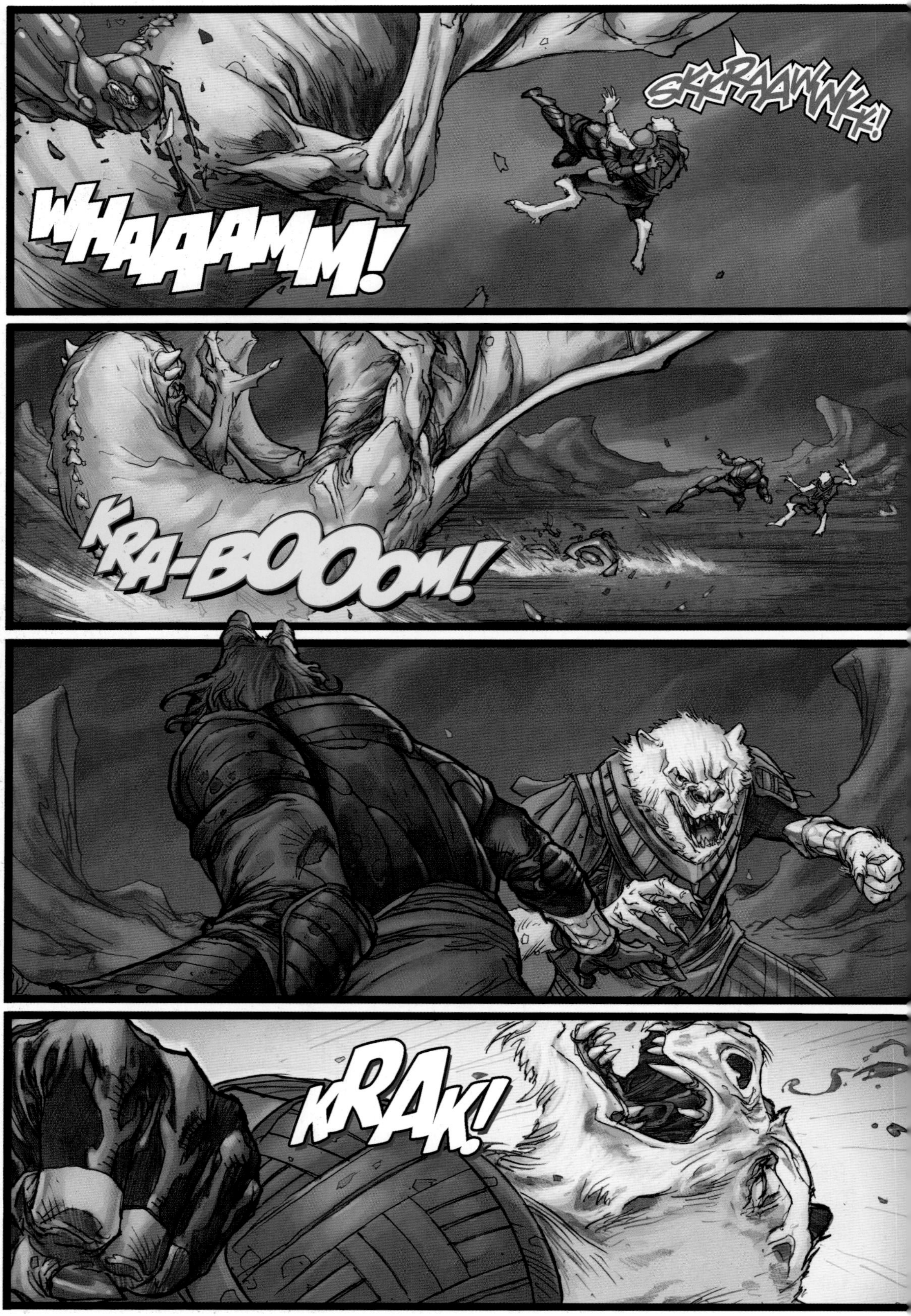

SKKRAAWWKK!
WHAAAAMM!
KRA-BOOOOM!
KRAK!

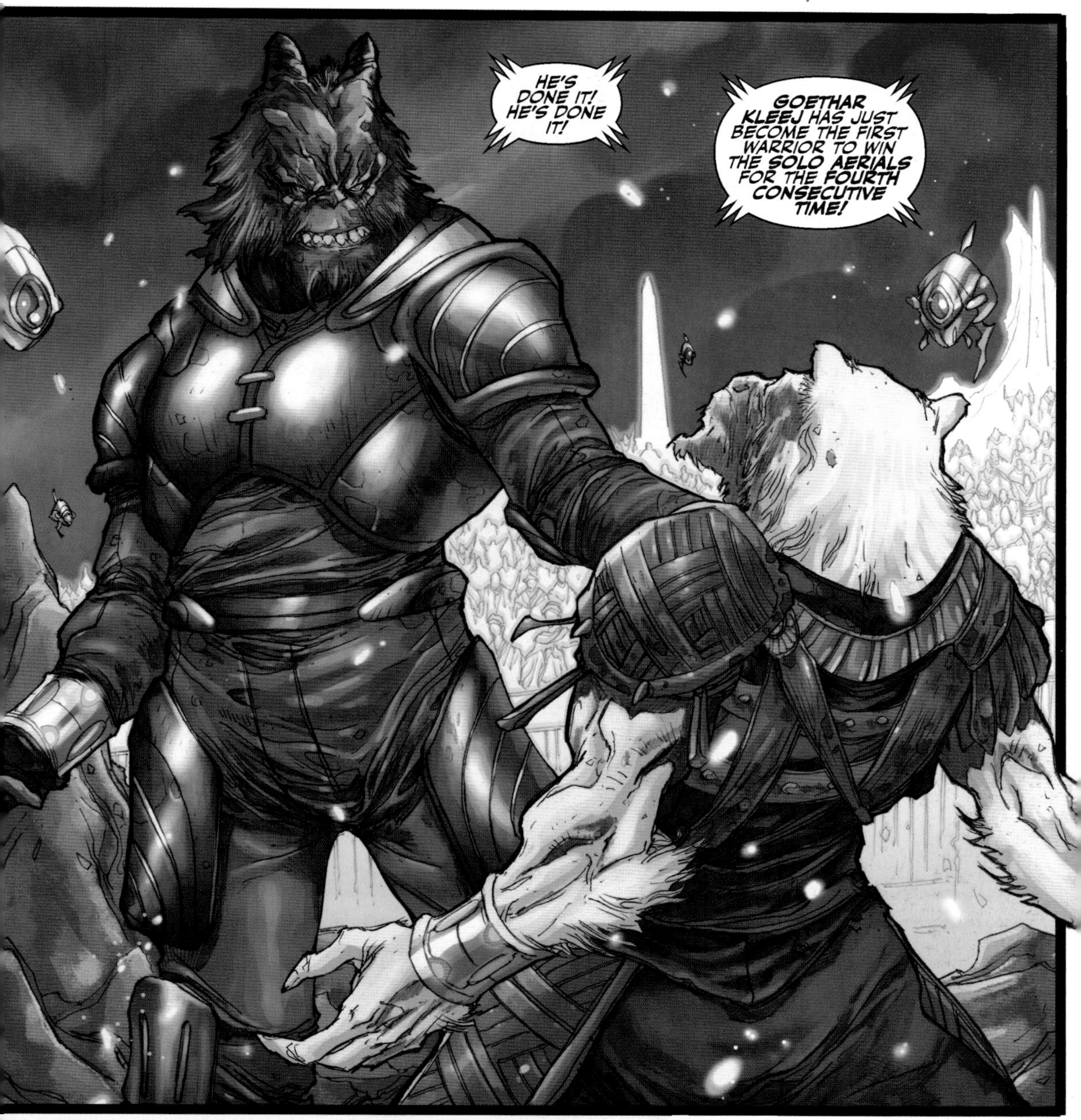
HE'S DONE IT! HE'S DONE IT!
GOETHAR KLEEJ HAS JUST BECOME THE FIRST WARRIOR TO WIN THE SOLO AERIALS FOR THE FOURTH CONSECUTIVE TIME!

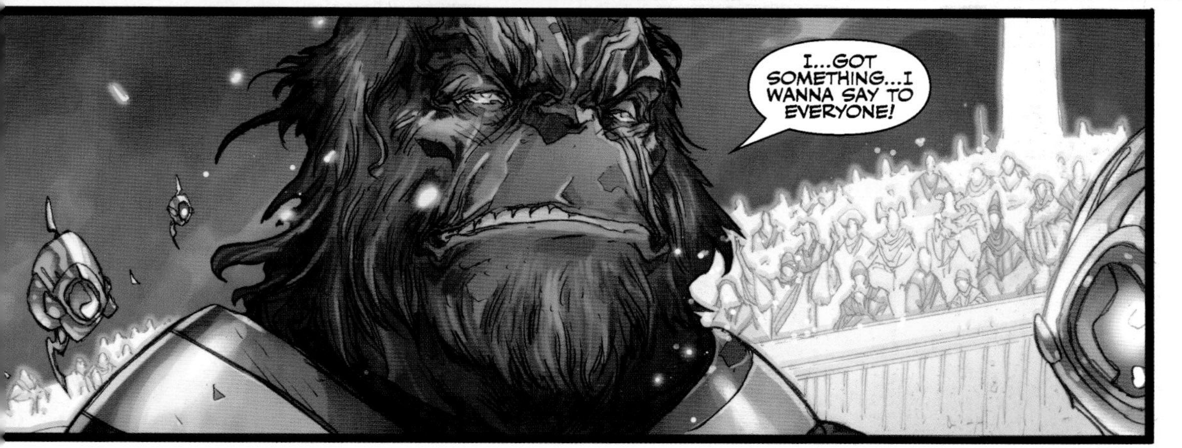
I...GOT SOMETHING...I WANNA SAY TO EVERYONE!

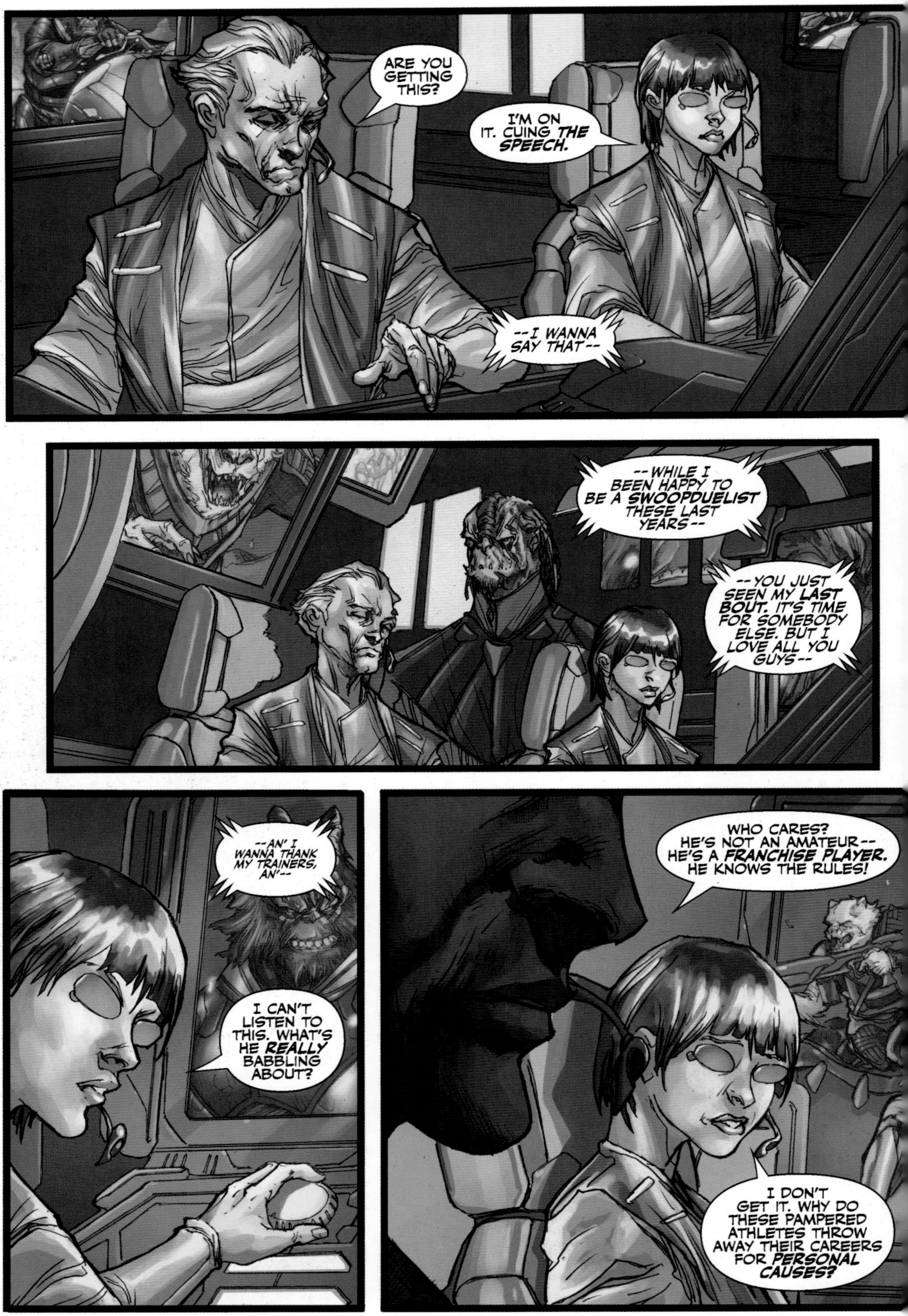
ARE YOU GETTING THIS?
I'M ON IT. CUING THE SPEECH.
--I WANNA SAY THAT--
--WHILE I BEEN HAPPY TO BE A SWOOPDUELIST THESE LAST YEARS--
--YOU JUST SEEN MY LAST BOUT. IT'S TIME FOR SOMEBODY ELSE. BUT I LOVE ALL YOU GUYS--
--AN' I WANNA THANK MY TRAINERS, AN'--
I CAN'T LISTEN TO THIS. WHAT'S HE REALLY BABBLING ABOUT?
WHO CARES? HE'S NOT AN AMATEUR--HE'S A FRANCHISE PLAYER. HE KNOWS THE RULES!
I DON'T GET IT. WHY DO THESE PAMPERED ATHLETES THROW AWAY THEIR CAREERS FOR PERSONAL CAUSES?

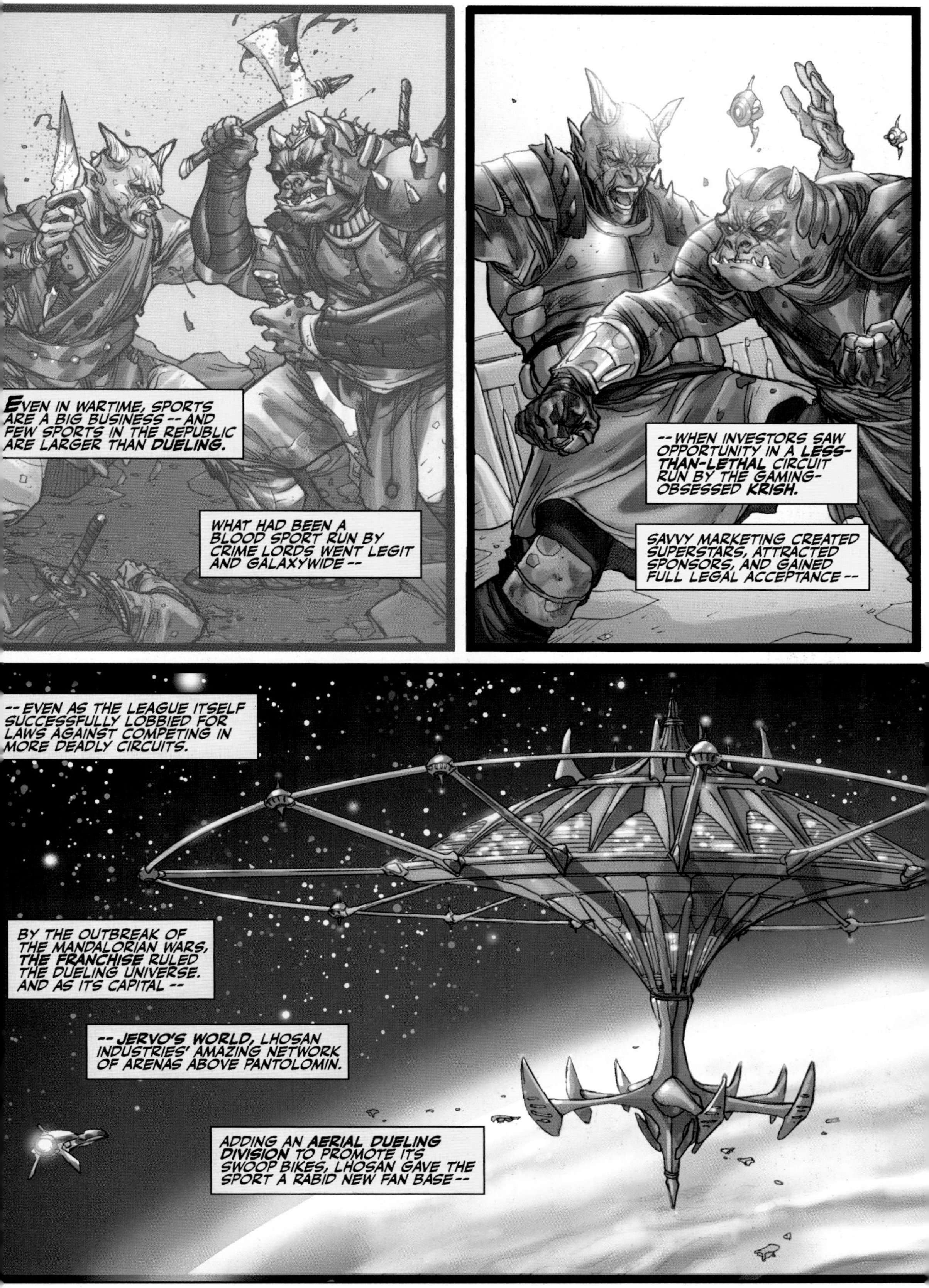
EVEN IN WARTIME, SPORTS ARE A BIG BUSINESS -- AND FEW SPORTS IN THE REPUBLIC ARE LARGER THAN DUELING.
WHAT HAD BEEN A BLOOD SPORT RUN BY CRIME LORDS WENT LEGIT AND GALAXYWIDE --
-- WHEN INVESTORS SAW OPPORTUNITY IN A LESS-THAN-LETHAL CIRCUIT RUN BY THE GAMING-OBSESSED KRISH.
SAVVY MARKETING CREATED SUPERSTARS, ATTRACTED SPONSORS, AND GAINED FULL LEGAL ACCEPTANCE --
-- EVEN AS THE LEAGUE ITSELF SUCCESSFULLY LOBBIED FOR LAWS AGAINST COMPETING IN MORE DEADLY CIRCUITS.
BY THE OUTBREAK OF THE MANDALORIAN WARS, THE FRANCHISE RULED THE DUELING UNIVERSE. AND AS ITS CAPITAL --
-- JERVO'S WORLD, LHOSAN INDUSTRIES' AMAZING NETWORK OF ARENAS ABOVE PANTOLOMIN.
ADDING AN AERIAL DUELING DIVISION TO PROMOTE ITS SWOOP BIKES, LHOSAN GAVE THE SPORT A RABID NEW FAN BASE --

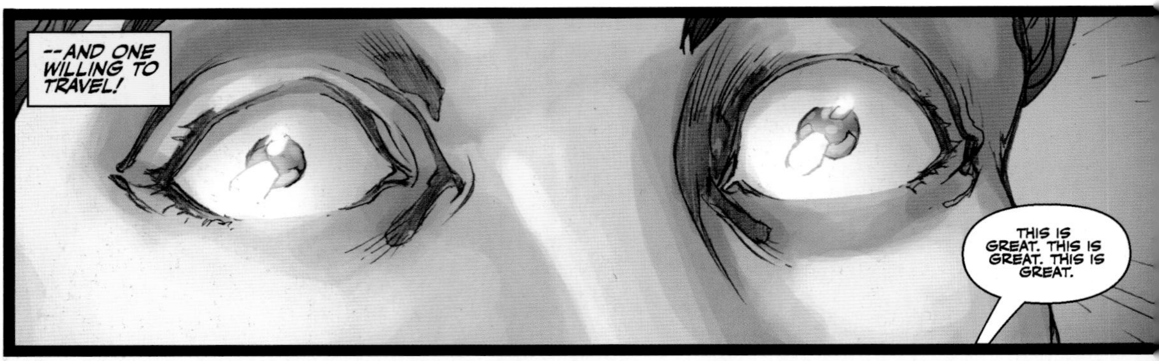
--AND ONE WILLING TO TRAVEL!
THIS IS GREAT. THIS IS GREAT. THIS IS GREAT.

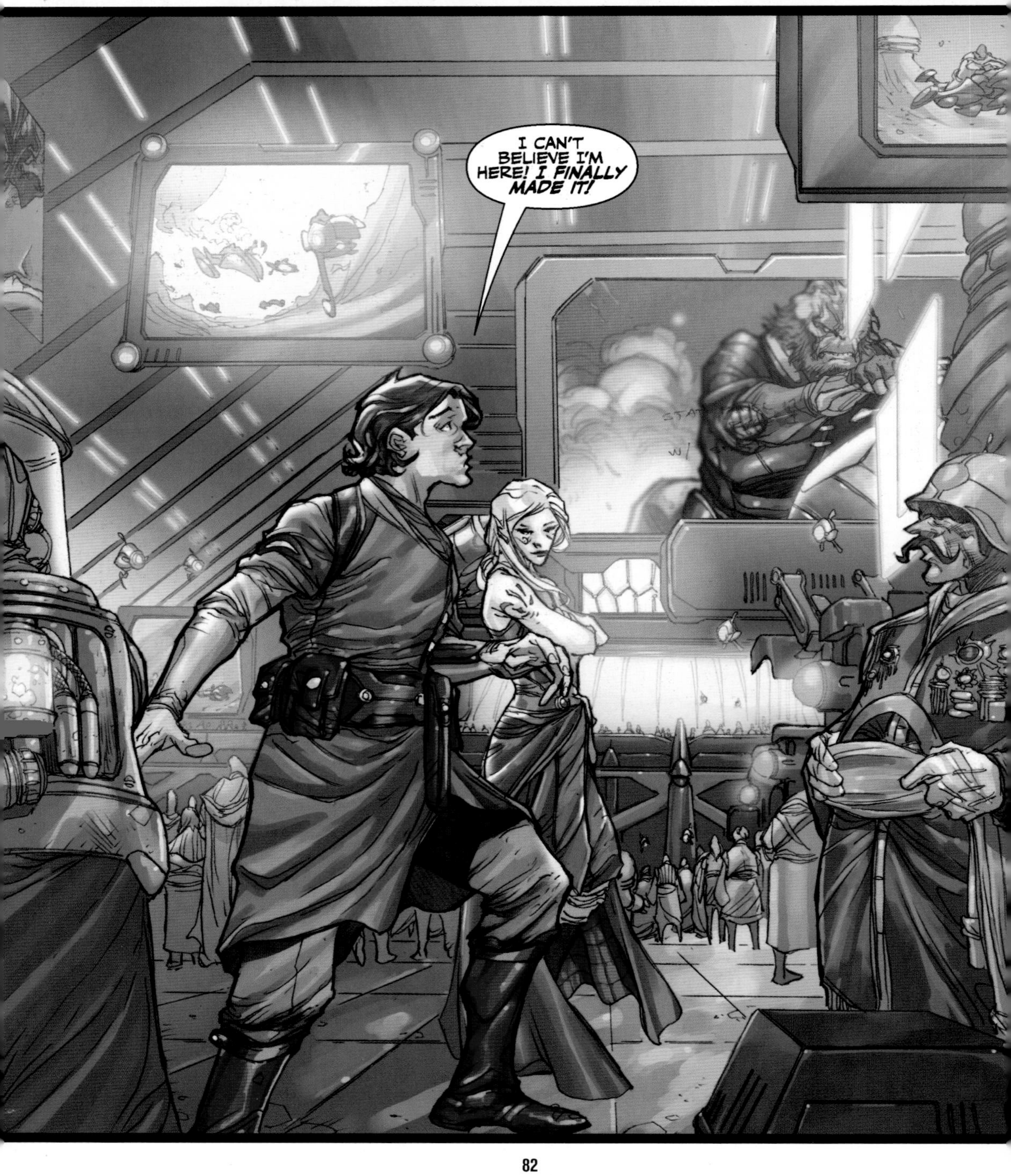
I CAN'T BELIEVE I'M HERE! I FINALLY MADE IT!

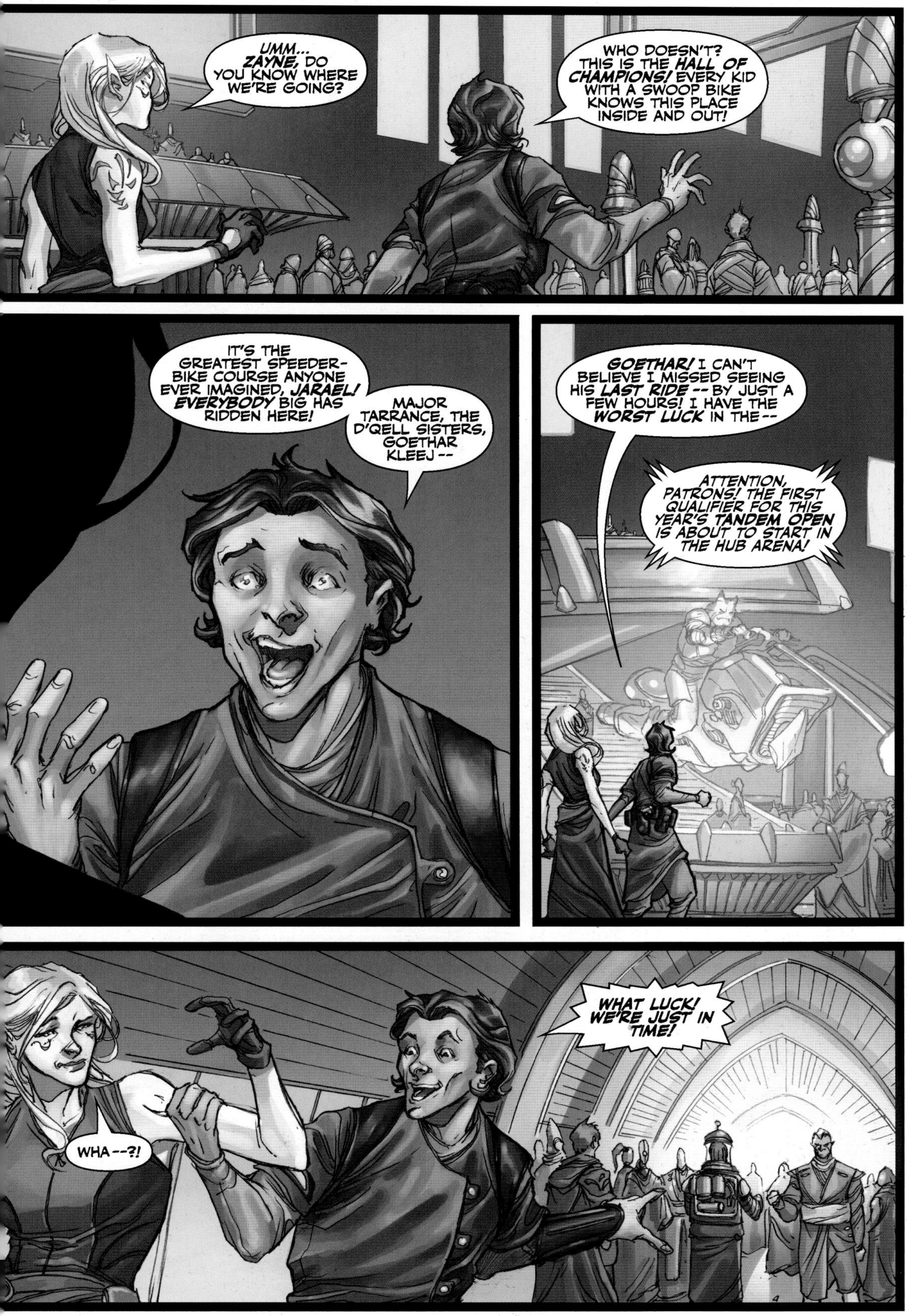
UMM... ZAYNE, DO YOU KNOW WHERE WE'RE GOING?
WHO DOESN'T? THIS IS THE HALL OF CHAMPIONS! EVERY KID WITH A SWOOP BIKE KNOWS THIS PLACE INSIDE AND OUT!
IT'S THE GREATEST SPEEDER-BIKE COURSE ANYONE EVER IMAGINED, JARAEL! EVERYBODY BIG HAS RIDDEN HERE!
MAJOR TARRANCE, THE D'QELL SISTERS, GOETHAR KLEEJ --
GOETHAR! I CAN'T BELIEVE I MISSED SEEING HIS LAST RIDE -- BY JUST A FEW HOURS! I HAVE THE WORST LUCK IN THE --
ATTENTION, PATRONS! THE FIRST QUALIFIER FOR THIS YEAR'S TANDEM OPEN IS ABOUT TO START IN THE HUB ARENA!
WHAT LUCK! WE'RE JUST IN TIME!
WHA --?!

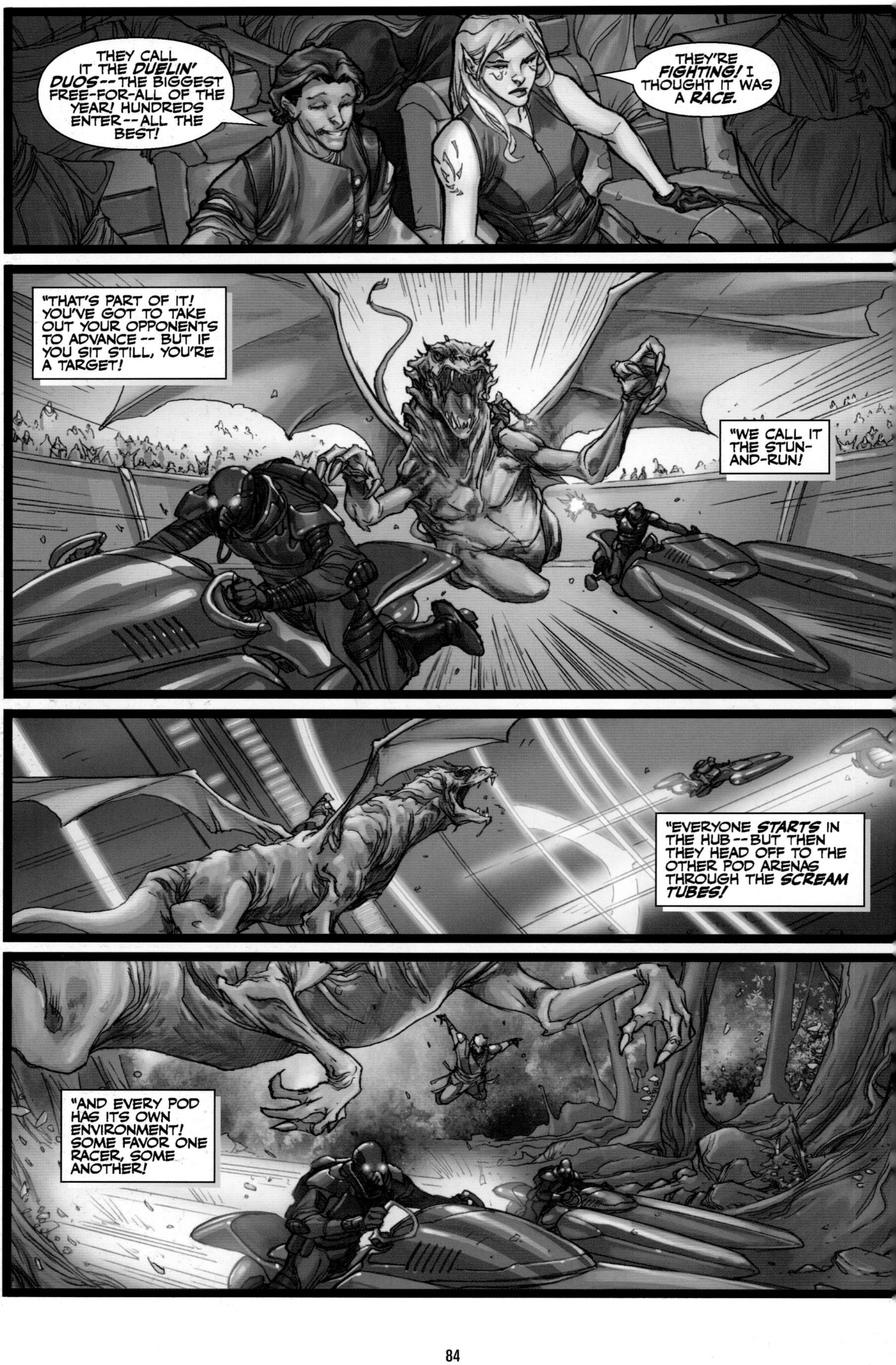
THEY CALL IT THE DUELIN' DUOS--THE BIGGEST FREE-FOR-ALL OF THE YEAR! HUNDREDS ENTER--ALL THE BEST!
THEY'RE FIGHTING! I THOUGHT IT WAS A RACE.
"THAT'S PART OF IT! YOU'VE GOT TO TAKE OUT YOUR OPPONENTS TO ADVANCE -- BUT IF YOU SIT STILL, YOU'RE A TARGET!
"WE CALL IT THE STUN-AND-RUN!
"EVERYONE STARTS IN THE HUB -- BUT THEN THEY HEAD OFF TO THE OTHER POD ARENAS THROUGH THE SCREAM TUBES!
"AND EVERY POD HAS ITS OWN ENVIRONMENT! SOME FAVOR ONE RACER, SOME ANOTHER!

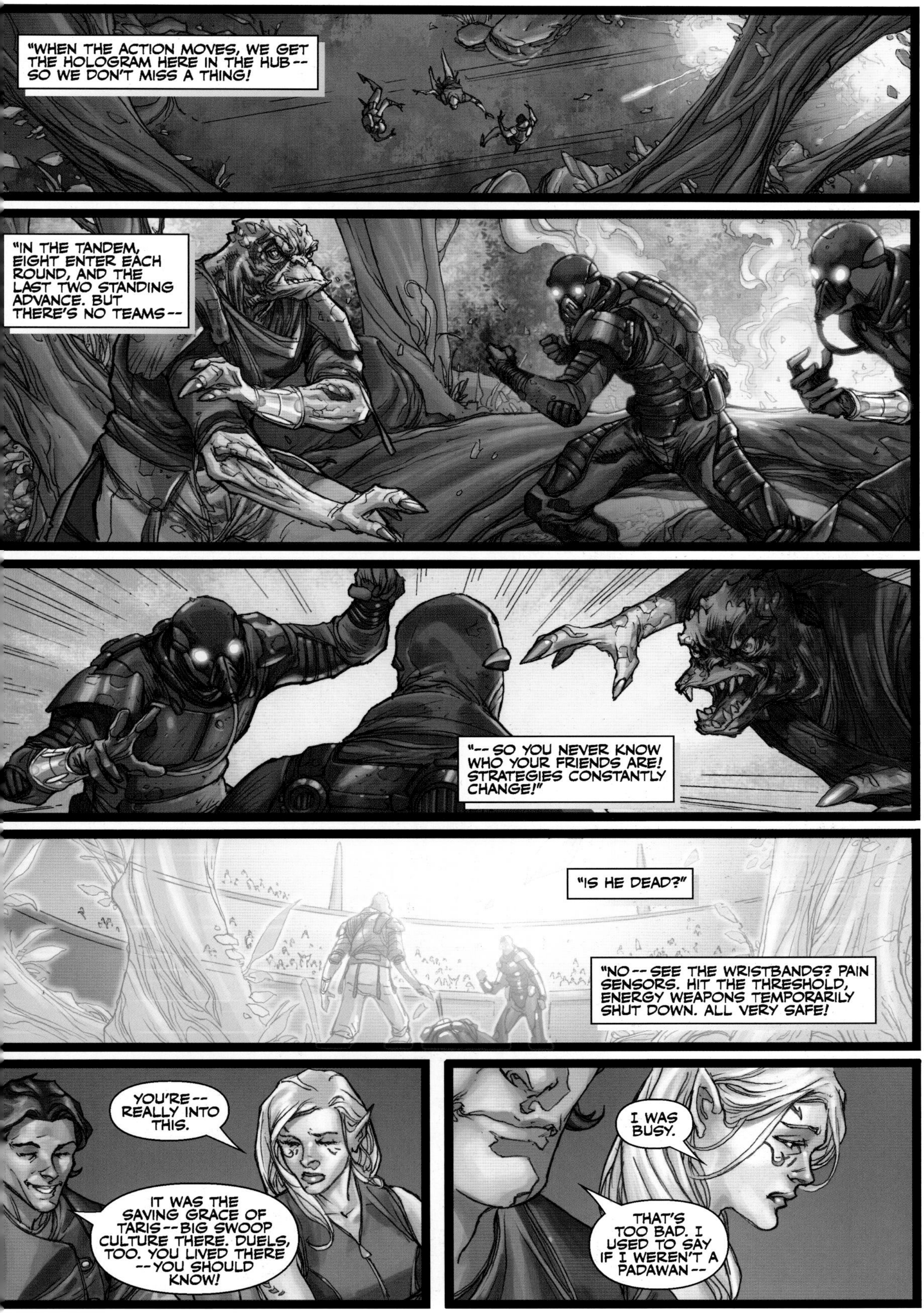
"WHEN THE ACTION MOVES, WE GET THE HOLOGRAM HERE IN THE HUB-- SO WE DON'T MISS A THING!
"IN THE TANDEM, EIGHT ENTER EACH ROUND, AND THE LAST TWO STANDING ADVANCE. BUT THERE'S NO TEAMS--
"--SO YOU NEVER KNOW WHO YOUR FRIENDS ARE! STRATEGIES CONSTANTLY CHANGE!"
"IS HE DEAD?"
"NO--SEE THE WRISTBANDS? PAIN SENSORS. HIT THE THRESHOLD, ENERGY WEAPONS TEMPORARILY SHUT DOWN. ALL VERY SAFE!
YOU'RE--REALLY INTO THIS.
IT WAS THE SAVING GRACE OF TARIS--BIG SWOOP CULTURE THERE. DUELS, TOO. YOU LIVED THERE--YOU SHOULD KNOW!
I WAS BUSY.
THAT'S TOO BAD. I USED TO SAY IF I WEREN'T A PADAWAN--

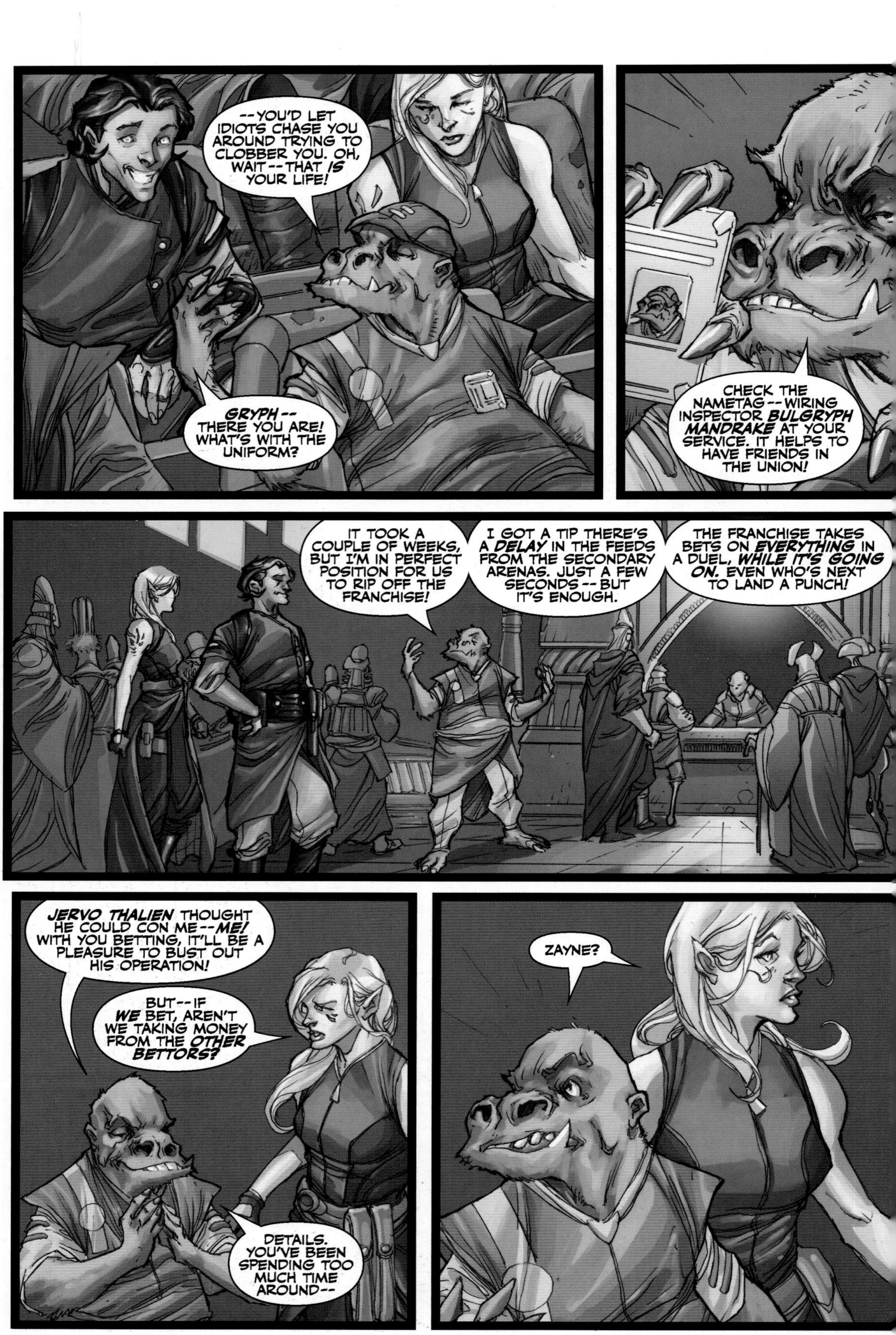
--YOU'D LET IDIOTS CHASE YOU AROUND TRYING TO CLOBBER YOU. OH, WAIT--THAT *IS* YOUR LIFE!
GRYPH-- THERE YOU ARE! WHAT'S WITH THE UNIFORM?
CHECK THE NAMETAG--WIRING INSPECTOR *BULGRYPH MANDRAKE* AT YOUR SERVICE. IT HELPS TO HAVE FRIENDS IN THE UNION!
IT TOOK A COUPLE OF WEEKS, BUT I'M IN PERFECT POSITION FOR US TO RIP OFF THE FRANCHISE!
I GOT A TIP THERE'S A *DELAY* IN THE FEEDS FROM THE SECONDARY ARENAS. JUST A FEW SECONDS--BUT IT'S ENOUGH.
THE FRANCHISE TAKES BETS ON *EVERYTHING* IN A DUEL, *WHILE IT'S GOING ON.* EVEN WHO'S NEXT TO LAND A PUNCH!
JERVO THALIEN THOUGHT HE COULD CON ME--*ME!* WITH YOU BETTING, IT'LL BE A PLEASURE TO BUST OUT HIS OPERATION!
BUT--IF *WE* BET, AREN'T WE TAKING MONEY FROM THE *OTHER BETTORS?*
DETAILS. YOU'VE BEEN SPENDING TOO MUCH TIME AROUND--
ZAYNE?

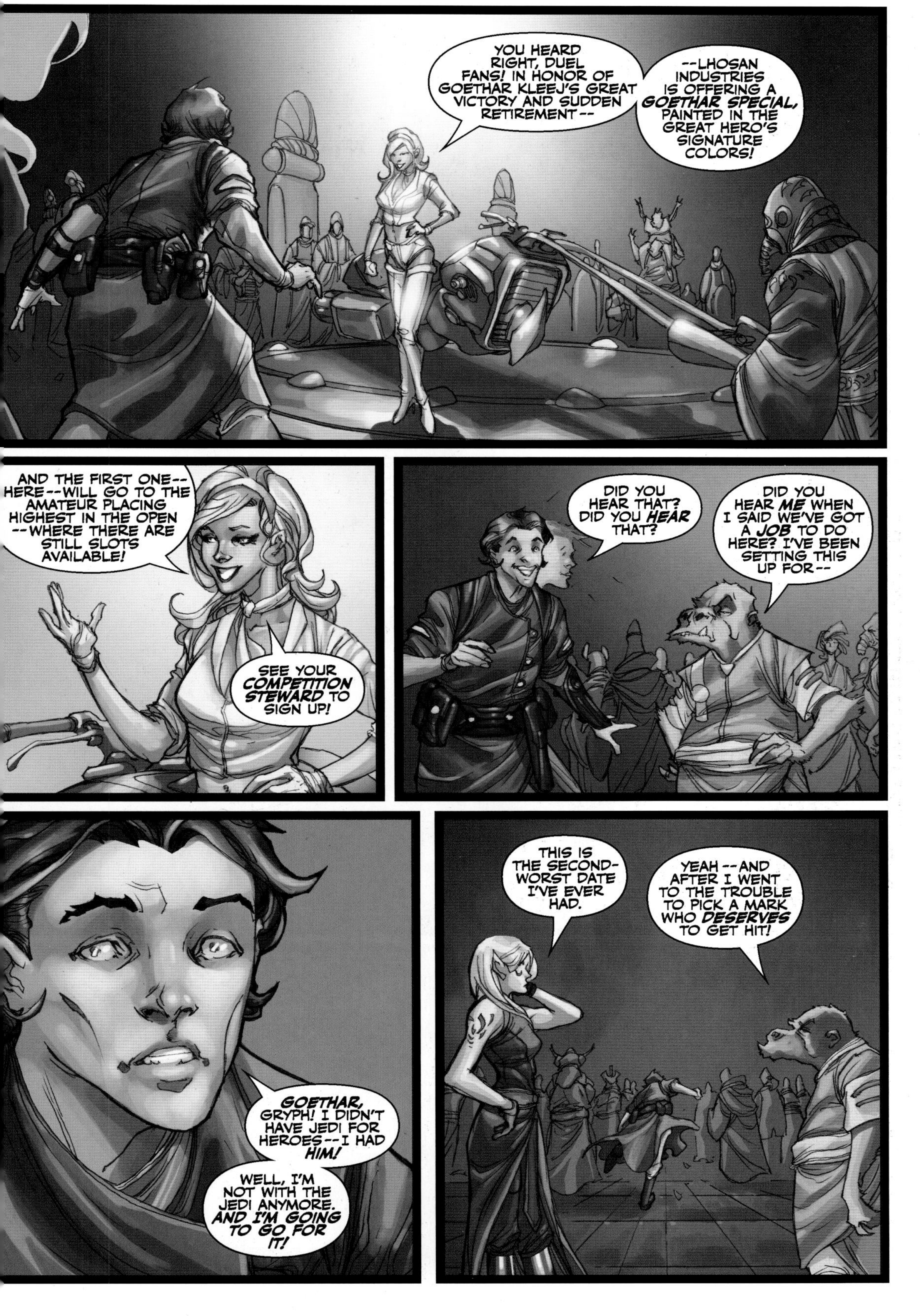
YOU HEARD RIGHT, DUEL FANS! IN HONOR OF GOETHAR KLEEJ'S GREAT VICTORY AND SUDDEN RETIREMENT--
--LHOSAN INDUSTRIES IS OFFERING A GOETHAR SPECIAL, PAINTED IN THE GREAT HERO'S SIGNATURE COLORS!
AND THE FIRST ONE-- HERE--WILL GO TO THE AMATEUR PLACING HIGHEST IN THE OPEN --WHERE THERE ARE STILL SLOTS AVAILABLE!
SEE YOUR COMPETITION STEWARD TO SIGN UP!
DID YOU HEAR THAT? DID YOU HEAR THAT?
DID YOU HEAR ME WHEN I SAID WE'VE GOT A JOB TO DO HERE? I'VE BEEN SETTING THIS UP FOR--
GOETHAR, GRYPH! I DIDN'T HAVE JEDI FOR HEROES--I HAD HIM!
WELL, I'M NOT WITH THE JEDI ANYMORE. AND I'M GOING TO GO FOR IT!
THIS IS THE SECOND-WORST DATE I'VE EVER HAD.
YEAH--AND AFTER I WENT TO THE TROUBLE TO PICK A MARK WHO DESERVES TO GET HIT!

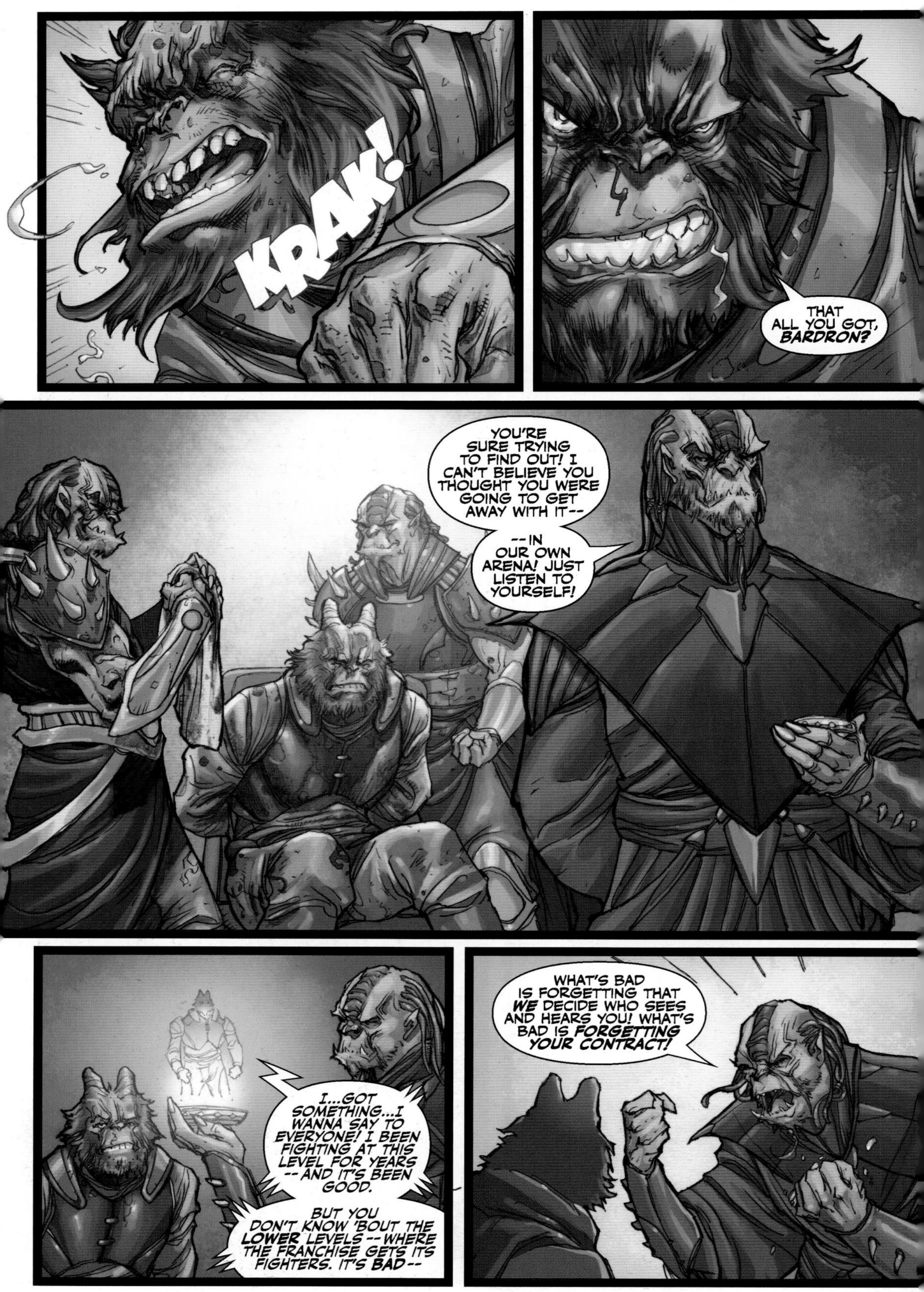
KRAK!
THAT ALL YOU GOT, BARDRON?
YOU'RE SURE TRYING TO FIND OUT! I CAN'T BELIEVE YOU THOUGHT YOU WERE GOING TO GET AWAY WITH IT--
--IN OUR OWN ARENA! JUST LISTEN TO YOURSELF!
I...GOT SOMETHING...I WANNA SAY TO EVERYONE! I BEEN FIGHTING AT THIS LEVEL FOR YEARS --AND IT'S BEEN GOOD.
BUT YOU DON'T KNOW 'BOUT THE LOWER LEVELS--WHERE THE FRANCHISE GETS ITS FIGHTERS. IT'S BAD--
WHAT'S BAD IS FORGETTING THAT WE DECIDE WHO SEES AND HEARS YOU! WHAT'S BAD IS FORGETTING YOUR CONTRACT!

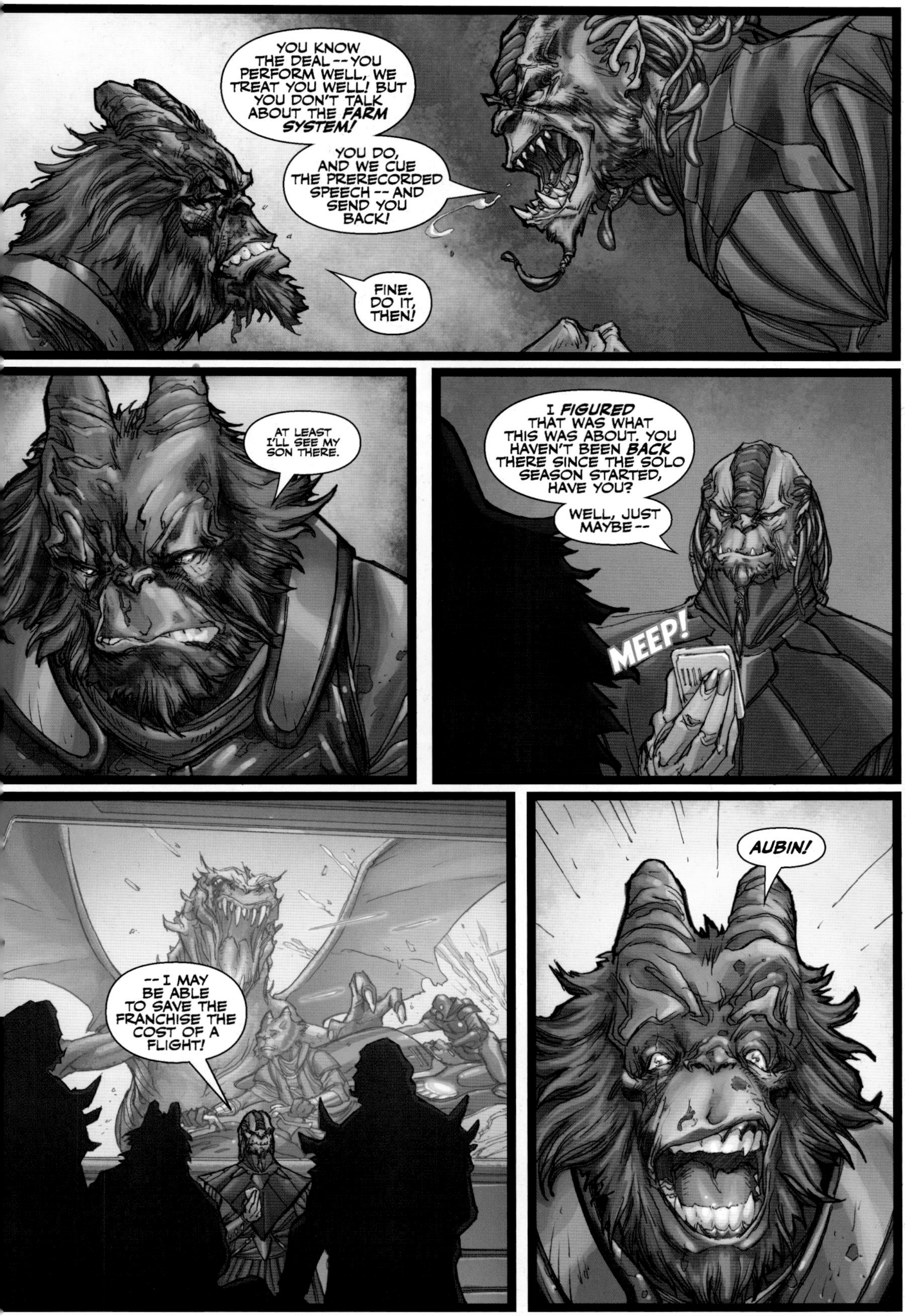
YOU KNOW THE DEAL--YOU PERFORM WELL, WE TREAT YOU WELL! BUT YOU DON'T TALK ABOUT THE FARM SYSTEM!
YOU DO, AND WE CUE THE PRERECORDED SPEECH--AND SEND YOU BACK!
FINE. DO IT, THEN!
AT LEAST I'LL SEE MY SON THERE.
I FIGURED THAT WAS WHAT THIS WAS ABOUT. YOU HAVEN'T BEEN BACK THERE SINCE THE SOLO SEASON STARTED, HAVE YOU?
WELL, JUST MAYBE--
MEEP!
--I MAY BE ABLE TO SAVE THE FRANCHISE THE COST OF A FLIGHT!
AUBIN!

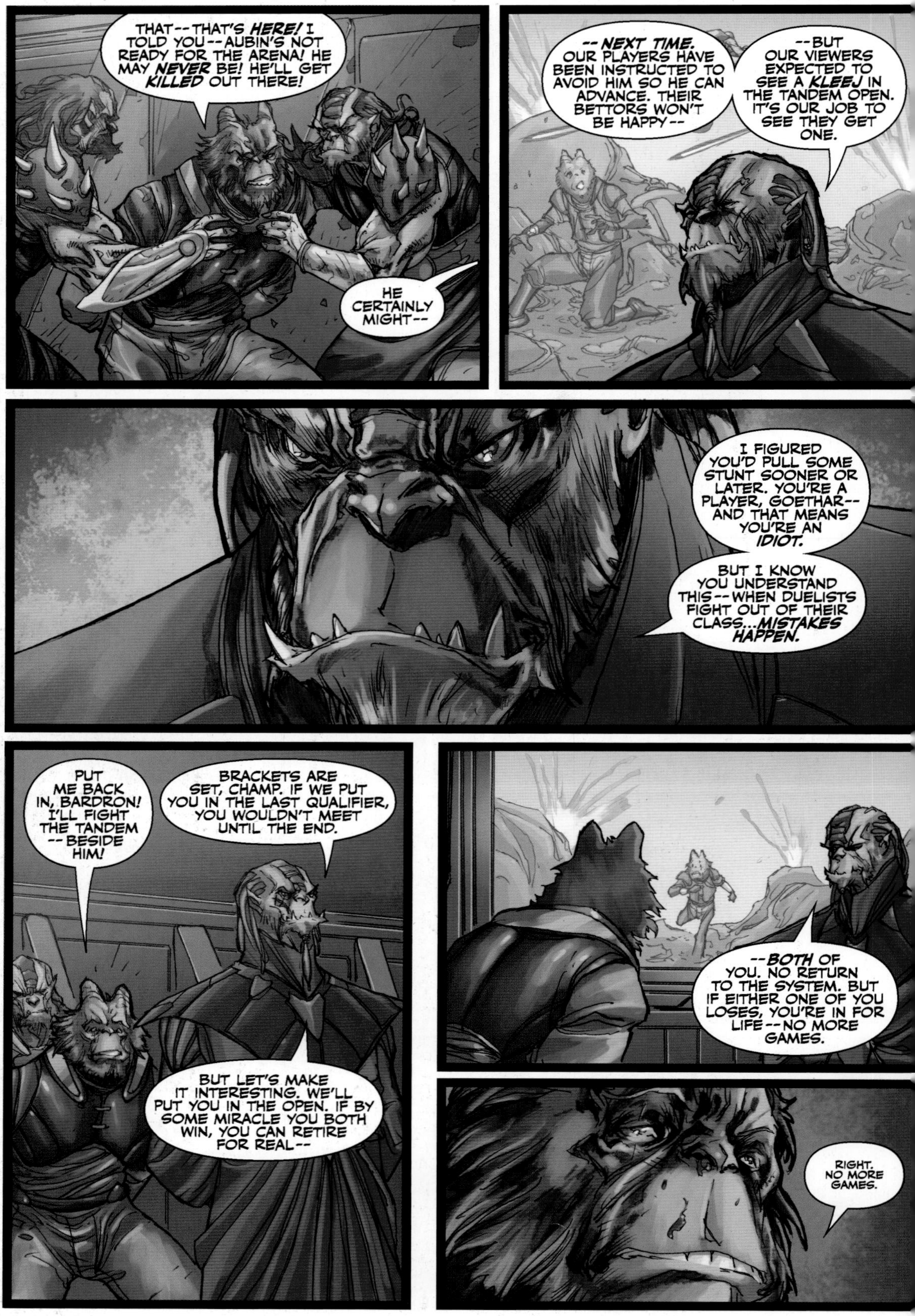
THAT--THAT'S HERE! I TOLD YOU--AUBIN'S NOT READY FOR THE ARENA! HE MAY NEVER BE! HE'LL GET KILLED OUT THERE!
HE CERTAINLY MIGHT--
--NEXT TIME. OUR PLAYERS HAVE BEEN INSTRUCTED TO AVOID HIM SO HE CAN ADVANCE. THEIR BETTORS WON'T BE HAPPY--
--BUT OUR VIEWERS EXPECTED TO SEE A KLEEJ IN THE TANDEM OPEN. IT'S OUR JOB TO SEE THEY GET ONE.
I FIGURED YOU'D PULL SOME STUNT SOONER OR LATER. YOU'RE A PLAYER, GOETHAR--AND THAT MEANS YOU'RE AN IDIOT.
BUT I KNOW YOU UNDERSTAND THIS--WHEN DUELISTS FIGHT OUT OF THEIR CLASS...MISTAKES HAPPEN.
PUT ME BACK IN, BARDRON! I'LL FIGHT THE TANDEM --BESIDE HIM!
BRACKETS ARE SET, CHAMP. IF WE PUT YOU IN THE LAST QUALIFIER, YOU WOULDN'T MEET UNTIL THE END.
BUT LET'S MAKE IT INTERESTING. WE'LL PUT YOU IN THE OPEN. IF BY SOME MIRACLE YOU BOTH WIN, YOU CAN RETIRE FOR REAL--
--BOTH OF YOU. NO RETURN TO THE SYSTEM. BUT IF EITHER ONE OF YOU LOSES, YOU'RE IN FOR LIFE--NO MORE GAMES.
RIGHT. NO MORE GAMES.

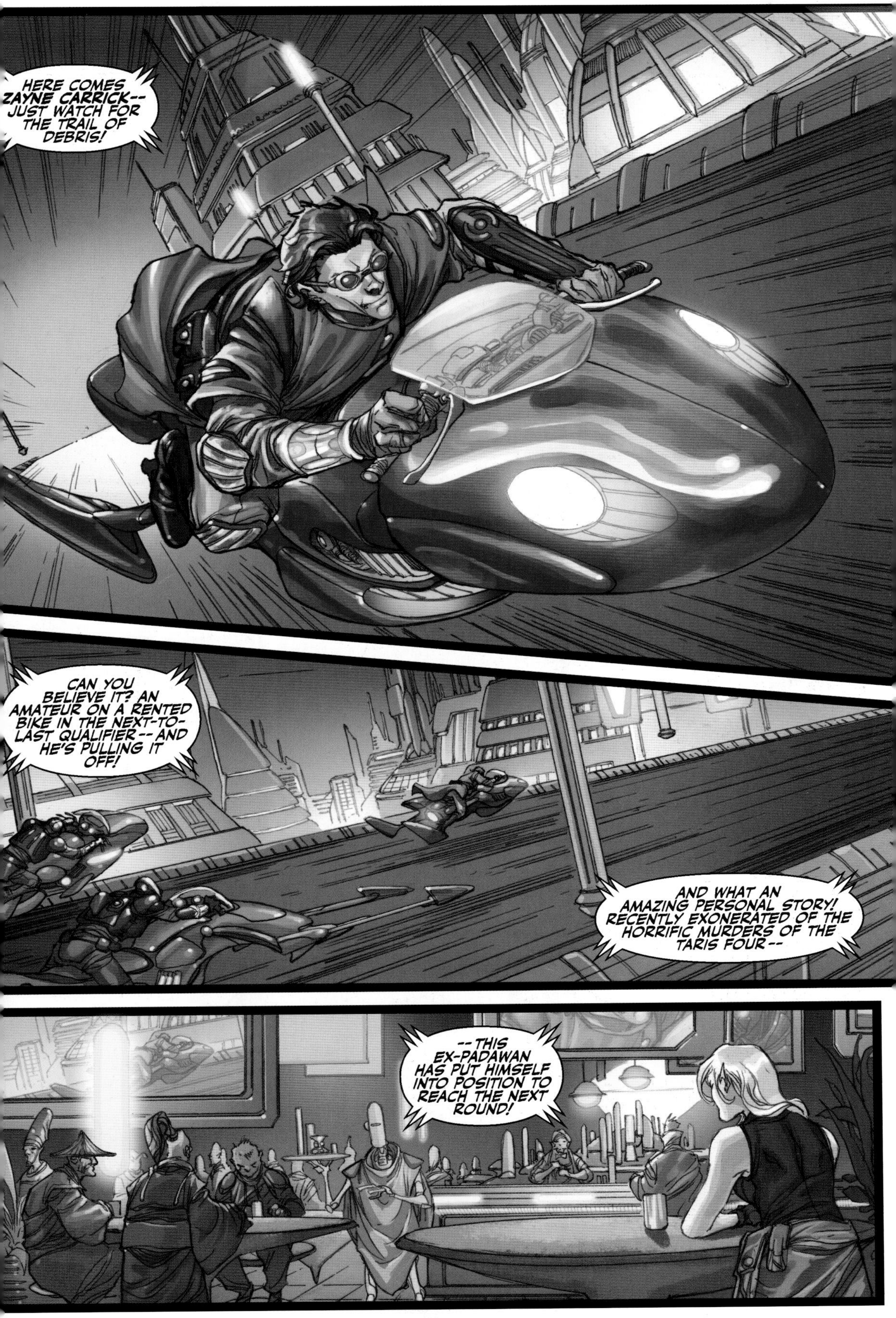
HERE COMES ZAYNE CARRICK-- JUST WATCH FOR THE TRAIL OF DEBRIS!
CAN YOU BELIEVE IT? AN AMATEUR ON A RENTED BIKE IN THE NEXT-TO-LAST QUALIFIER-- AND HE'S PULLING IT OFF!
AND WHAT AN AMAZING PERSONAL STORY! RECENTLY EXONERATED OF THE HORRIFIC MURDERS OF THE TARIS FOUR--
--THIS EX-PADAWAN HAS PUT HIMSELF INTO POSITION TO REACH THE NEXT ROUND!

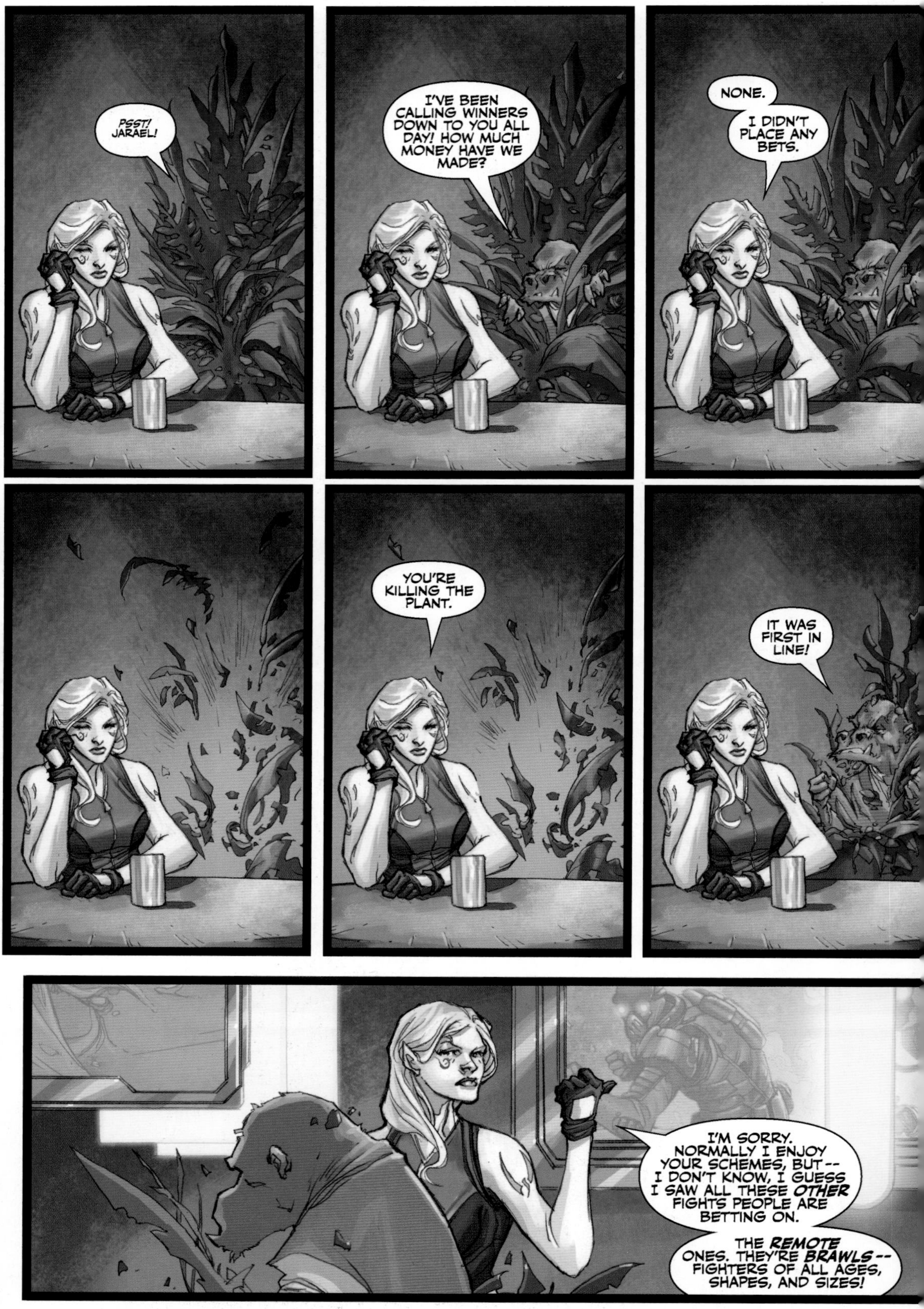
PSST! JARAEL!
I'VE BEEN CALLING WINNERS DOWN TO YOU ALL DAY! HOW MUCH MONEY HAVE WE MADE?
NONE.
I DIDN'T PLACE ANY BETS.
YOU'RE KILLING THE PLANT.
IT WAS FIRST IN LINE!
I'M SORRY. NORMALLY I ENJOY YOUR SCHEMES, BUT-- I DON'T KNOW, I GUESS I SAW ALL THESE *OTHER* FIGHTS PEOPLE ARE BETTING ON.
THE *REMOTE* ONES. THEY'RE *BRAWLS*-- FIGHTERS OF ALL AGES, SHAPES, AND SIZES!

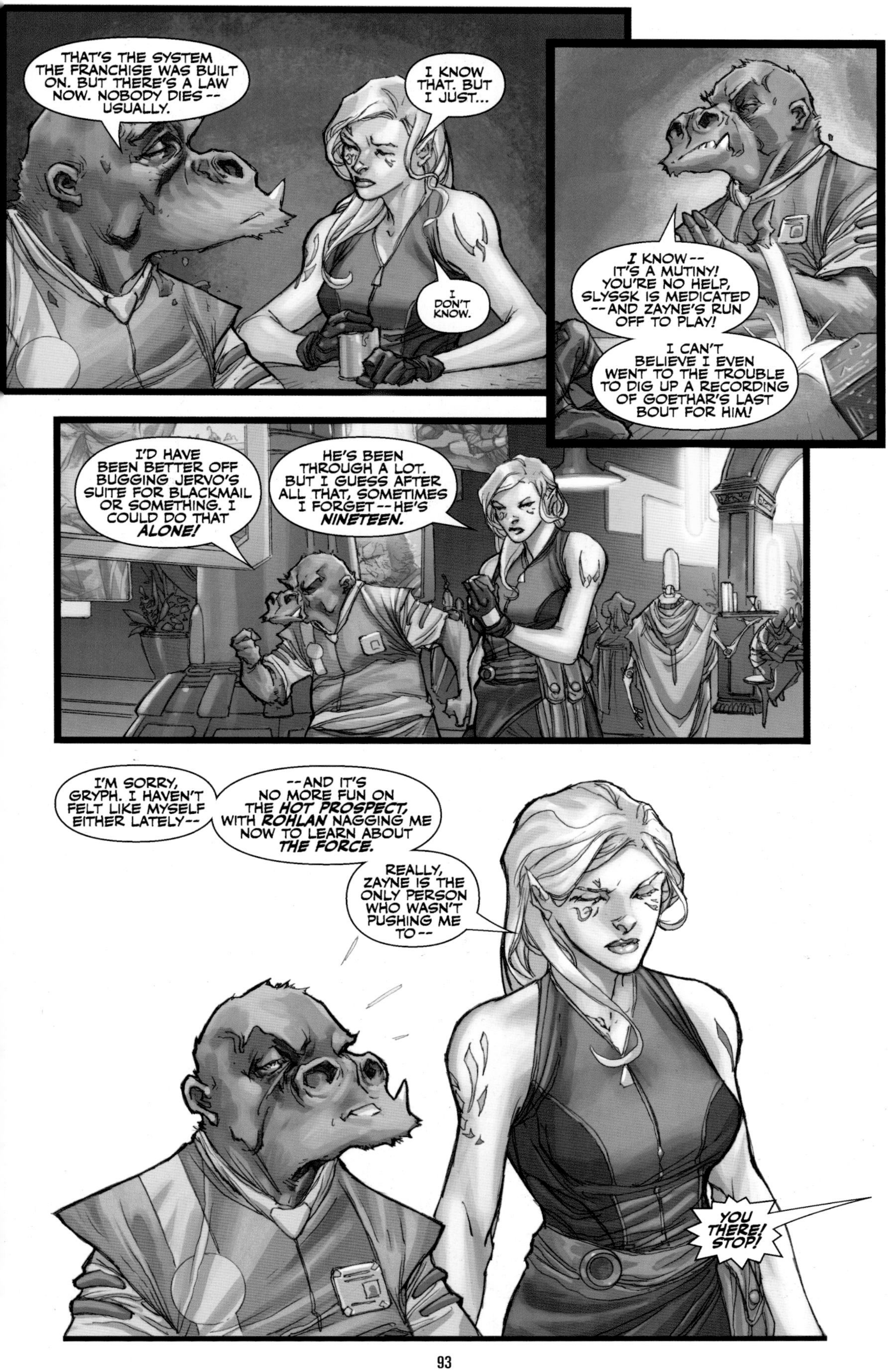
THAT'S THE SYSTEM THE FRANCHISE WAS BUILT ON. BUT THERE'S A LAW NOW. NOBODY DIES -- USUALLY.
I KNOW THAT. BUT I JUST...
I DON'T KNOW.
I KNOW -- IT'S A MUTINY! YOU'RE NO HELP, SLYSSK IS MEDICATED -- AND ZAYNE'S RUN OFF TO PLAY!
I CAN'T BELIEVE I EVEN WENT TO THE TROUBLE TO DIG UP A RECORDING OF GOETHAR'S LAST BOUT FOR HIM!
I'D HAVE BEEN BETTER OFF BUGGING JERVO'S SUITE FOR BLACKMAIL OR SOMETHING. I COULD DO THAT ALONE!
HE'S BEEN THROUGH A LOT. BUT I GUESS AFTER ALL THAT, SOMETIMES I FORGET -- HE'S NINETEEN.
I'M SORRY, GRYPH. I HAVEN'T FELT LIKE MYSELF EITHER LATELY--
--AND IT'S NO MORE FUN ON THE HOT PROSPECT, WITH ROHLAN NAGGING ME NOW TO LEARN ABOUT THE FORCE.
REALLY, ZAYNE IS THE ONLY PERSON WHO WASN'T PUSHING ME TO --
YOU THERE! STOP!

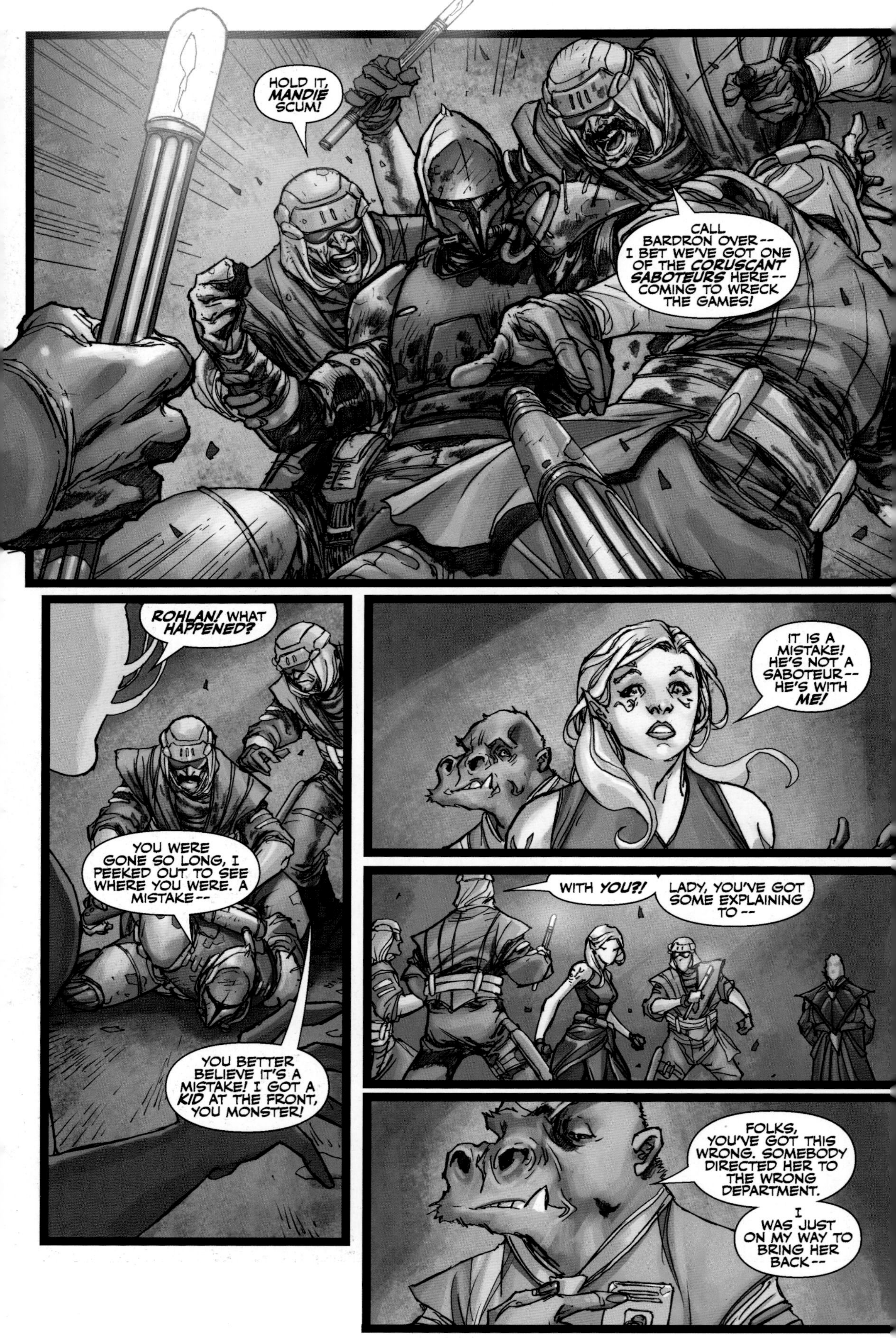

HOLD IT, MANDIE SCUM!
CALL BARDRON OVER-- I BET WE'VE GOT ONE OF THE CORUSCANT SABOTEURS HERE-- COMING TO WRECK THE GAMES!
ROHLAN! WHAT HAPPENED?
YOU WERE GONE SO LONG, I PEEKED OUT TO SEE WHERE YOU WERE. A MISTAKE--
YOU BETTER BELIEVE IT'S A MISTAKE! I GOT A KID AT THE FRONT, YOU MONSTER!
IT IS A MISTAKE! HE'S NOT A SABOTEUR-- HE'S WITH ME!
WITH YOU?!
LADY, YOU'VE GOT SOME EXPLAINING TO--
FOLKS, YOU'VE GOT THIS WRONG. SOMEBODY DIRECTED HER TO THE WRONG DEPARTMENT.
I WAS JUST ON MY WAY TO BRING HER BACK--

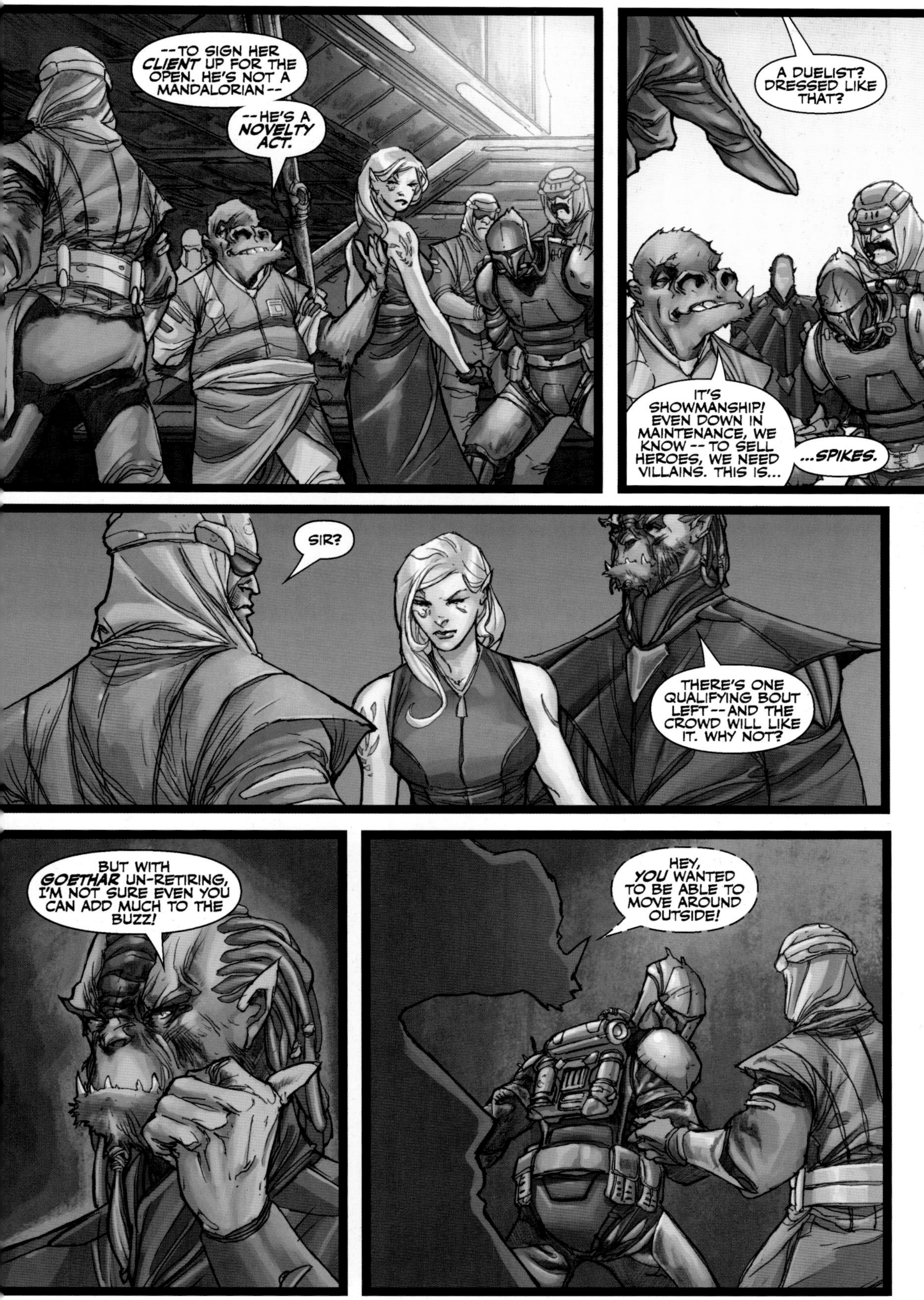
--TO SIGN HER CLIENT UP FOR THE OPEN. HE'S NOT A MANDALORIAN--
--HE'S A NOVELTY ACT.
A DUELIST? DRESSED LIKE THAT?
IT'S SHOWMANSHIP! EVEN DOWN IN MAINTENANCE, WE KNOW -- TO SELL HEROES, WE NEED VILLAINS. THIS IS...
...SPIKES.
SIR?
THERE'S ONE QUALIFYING BOUT LEFT -- AND THE CROWD WILL LIKE IT. WHY NOT?
BUT WITH GOETHAR UN-RETIRING, I'M NOT SURE EVEN YOU CAN ADD MUCH TO THE BUZZ!
HEY, YOU WANTED TO BE ABLE TO MOVE AROUND OUTSIDE!

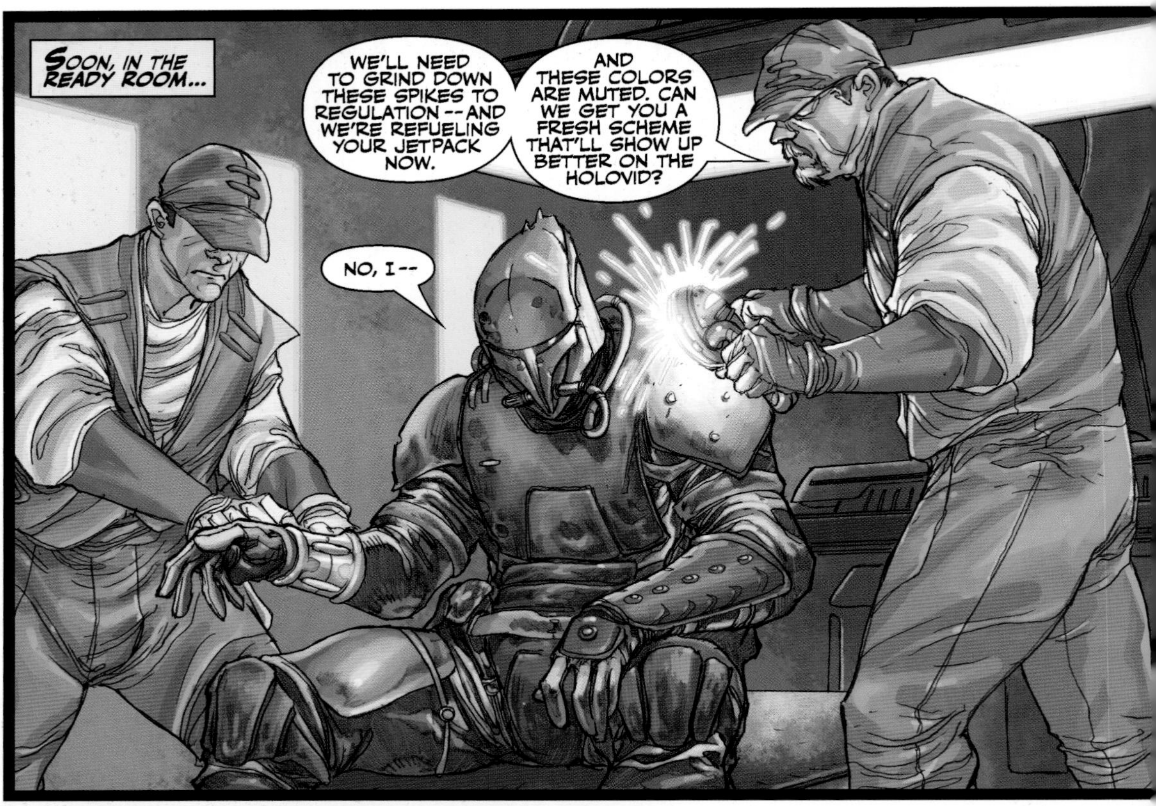
SOON, IN THE READY ROOM...
WE'LL NEED TO GRIND DOWN THESE SPIKES TO REGULATION --AND WE'RE REFUELING YOUR JETPACK NOW.
AND THESE COLORS ARE MUTED. CAN WE GET YOU A FRESH SCHEME THAT'LL SHOW UP BETTER ON THE HOLOVID?
NO, I--

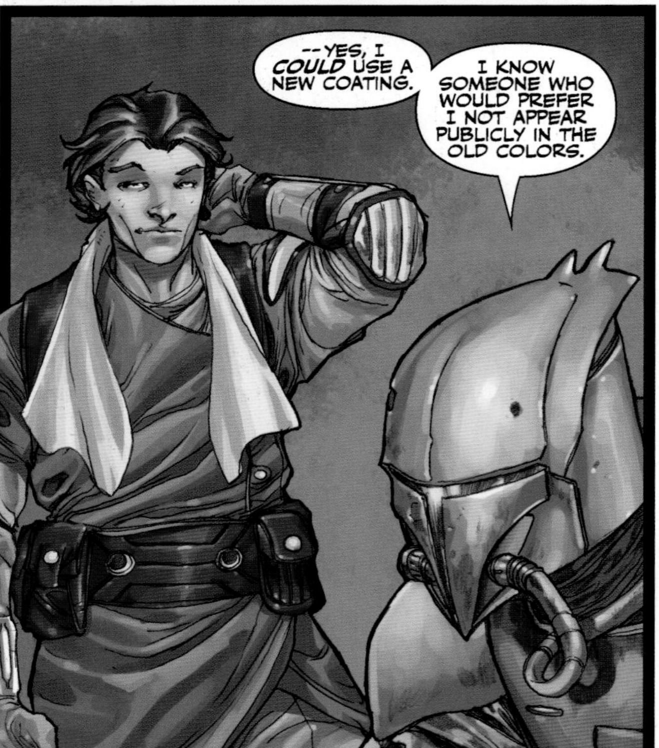
--YES, I COULD USE A NEW COATING.
I KNOW SOMEONE WHO WOULD PREFER I NOT APPEAR PUBLICLY IN THE OLD COLORS.

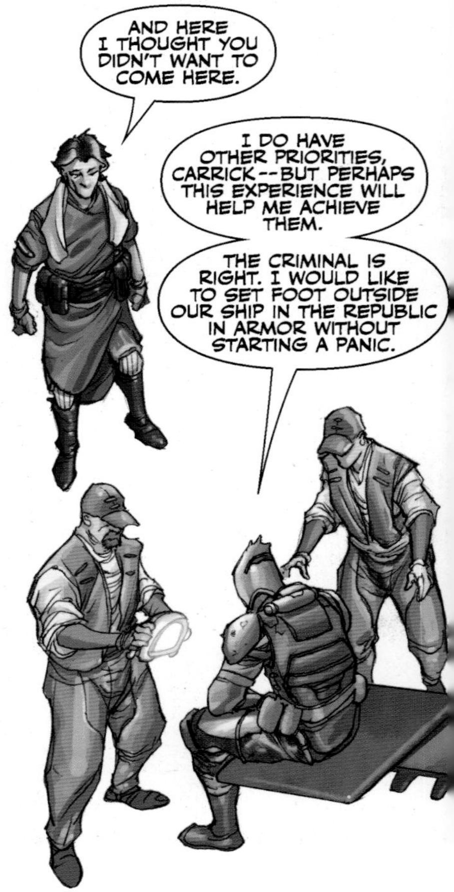
AND HERE I THOUGHT YOU DIDN'T WANT TO COME HERE.
I DO HAVE OTHER PRIORITIES, CARRICK--BUT PERHAPS THIS EXPERIENCE WILL HELP ME ACHIEVE THEM.
THE CRIMINAL IS RIGHT. I WOULD LIKE TO SET FOOT OUTSIDE OUR SHIP IN THE REPUBLIC IN ARMOR WITHOUT STARTING A PANIC.

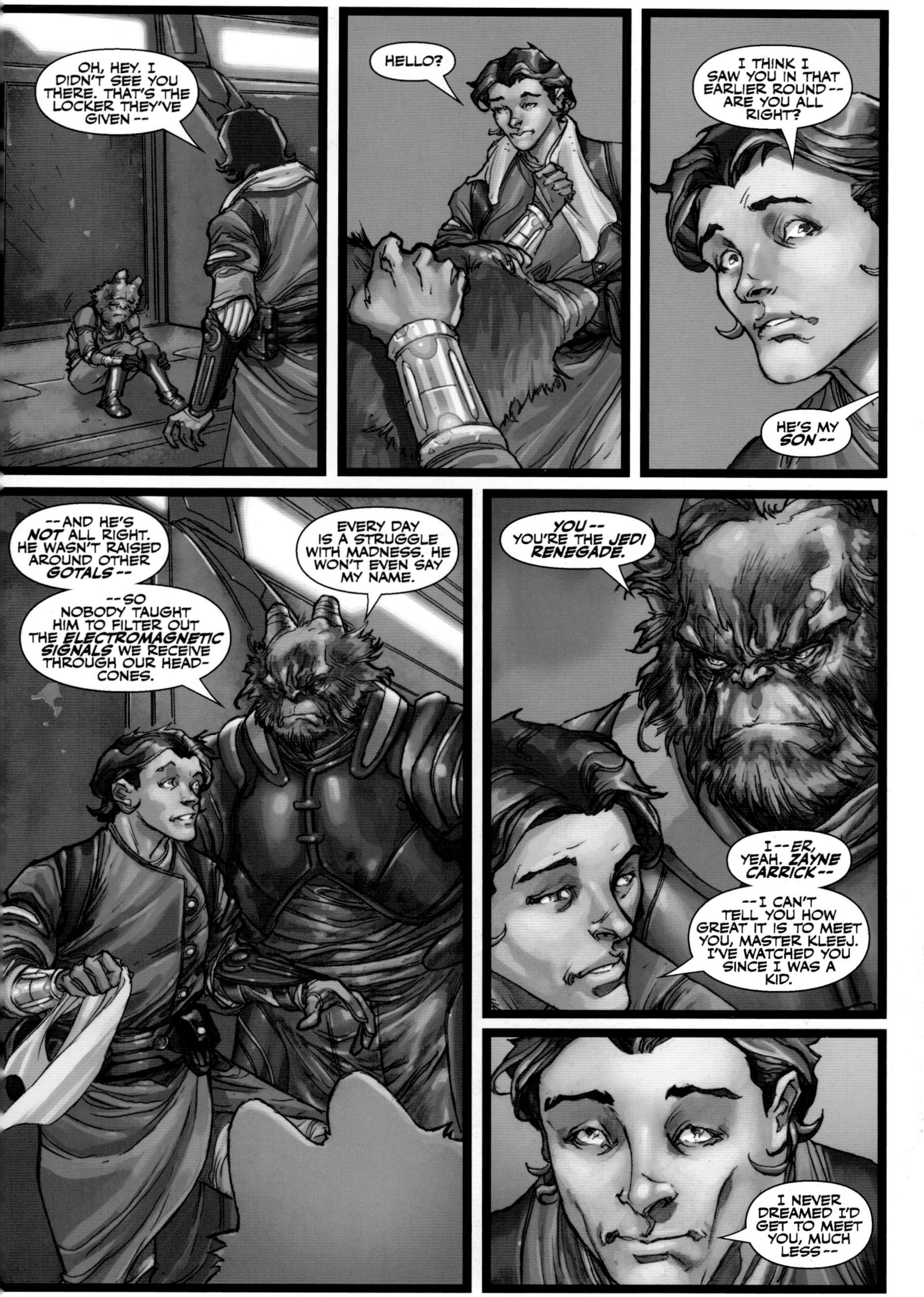

OH, HEY. I DIDN'T SEE YOU THERE. THAT'S THE LOCKER THEY'VE GIVEN --
HELLO?
I THINK I SAW YOU IN THAT EARLIER ROUND -- ARE YOU ALL RIGHT?
HE'S MY *SON* --
-- AND HE'S *NOT* ALL RIGHT. HE WASN'T RAISED AROUND OTHER *GOTALS* --
-- SO NOBODY TAUGHT HIM TO FILTER OUT THE *ELECTROMAGNETIC SIGNALS* WE RECEIVE THROUGH OUR HEAD-CONES.
EVERY DAY IS A STRUGGLE WITH MADNESS. HE WON'T EVEN SAY MY NAME.
YOU -- YOU'RE THE *JEDI RENEGADE.*
I -- ER, YEAH. *ZAYNE CARRICK* --
-- I CAN'T TELL YOU HOW GREAT IT IS TO MEET YOU, MASTER KLEEJ. I'VE WATCHED YOU SINCE I WAS A KID.
I NEVER DREAMED I'D GET TO MEET YOU, MUCH LESS --

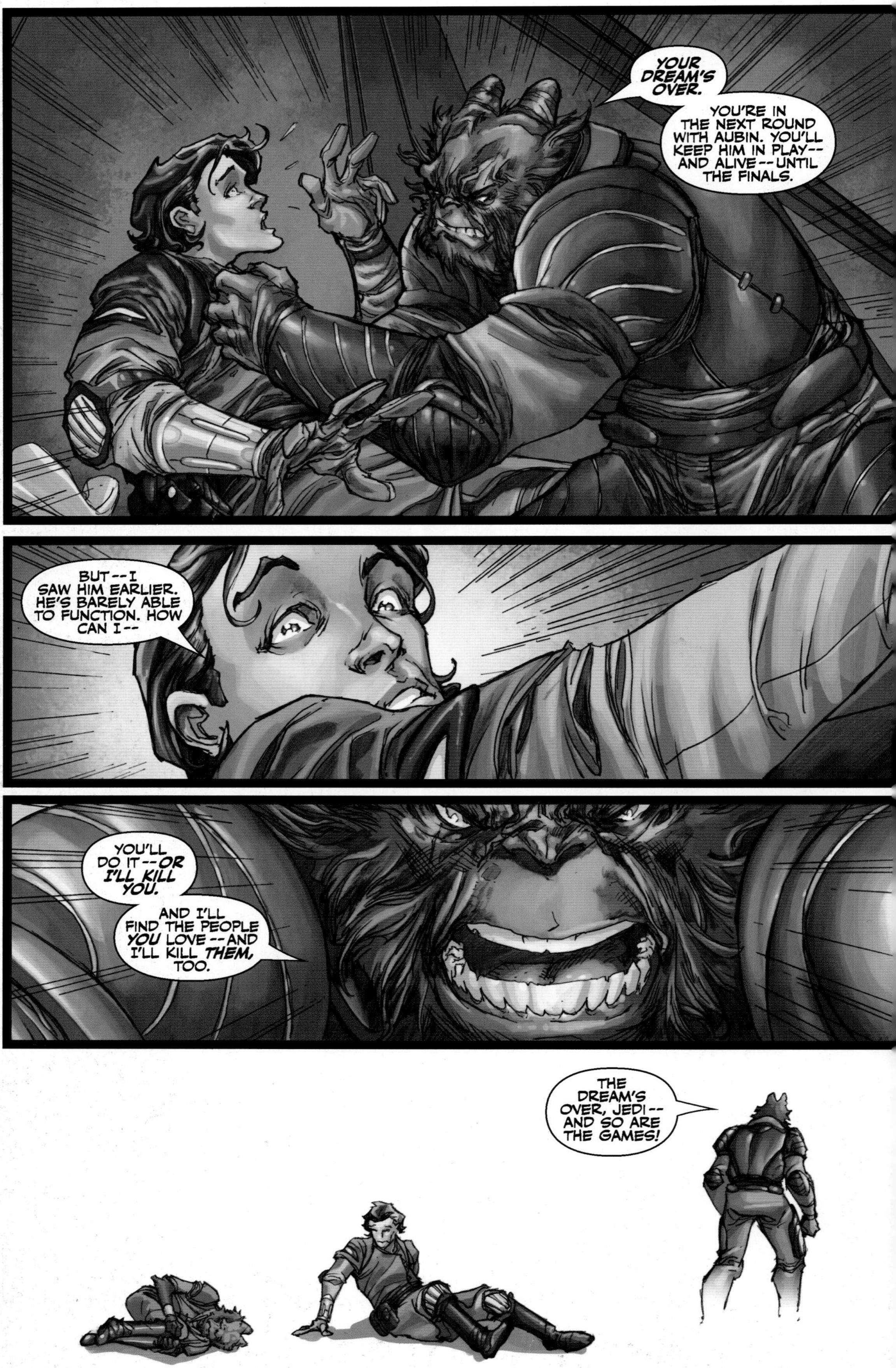
YOUR DREAM'S OVER.
YOU'RE IN THE NEXT ROUND WITH AUBIN. YOU'LL KEEP HIM IN PLAY-- AND ALIVE--UNTIL THE FINALS.
BUT--I SAW HIM EARLIER. HE'S BARELY ABLE TO FUNCTION. HOW CAN I--
YOU'LL DO IT--OR I'LL KILL YOU.
AND I'LL FIND THE PEOPLE YOU LOVE--AND I'LL KILL THEM, TOO.
THE DREAM'S OVER, JEDI-- AND SO ARE THE GAMES!

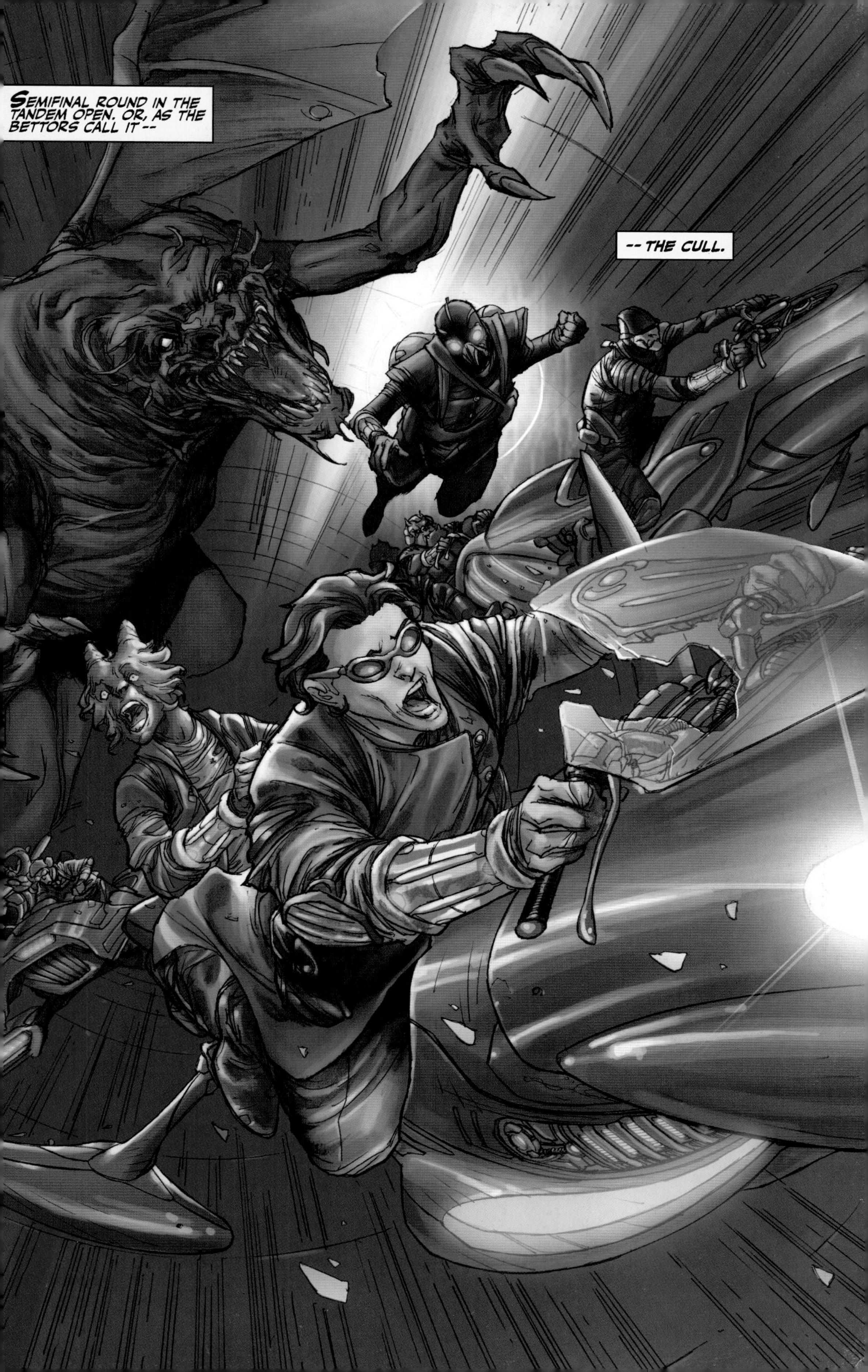
SEMIFINAL ROUND IN THE TANDEM OPEN. OR, AS THE BETTORS CALL IT --
-- THE CULL.

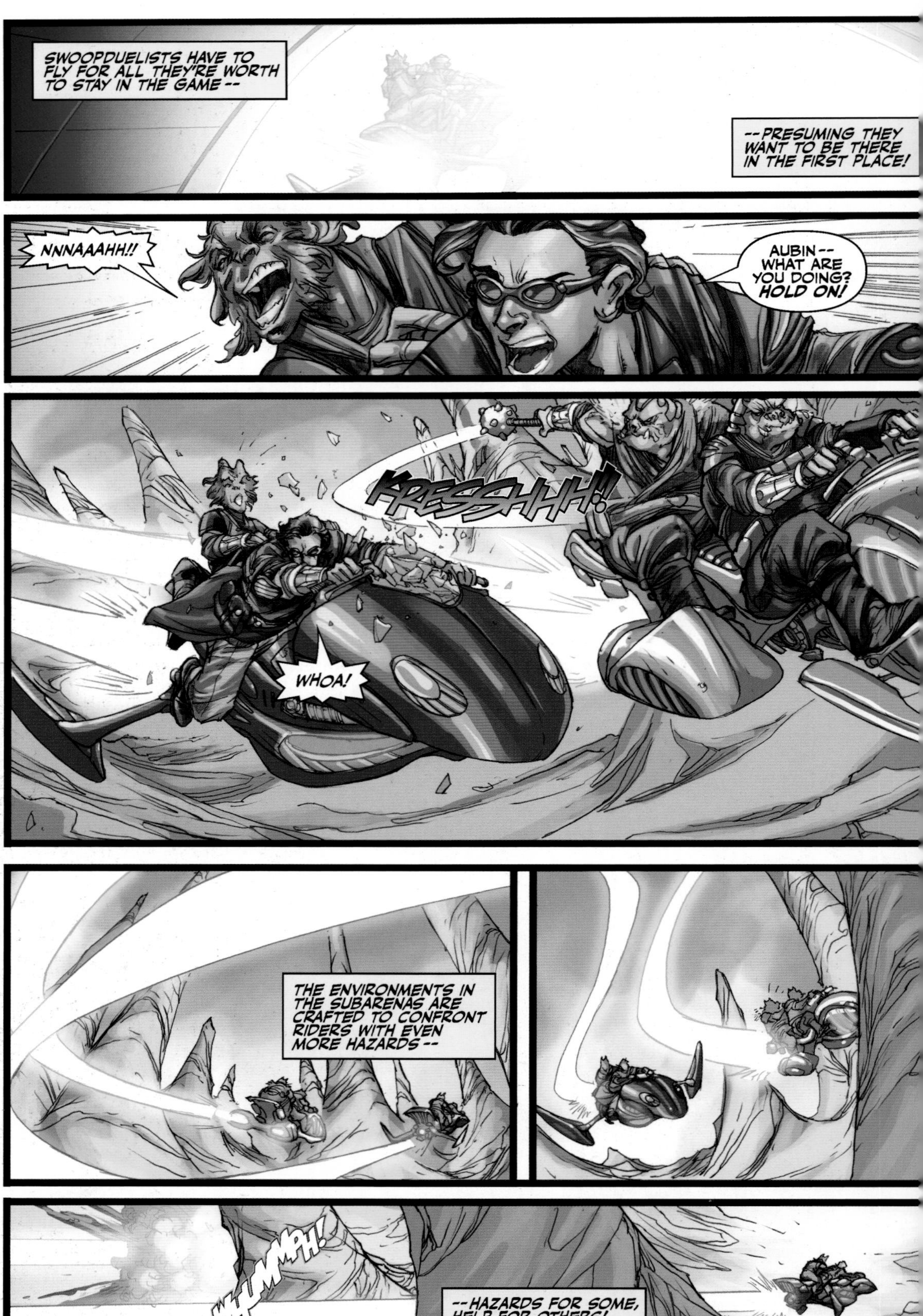
SWOOPDUELISTS HAVE TO FLY FOR ALL THEY'RE WORTH TO STAY IN THE GAME --
--PRESUMING THEY WANT TO BE THERE IN THE FIRST PLACE!
NNNAAAHH!!
AUBIN -- WHAT ARE YOU DOING? HOLD ON!
KRESSHHH!!
WHOA!
THE ENVIRONMENTS IN THE SUBARENAS ARE CRAFTED TO CONFRONT RIDERS WITH EVEN MORE HAZARDS --
WHUMMPH!
--HAZARDS FOR SOME, HELP FOR OTHERS!

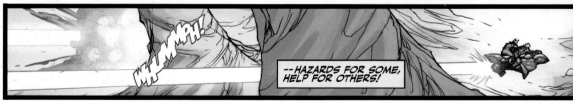

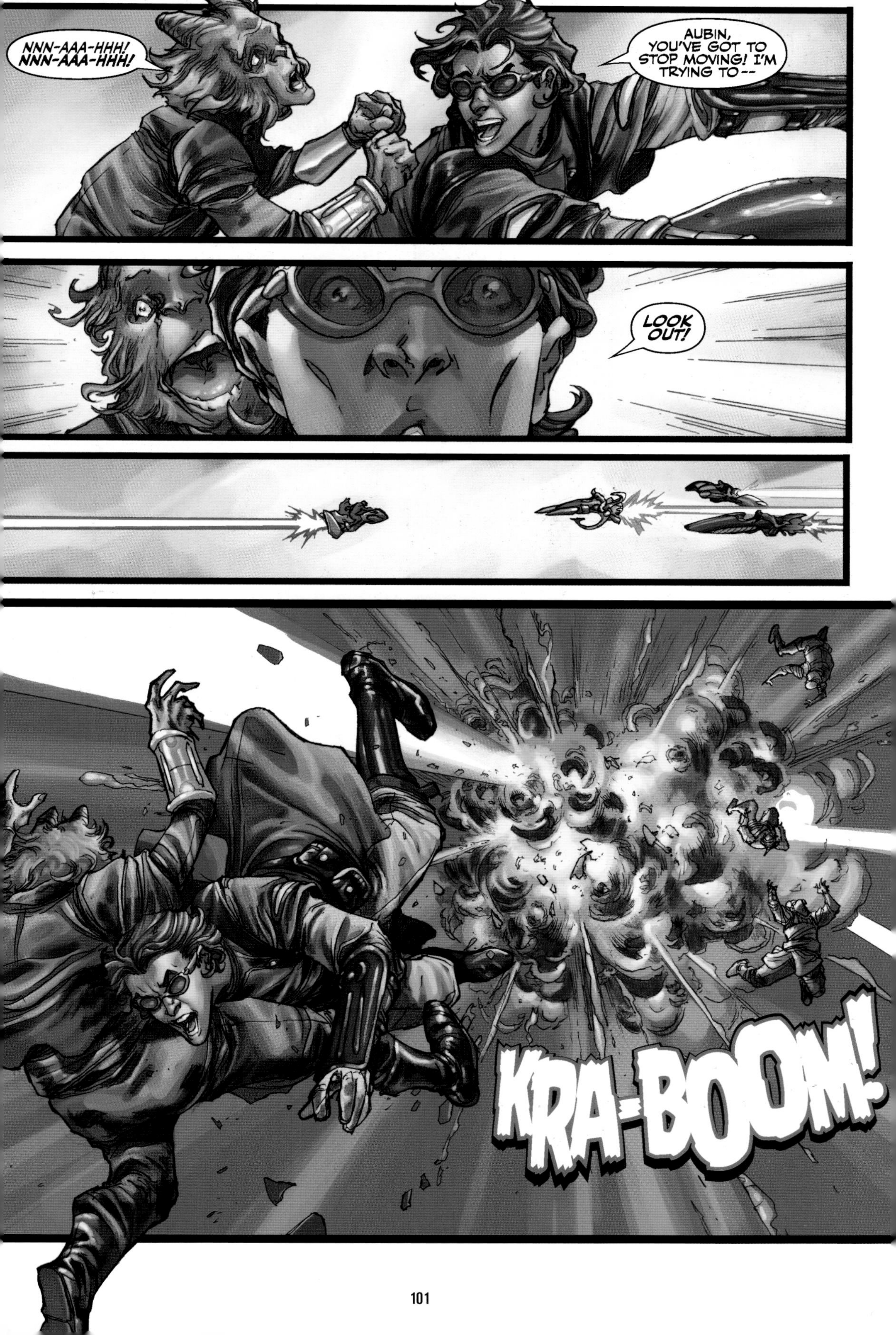
NNN-AAA-HHH! NNN-AAA-HHH!
AUBIN, YOU'VE GOT TO STOP MOVING! I'M TRYING TO --
LOOK OUT!
KRA-BOOM!

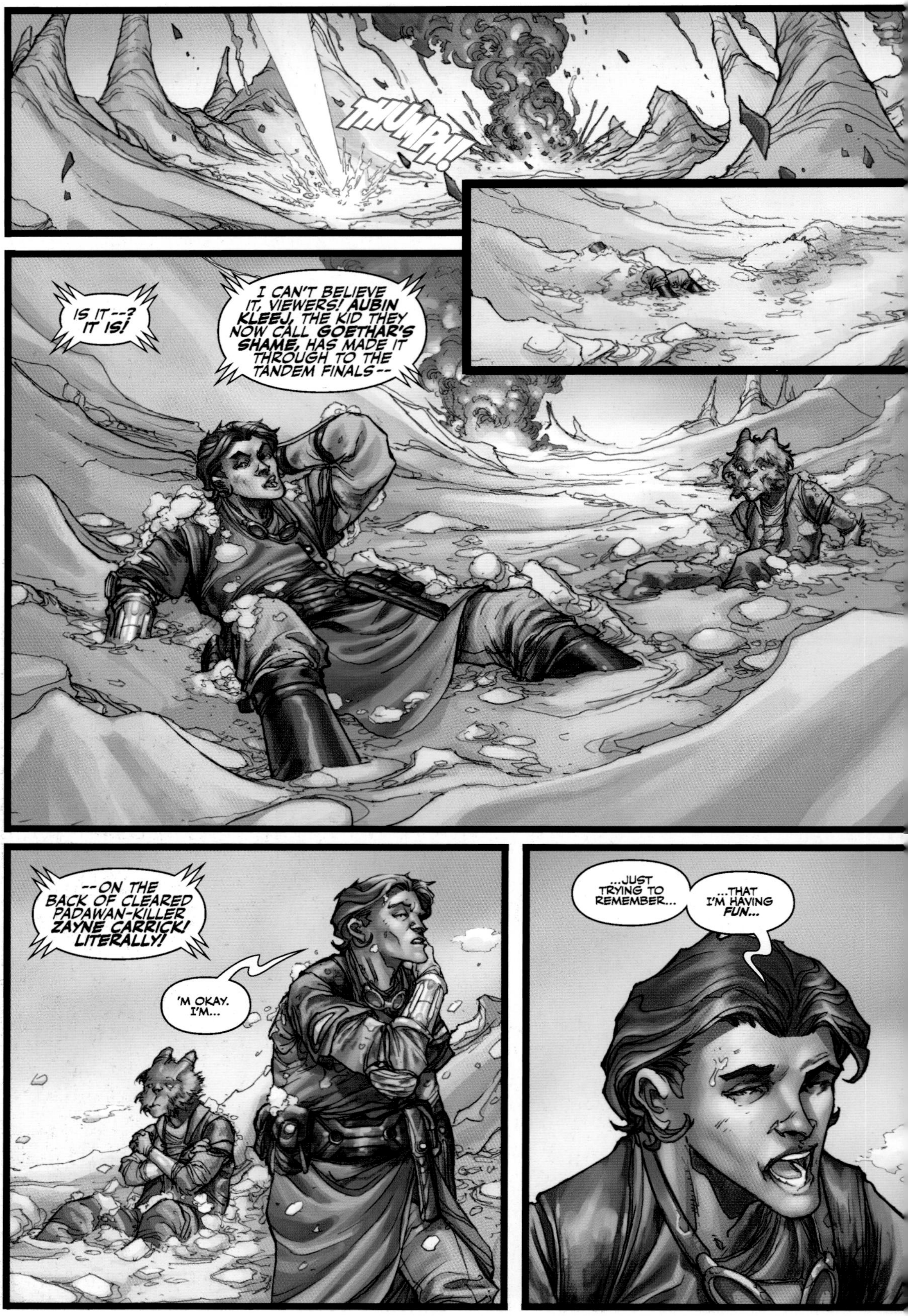
THUMPH!
IS IT--? IT IS!
I CAN'T BELIEVE IT, VIEWERS! AUBIN KLEEJ, THE KID THEY NOW CALL GOETHAR'S SHAME, HAS MADE IT THROUGH TO THE TANDEM FINALS--
--ON THE BACK OF CLEARED PADAWAN-KILLER ZAYNE CARRICK! LITERALLY!
'M OKAY. I'M...
...JUST TRYING TO REMEMBER...
...THAT I'M HAVING FUN...

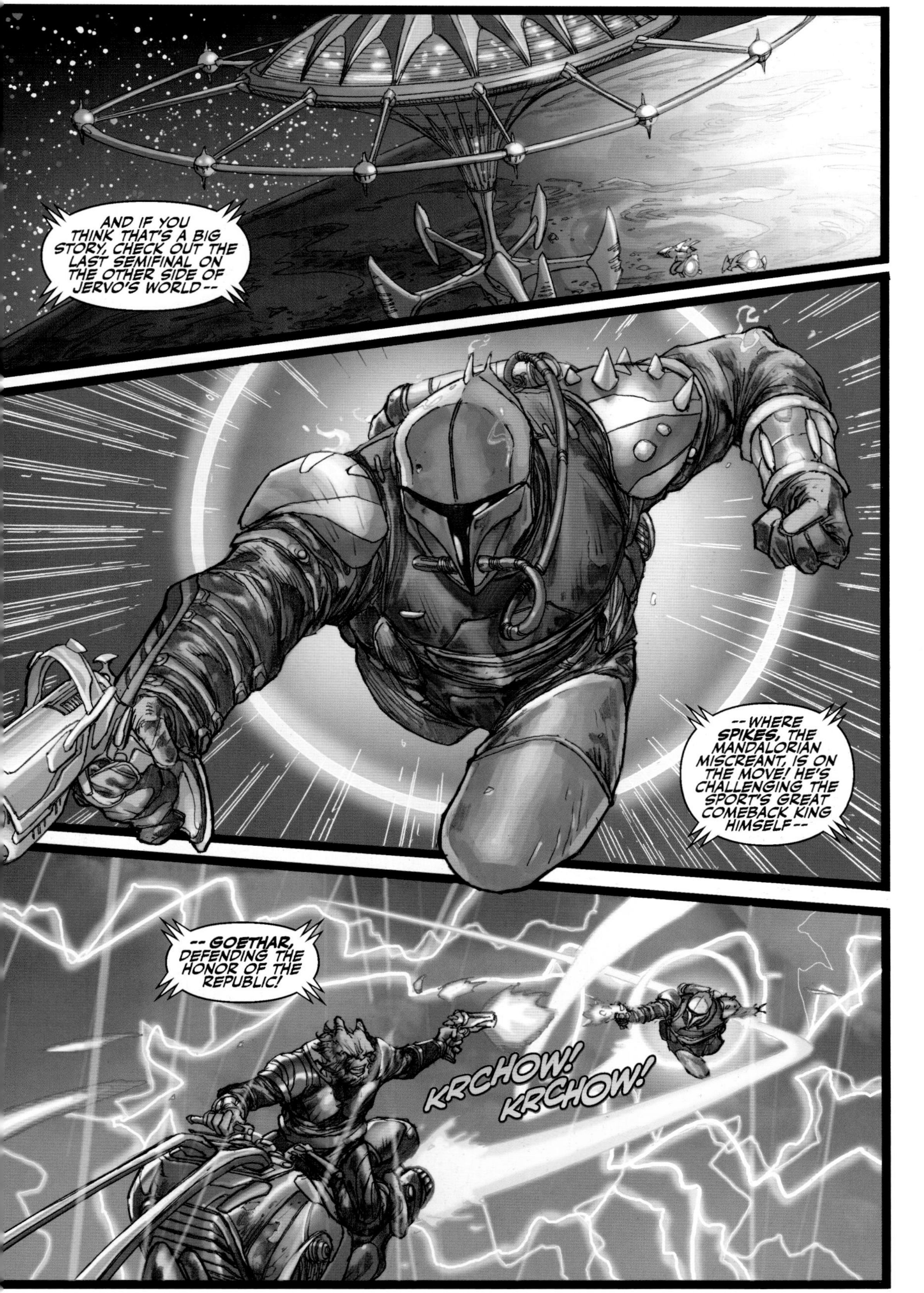
AND IF YOU THINK THAT'S A BIG STORY, CHECK OUT THE LAST SEMIFINAL ON THE OTHER SIDE OF JERVO'S WORLD--
--WHERE SPIKES, THE MANDALORIAN MISCREANT, IS ON THE MOVE! HE'S CHALLENGING THE SPORT'S GREAT COMEBACK KING HIMSELF--
--GOETHAR, DEFENDING THE HONOR OF THE REPUBLIC!
KRCHOW! KRCHOW!

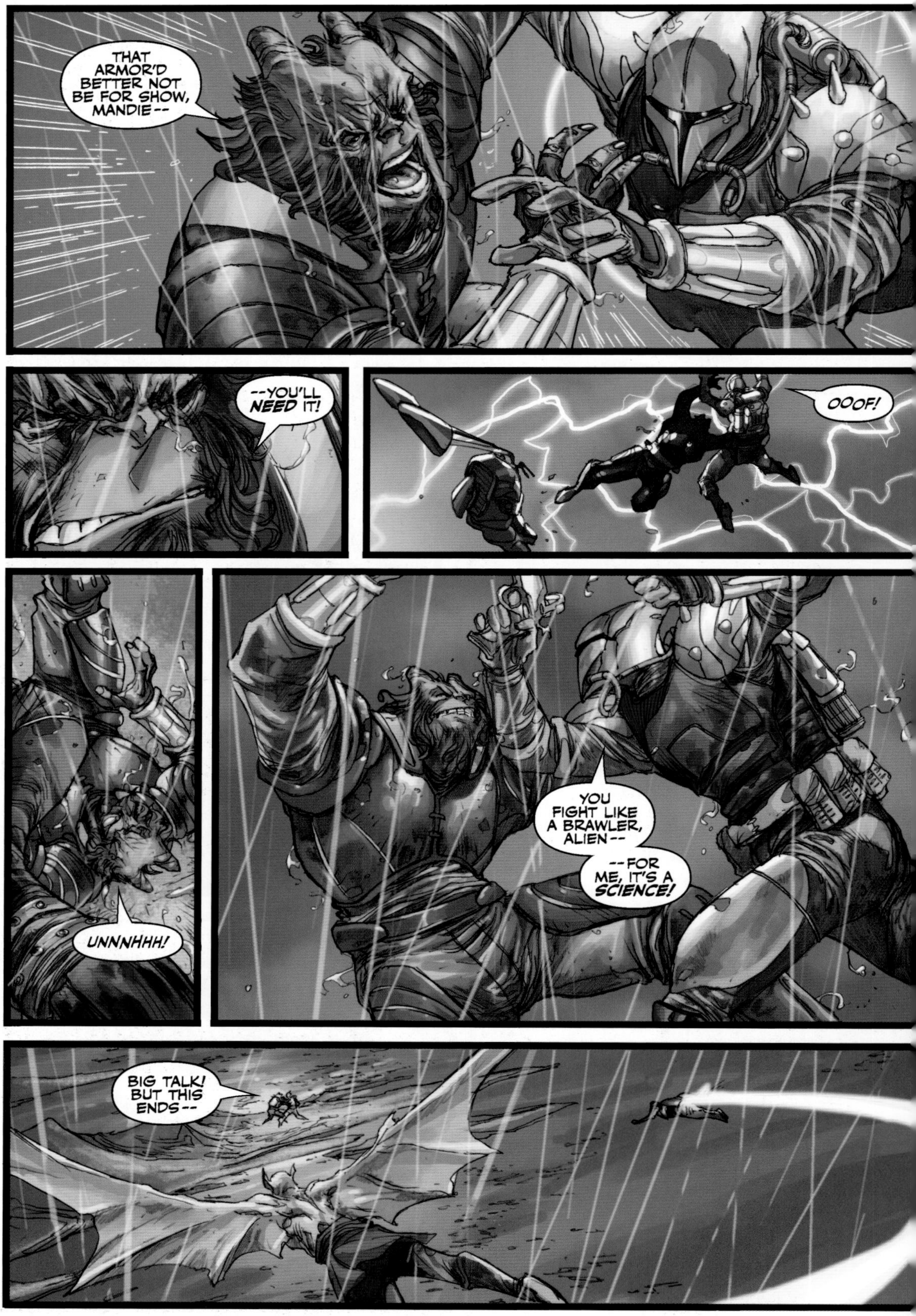
THAT ARMOR'D BETTER NOT BE FOR SHOW, MANDIE--
--YOU'LL NEED IT!
OOOF!
UNNNHHH!
YOU FIGHT LIKE A BRAWLER, ALIEN--
--FOR ME, IT'S A SCIENCE!
BIG TALK! BUT THIS ENDS--

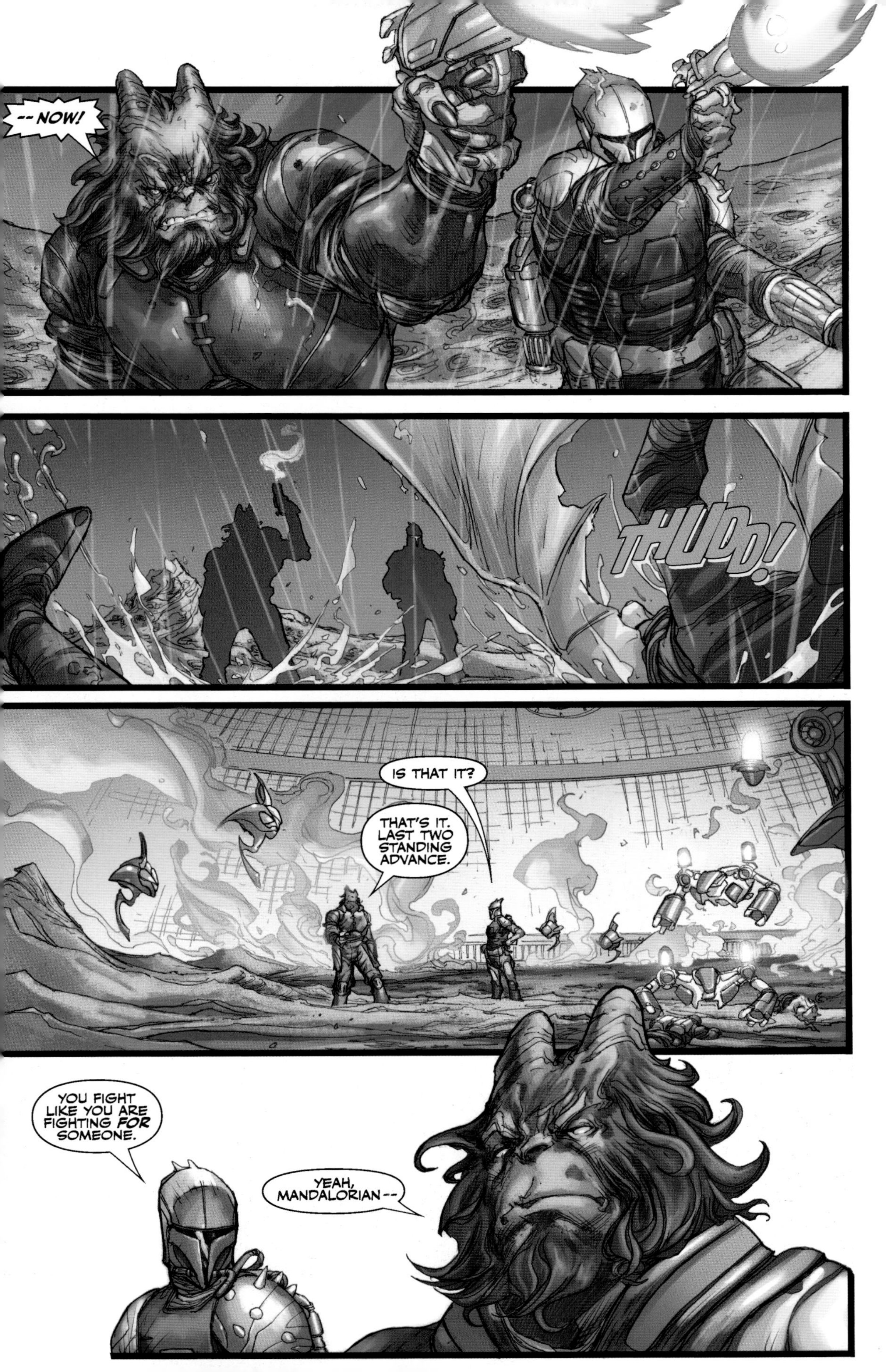
--NOW!
THUDD!
IS THAT IT?
THAT'S IT. LAST TWO STANDING ADVANCE.
YOU FIGHT LIKE YOU ARE FIGHTING *FOR* SOMEONE.
YEAH, MANDALORIAN--

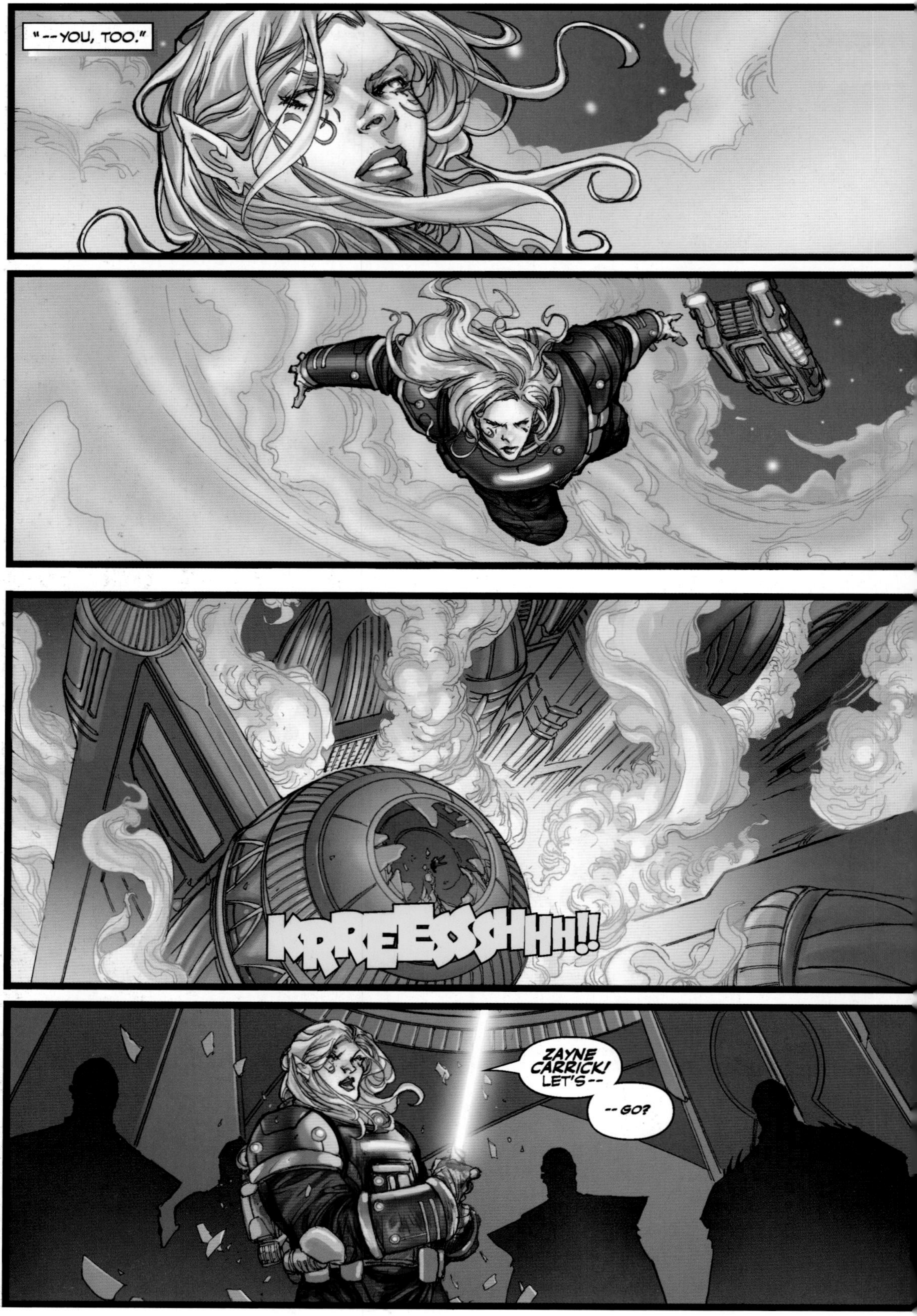
"--YOU, TOO."
KRREESSHHH!!
ZAYNE CARRICK! LET'S--
--GO?

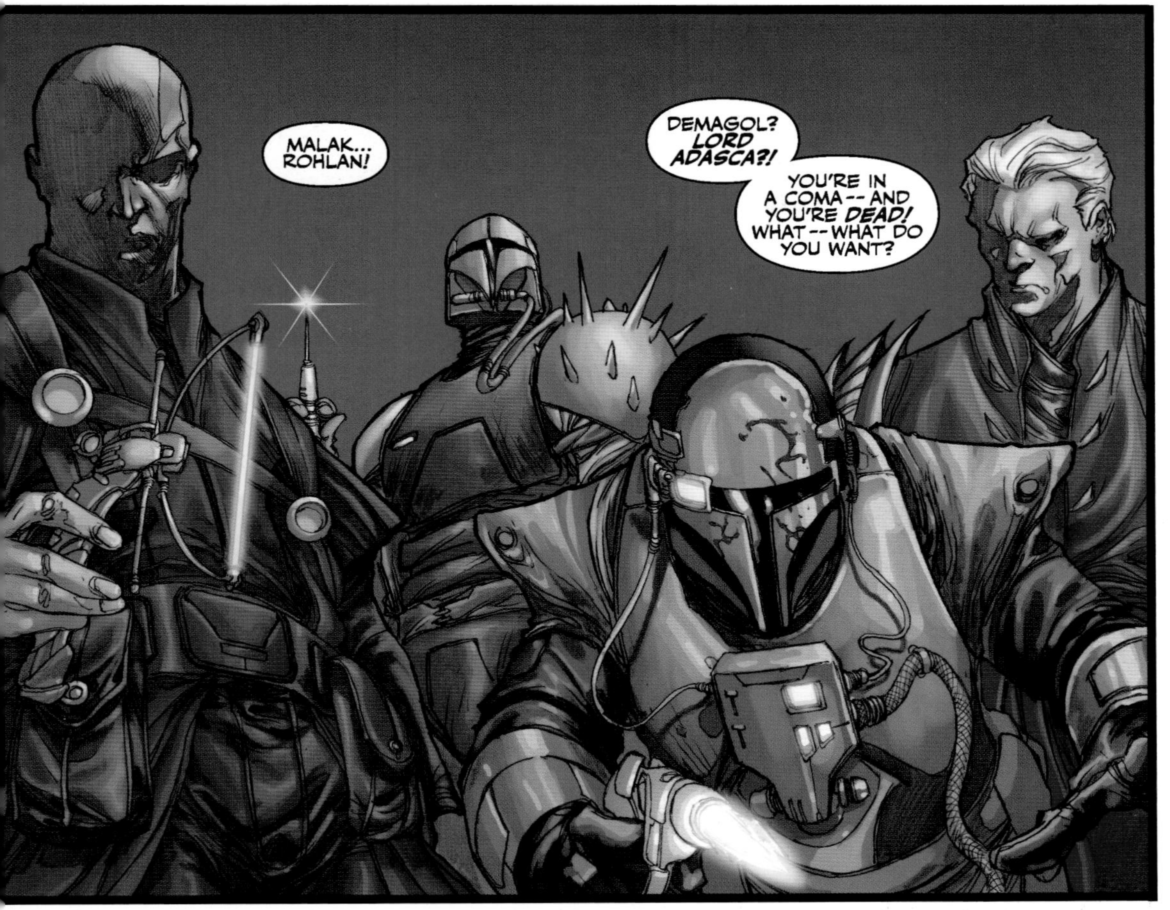
MALAK... ROHLAN!
DEMAGOL? LORD ADASCA?!
YOU'RE IN A COMA -- AND YOU'RE DEAD! WHAT -- WHAT DO YOU WANT?

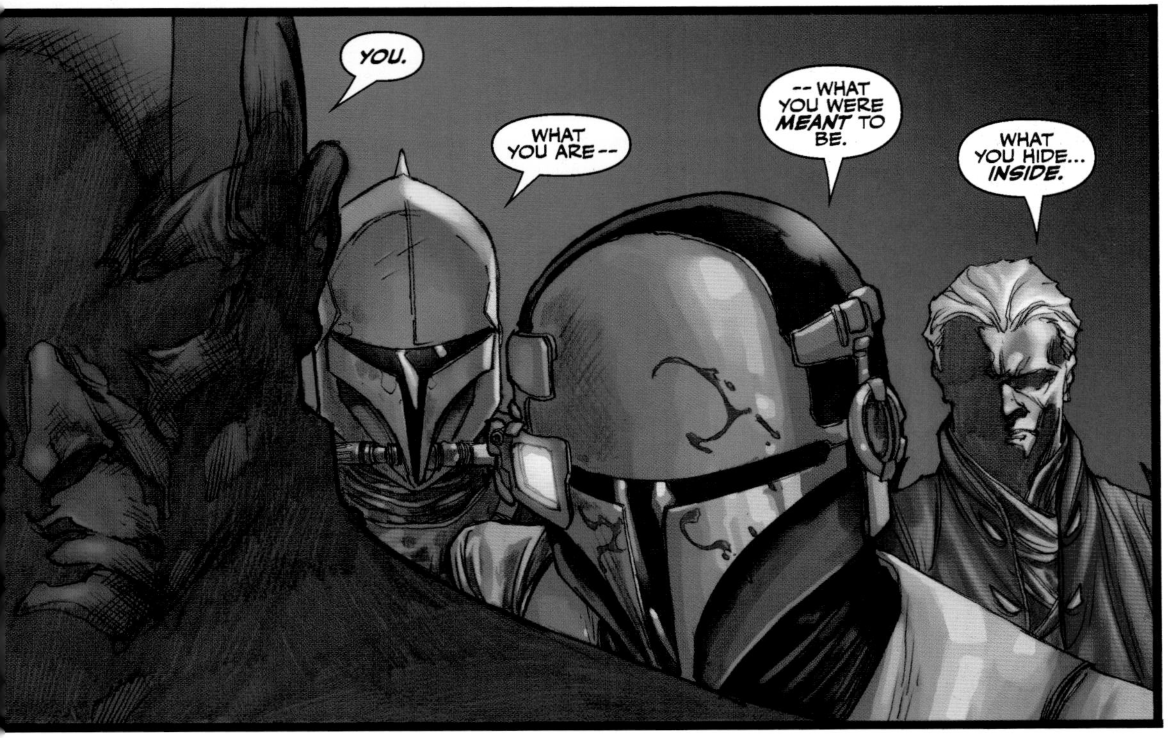
YOU.
WHAT YOU ARE --
-- WHAT YOU WERE MEANT TO BE.
WHAT YOU HIDE... INSIDE.

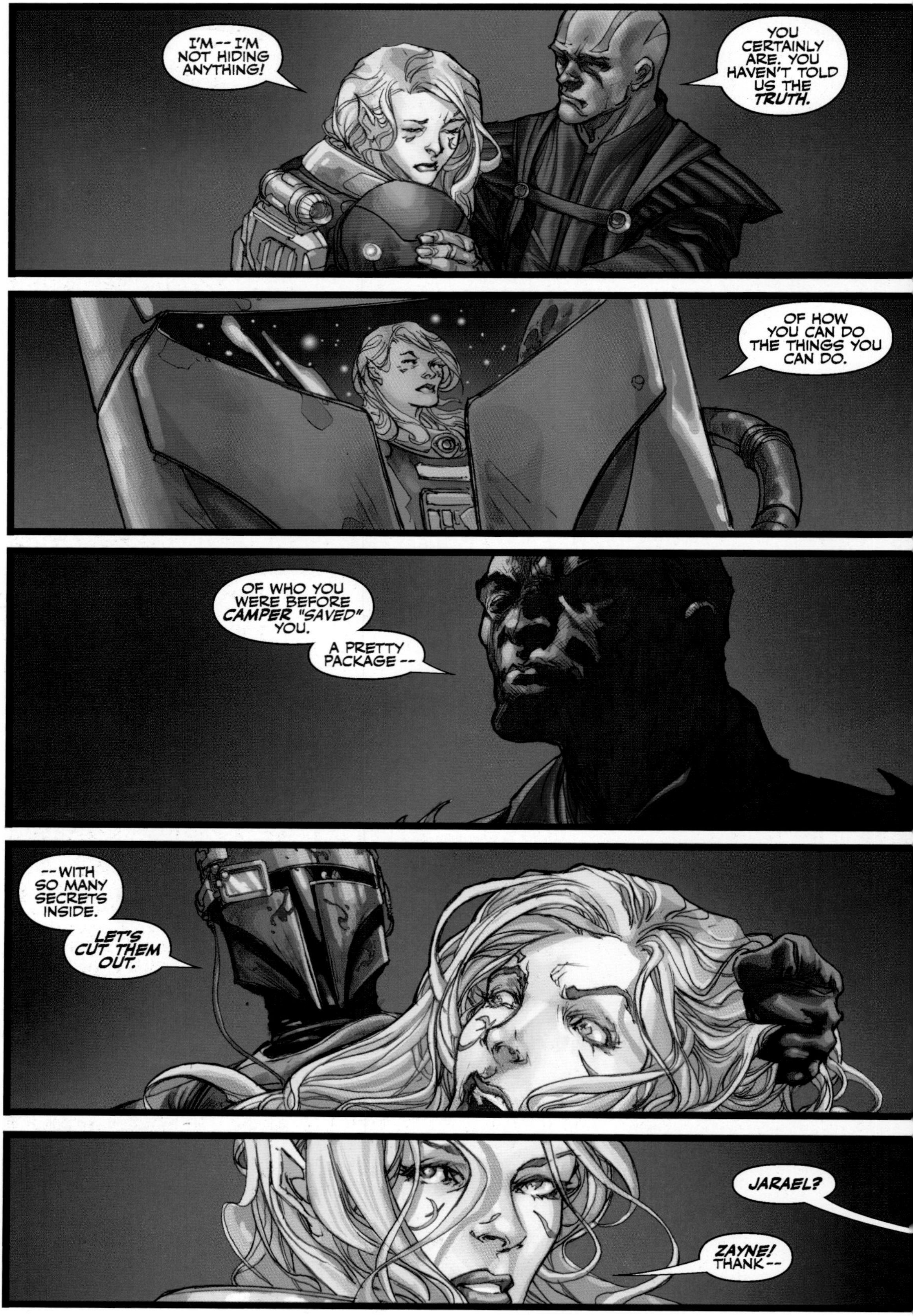
I'M -- I'M NOT HIDING ANYTHING!
YOU CERTAINLY ARE. YOU HAVEN'T TOLD US THE TRUTH.
OF HOW YOU CAN DO THE THINGS YOU CAN DO.
OF WHO YOU WERE BEFORE CAMPER "SAVED" YOU.
A PRETTY PACKAGE --
-- WITH SO MANY SECRETS INSIDE.
LET'S CUT THEM OUT.
JARAEL?
ZAYNE! THANK --

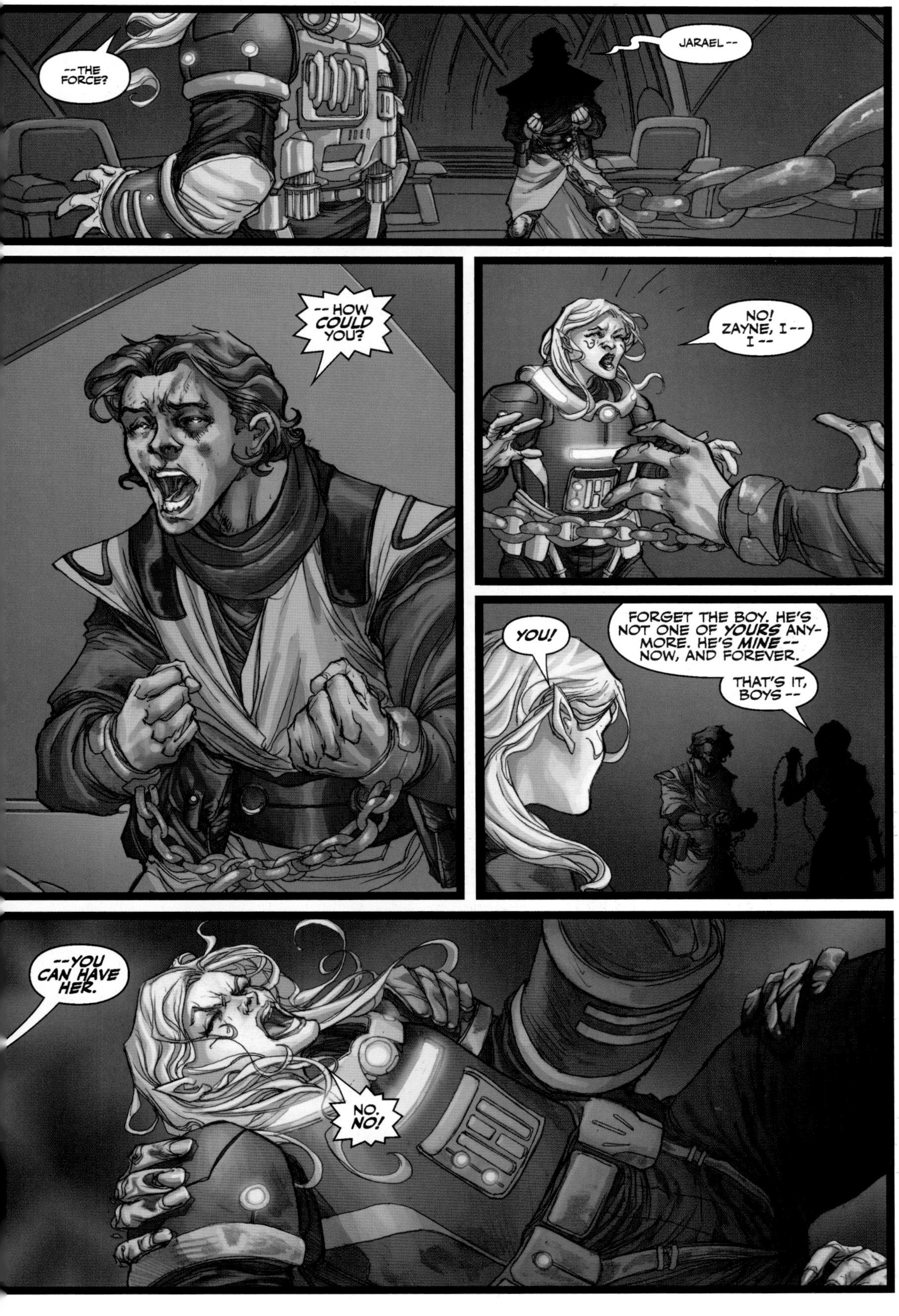
--THE FORCE?
JARAEL--
--HOW COULD YOU?
NO! ZAYNE, I-- I--
YOU!
FORGET THE BOY. HE'S NOT ONE OF YOURS ANYMORE. HE'S MINE-- NOW, AND FOREVER.
THAT'S IT, BOYS--
--YOU CAN HAVE HER.
NO. NO!

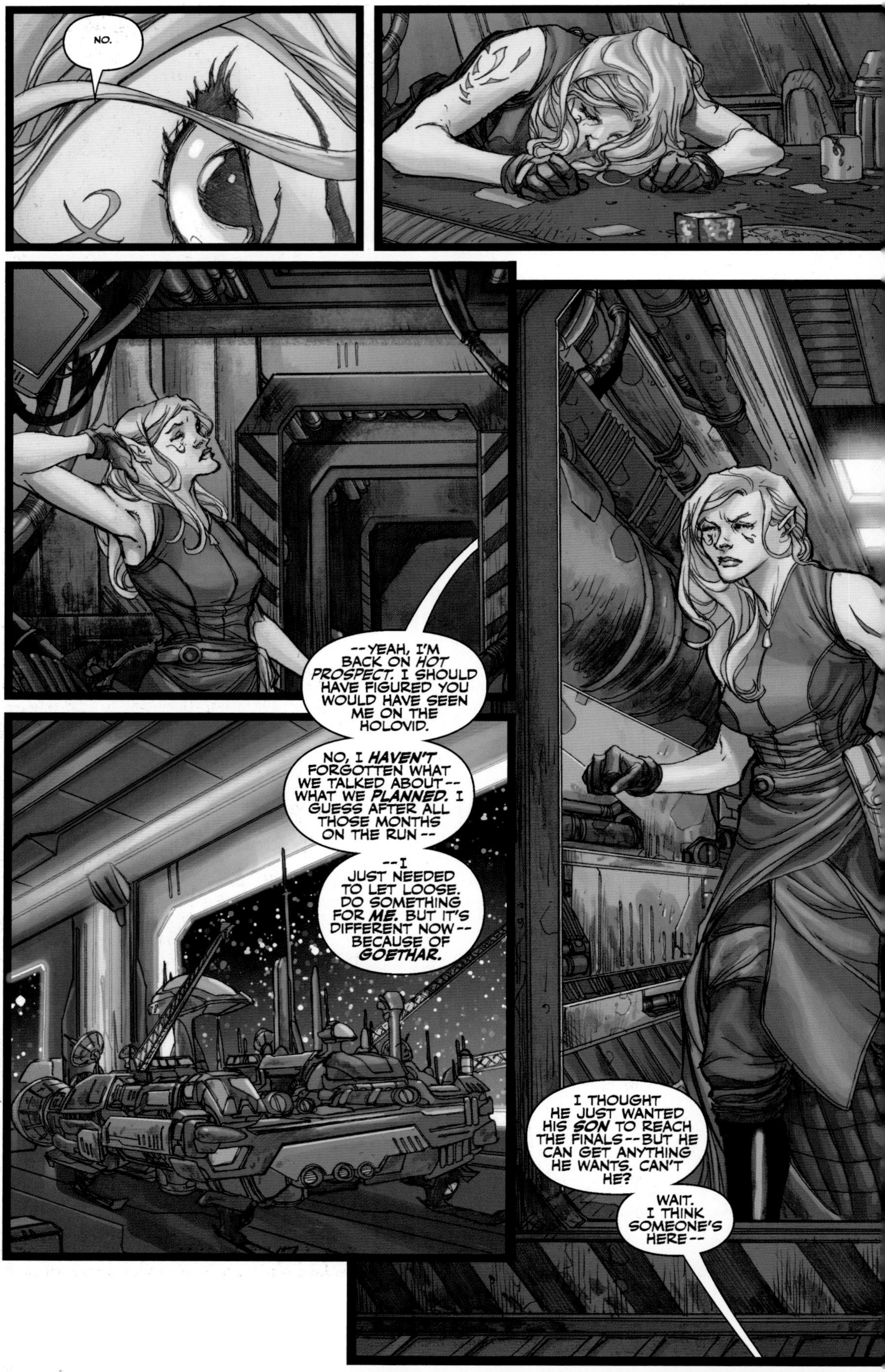
NO.
--YEAH, I'M BACK ON *HOT PROSPECT.* I SHOULD HAVE FIGURED YOU WOULD HAVE SEEN ME ON THE HOLOVID.
NO, I ***HAVEN'T*** FORGOTTEN WHAT WE TALKED ABOUT-- WHAT WE ***PLANNED.*** I GUESS AFTER ALL THOSE MONTHS ON THE RUN--
--I JUST NEEDED TO LET LOOSE. DO SOMETHING FOR ***ME.*** BUT IT'S DIFFERENT NOW-- BECAUSE OF ***GOETHAR.***
I THOUGHT HE JUST WANTED HIS ***SON*** TO REACH THE FINALS--BUT HE CAN GET ANYTHING HE WANTS. CAN'T HE?
WAIT. I THINK SOMEONE'S HERE--

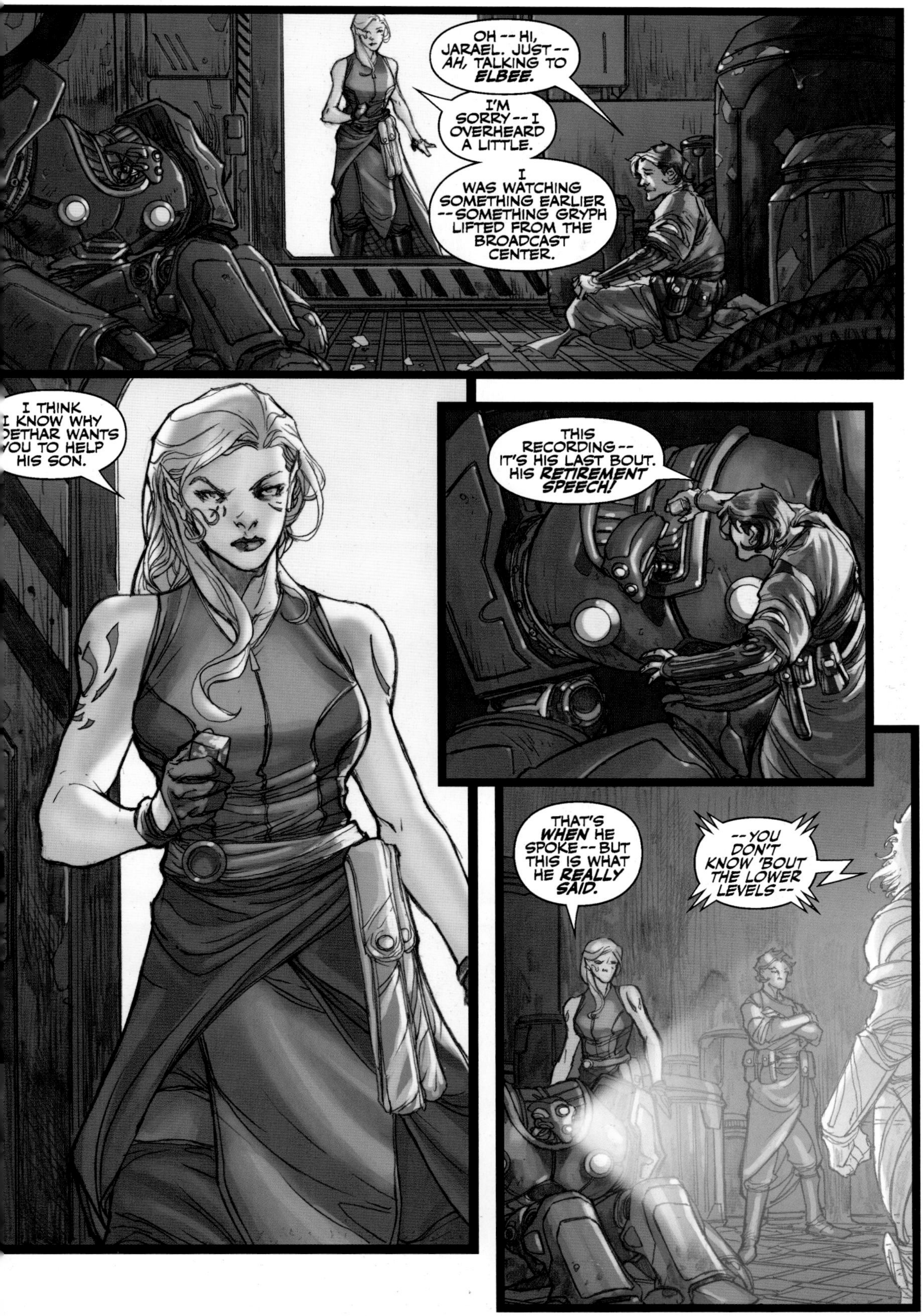
OH -- HI, JARAEL. JUST -- *AH,* TALKING TO ***ELBEE.***
I'M SORRY -- I OVERHEARD A LITTLE.
I WAS WATCHING SOMETHING EARLIER -- SOMETHING GRYPH LIFTED FROM THE BROADCAST CENTER.
I THINK I KNOW WHY DETHAR WANTS YOU TO HELP HIS SON.
THIS RECORDING -- IT'S HIS LAST BOUT. HIS ***RETIREMENT SPEECH!***
THAT'S ***WHEN*** HE SPOKE -- BUT THIS IS WHAT HE ***REALLY SAID.***
-- YOU DON'T KNOW 'BOUT THE LOWER LEVELS --

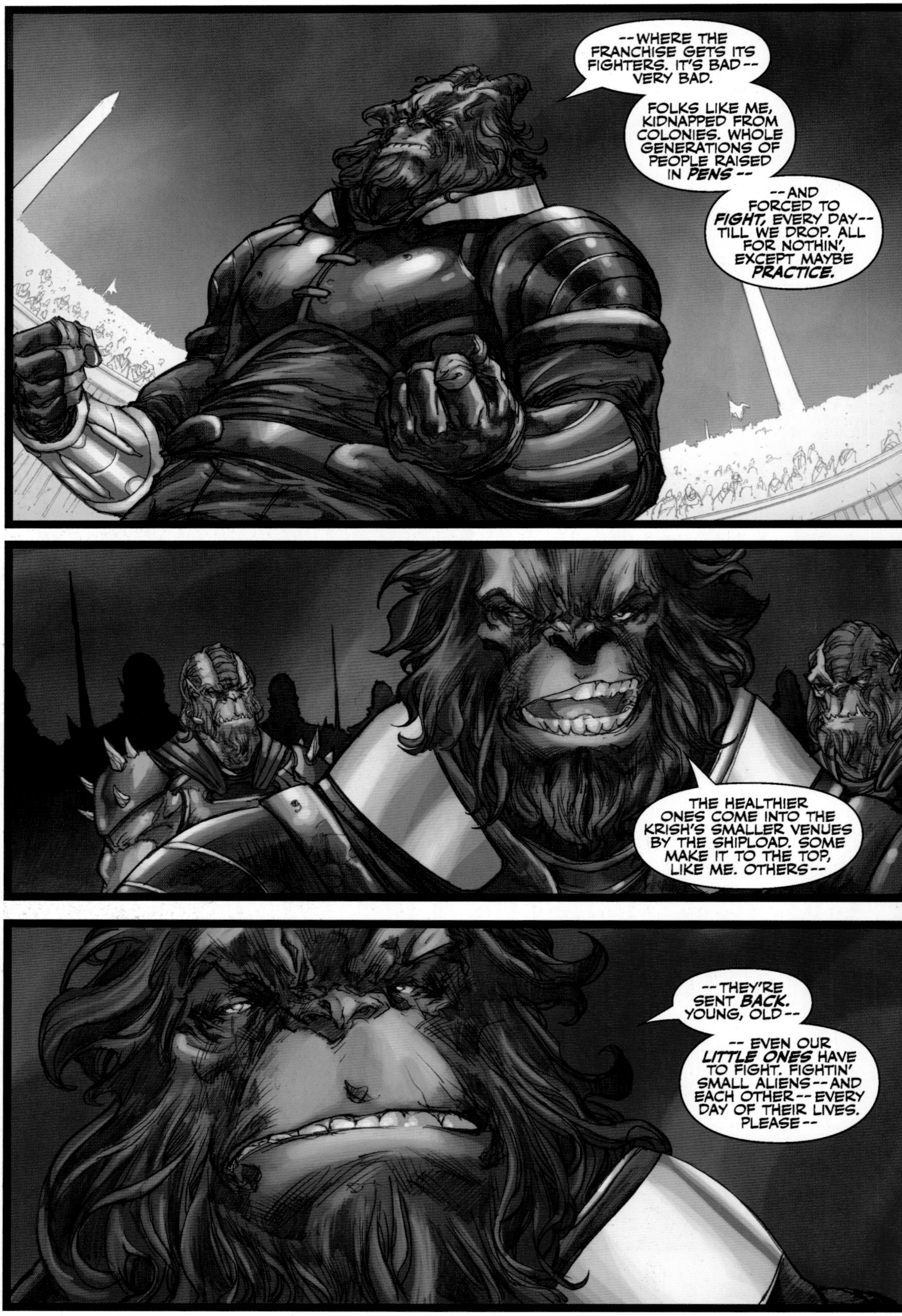
--WHERE THE FRANCHISE GETS ITS FIGHTERS. IT'S BAD--VERY BAD.
FOLKS LIKE ME, KIDNAPPED FROM COLONIES. WHOLE GENERATIONS OF PEOPLE RAISED IN *PENS*--
--AND FORCED TO *FIGHT,* EVERY DAY--TILL WE DROP. ALL FOR NOTHIN', EXCEPT MAYBE *PRACTICE.*
THE HEALTHIER ONES COME INTO THE KRISH'S SMALLER VENUES BY THE SHIPLOAD. SOME MAKE IT TO THE TOP, LIKE ME. OTHERS--
--THEY'RE SENT *BACK.* YOUNG, OLD--
-- EVEN OUR *LITTLE ONES* HAVE TO FIGHT. FIGHTIN' SMALL ALIENS--AND EACH OTHER--EVERY DAY OF THEIR LIVES. PLEASE--

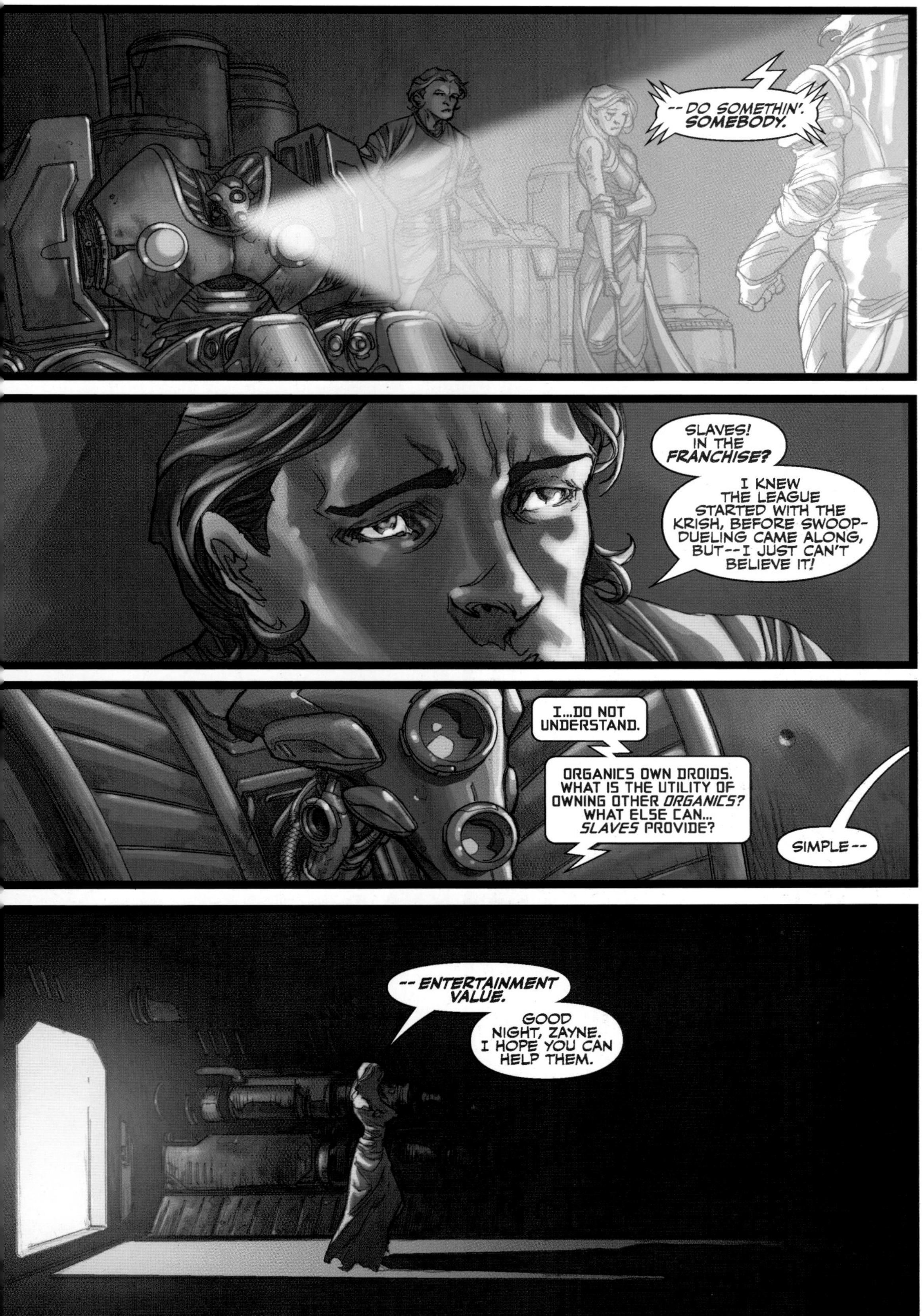
--DO SOMETHIN'. SOMEBODY.
SLAVES! IN THE FRANCHISE?
I KNEW THE LEAGUE STARTED WITH THE KRISH, BEFORE SWOOP-DUELING CAME ALONG, BUT--I JUST CAN'T BELIEVE IT!
I...DO NOT UNDERSTAND.
ORGANICS OWN DROIDS. WHAT IS THE UTILITY OF OWNING OTHER ORGANICS? WHAT ELSE CAN... SLAVES PROVIDE?
SIMPLE--
--ENTERTAINMENT VALUE.
GOOD NIGHT, ZAYNE. I HOPE YOU CAN HELP THEM.

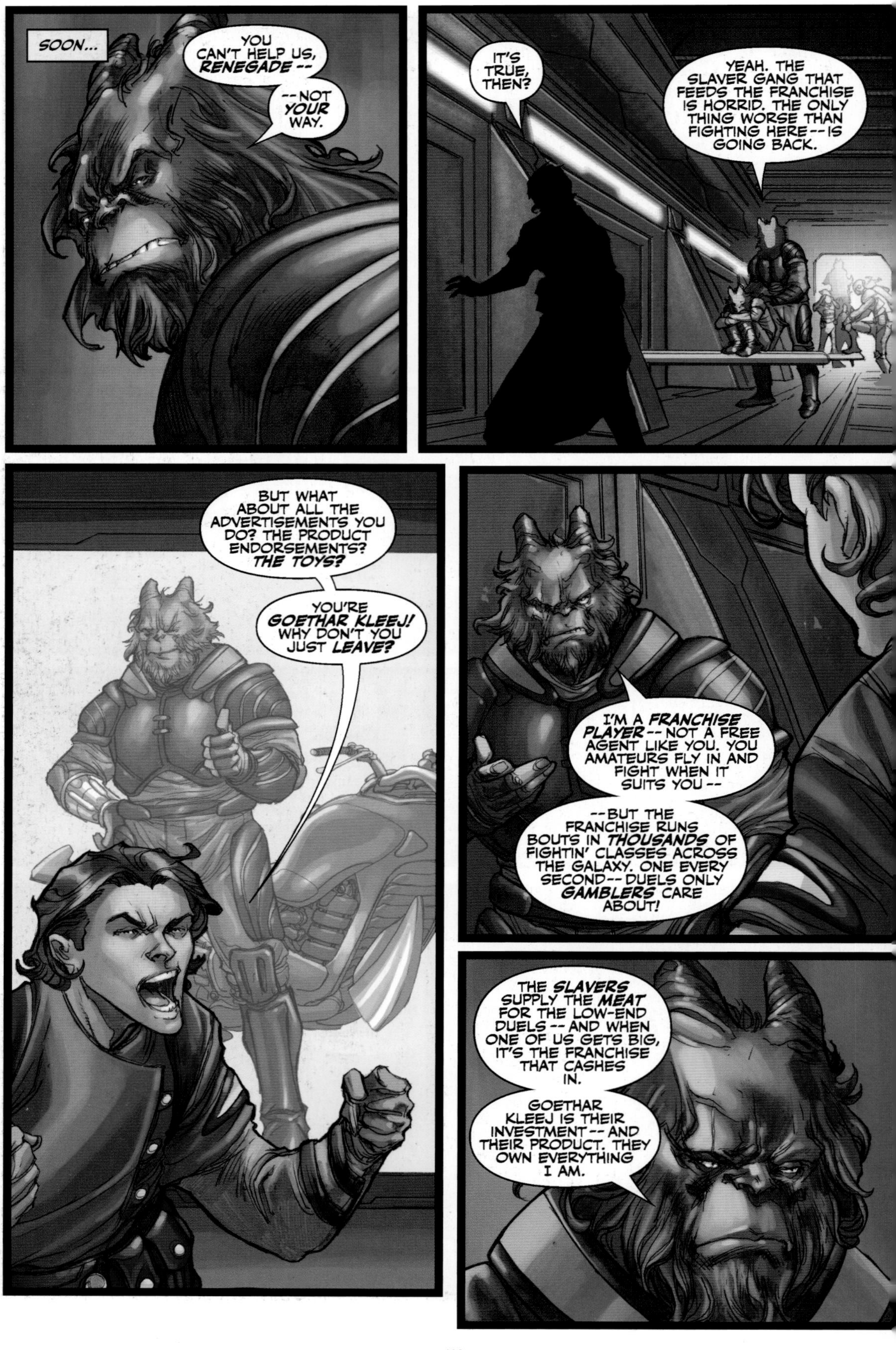
SOON...
YOU CAN'T HELP US, RENEGADE --
--NOT YOUR WAY.
IT'S TRUE, THEN?
YEAH. THE SLAVER GANG THAT FEEDS THE FRANCHISE IS HORRID. THE ONLY THING WORSE THAN FIGHTING HERE--IS GOING BACK.
BUT WHAT ABOUT ALL THE ADVERTISEMENTS YOU DO? THE PRODUCT ENDORSEMENTS? THE TOYS?
YOU'RE GOETHAR KLEEJ! WHY DON'T YOU JUST LEAVE?
I'M A FRANCHISE PLAYER -- NOT A FREE AGENT LIKE YOU. YOU AMATEURS FLY IN AND FIGHT WHEN IT SUITS YOU --
--BUT THE FRANCHISE RUNS BOUTS IN THOUSANDS OF FIGHTIN' CLASSES ACROSS THE GALAXY. ONE EVERY SECOND-- DUELS ONLY GAMBLERS CARE ABOUT!
THE SLAVERS SUPPLY THE MEAT FOR THE LOW-END DUELS -- AND WHEN ONE OF US GETS BIG, IT'S THE FRANCHISE THAT CASHES IN.
GOETHAR KLEEJ IS THEIR INVESTMENT -- AND THEIR PRODUCT. THEY OWN EVERYTHING I AM.

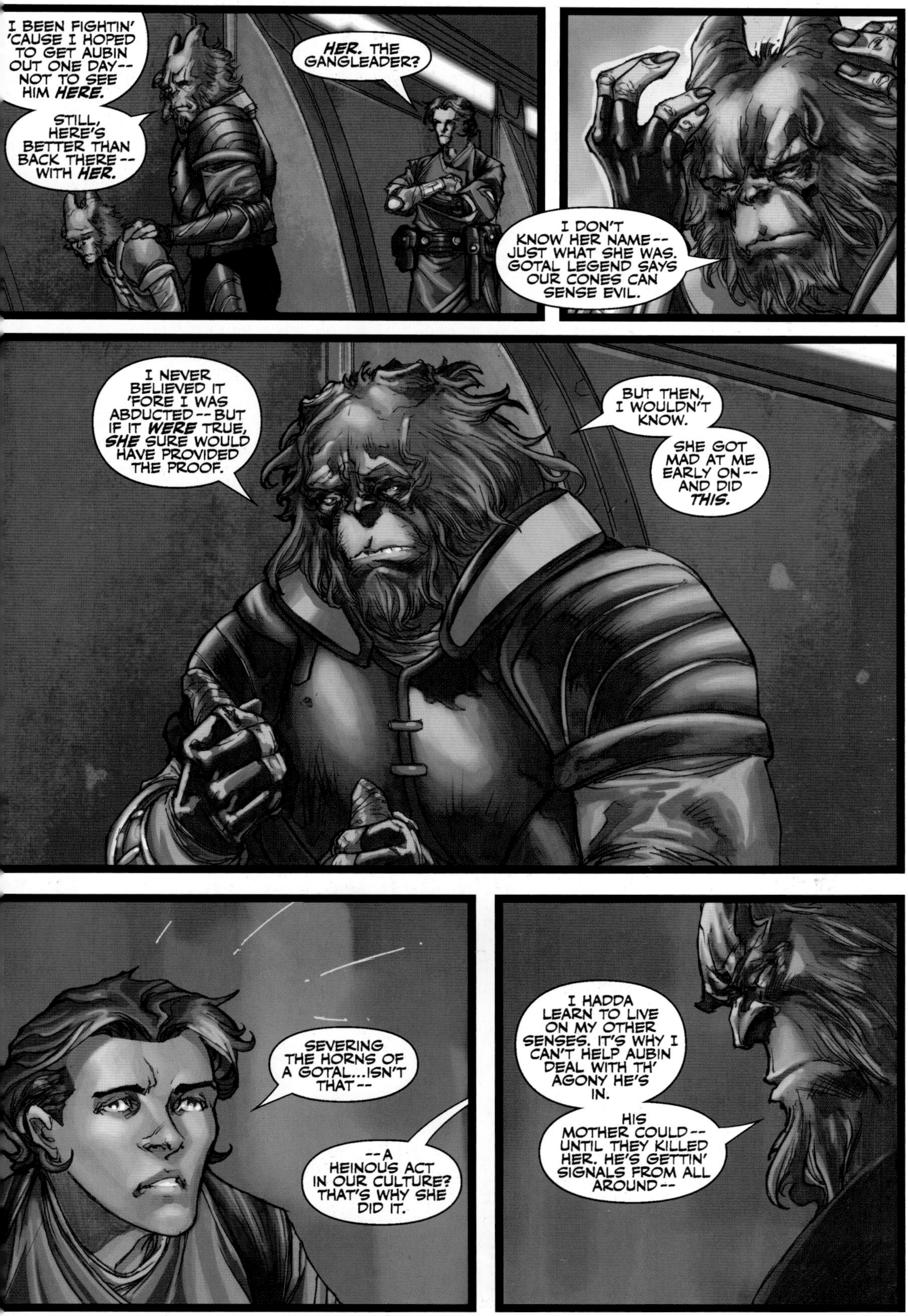

I BEEN FIGHTIN' 'CAUSE I HOPED TO GET AUBIN OUT ONE DAY-- NOT TO SEE HIM HERE.
STILL, HERE'S BETTER THAN BACK THERE-- WITH HER.
HER. THE GANGLEADER?
I DON'T KNOW HER NAME-- JUST WHAT SHE WAS. GOTAL LEGEND SAYS OUR CONES CAN SENSE EVIL.
I NEVER BELIEVED IT 'FORE I WAS ABDUCTED-- BUT IF IT WERE TRUE, SHE SURE WOULD HAVE PROVIDED THE PROOF.
BUT THEN, I WOULDN'T KNOW.
SHE GOT MAD AT ME EARLY ON-- AND DID THIS.
SEVERING THE HORNS OF A GOTAL...ISN'T THAT--
--A HEINOUS ACT IN OUR CULTURE? THAT'S WHY SHE DID IT.
I HADDA LEARN TO LIVE ON MY OTHER SENSES. IT'S WHY I CAN'T HELP AUBIN DEAL WITH TH' AGONY HE'S IN.
HIS MOTHER COULD-- UNTIL THEY KILLED HER. HE'S GETTIN' SIGNALS FROM ALL AROUND--

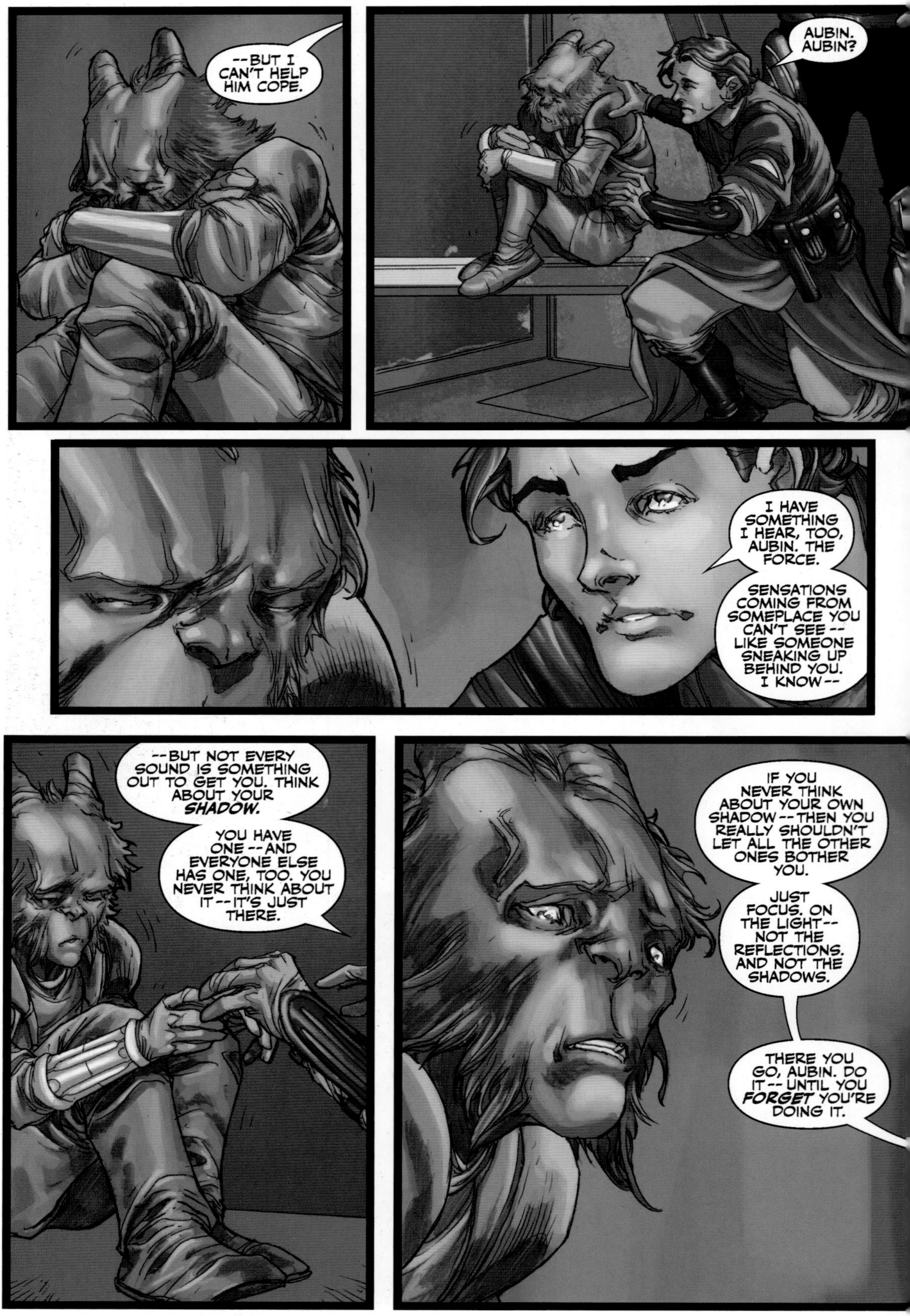
--BUT I CAN'T HELP HIM COPE.
AUBIN. AUBIN?
I HAVE SOMETHING I HEAR, TOO, AUBIN. THE FORCE.
SENSATIONS COMING FROM SOMEPLACE YOU CAN'T SEE--LIKE SOMEONE SNEAKING UP BEHIND YOU. I KNOW--
--BUT NOT EVERY SOUND IS SOMETHING OUT TO GET YOU. THINK ABOUT YOUR *SHADOW.*
YOU HAVE ONE--AND EVERYONE ELSE HAS ONE, TOO. YOU NEVER THINK ABOUT IT--IT'S JUST THERE.
IF YOU NEVER THINK ABOUT YOUR OWN SHADOW--THEN YOU REALLY SHOULDN'T LET ALL THE OTHER ONES BOTHER YOU.
JUST FOCUS. ON THE LIGHT--NOT THE REFLECTIONS. AND NOT THE SHADOWS.
THERE YOU GO, AUBIN. DO IT--UNTIL YOU *FORGET* YOU'RE DOING IT.

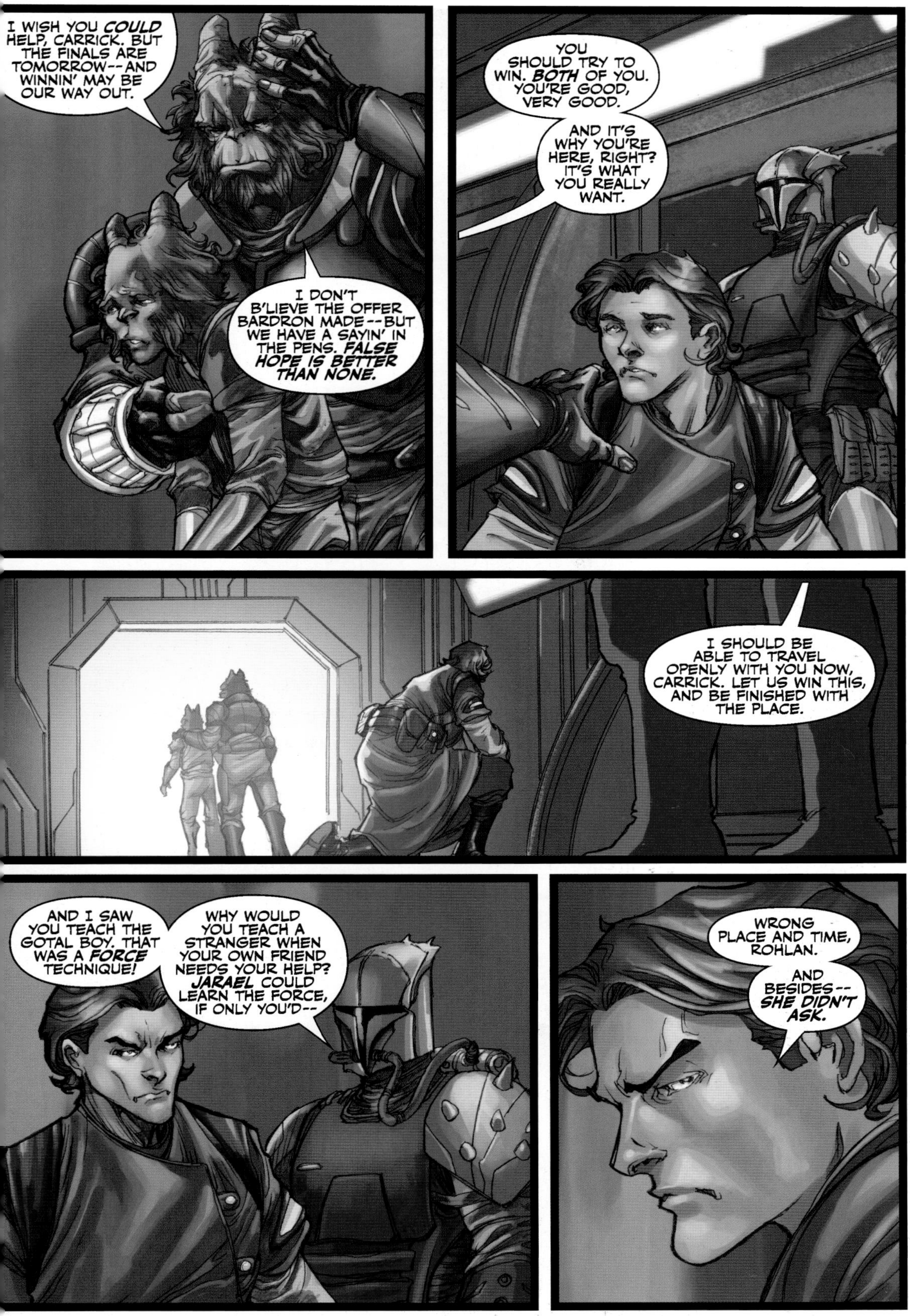
I WISH YOU COULD HELP, CARRICK. BUT THE FINALS ARE TOMORROW--AND WINNIN' MAY BE OUR WAY OUT.
I DON'T B'LIEVE THE OFFER BARDRON MADE--BUT WE HAVE A SAYIN' IN THE PENS. FALSE HOPE IS BETTER THAN NONE.
YOU SHOULD TRY TO WIN. BOTH OF YOU. YOU'RE GOOD, VERY GOOD.
AND IT'S WHY YOU'RE HERE, RIGHT? IT'S WHAT YOU REALLY WANT.
I SHOULD BE ABLE TO TRAVEL OPENLY WITH YOU NOW, CARRICK. LET US WIN THIS, AND BE FINISHED WITH THE PLACE.
AND I SAW YOU TEACH THE GOTAL BOY. THAT WAS A FORCE TECHNIQUE!
WHY WOULD YOU TEACH A STRANGER WHEN YOUR OWN FRIEND NEEDS YOUR HELP? JARAEL COULD LEARN THE FORCE, IF ONLY YOU'D--
WRONG PLACE AND TIME, ROHLAN.
AND BESIDES--SHE DIDN'T ASK.

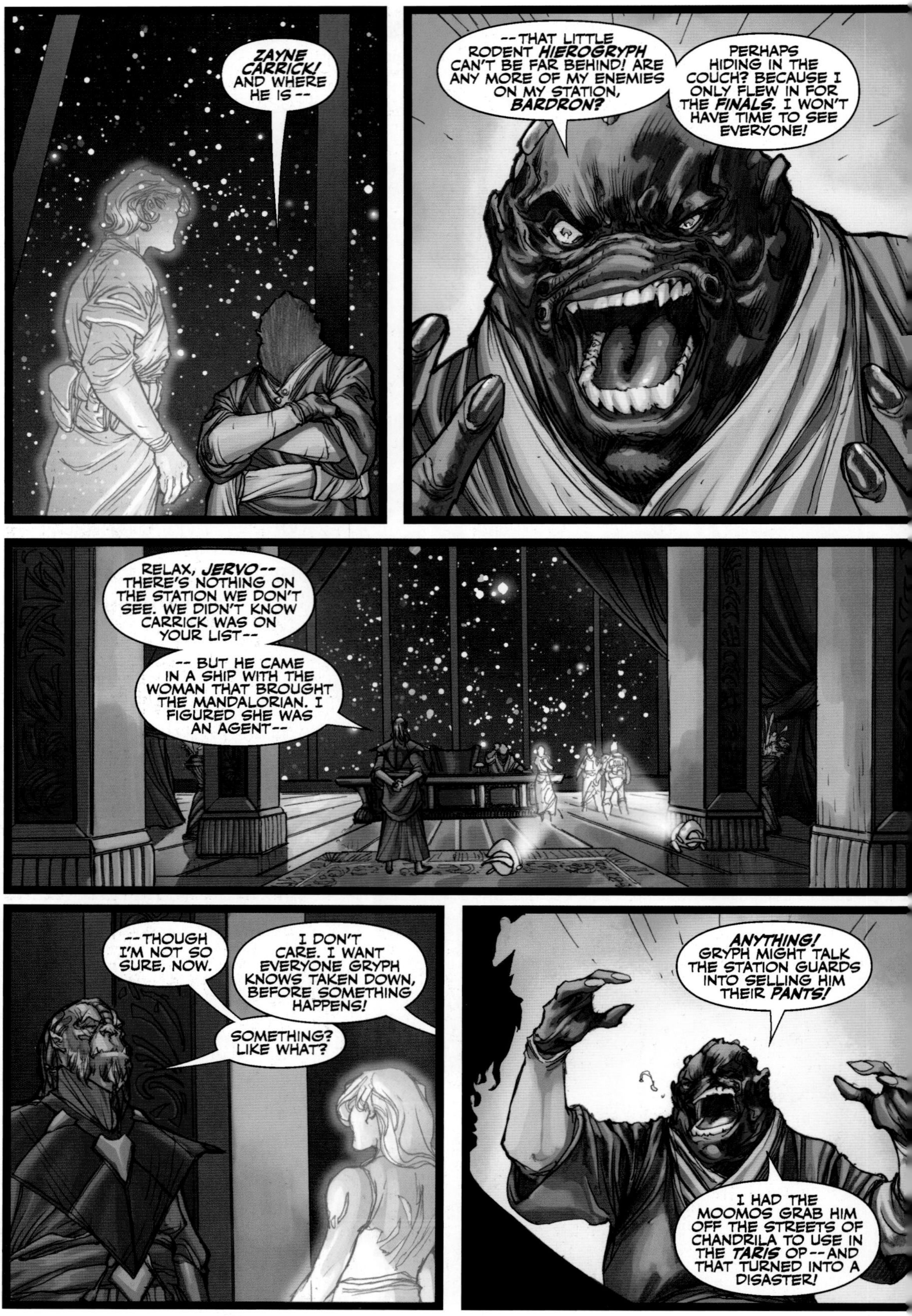
ZAYNE CARRICK! AND WHERE HE IS --
--THAT LITTLE RODENT HIEROGRYPH CAN'T BE FAR BEHIND! ARE ANY MORE OF MY ENEMIES ON MY STATION, BARDRON?
PERHAPS HIDING IN THE COUCH? BECAUSE I ONLY FLEW IN FOR THE FINALS. I WON'T HAVE TIME TO SEE EVERYONE!
RELAX, JERVO-- THERE'S NOTHING ON THE STATION WE DON'T SEE. WE DIDN'T KNOW CARRICK WAS ON YOUR LIST--
-- BUT HE CAME IN A SHIP WITH THE WOMAN THAT BROUGHT THE MANDALORIAN. I FIGURED SHE WAS AN AGENT--
--THOUGH I'M NOT SO SURE, NOW.
I DON'T CARE. I WANT EVERYONE GRYPH KNOWS TAKEN DOWN, BEFORE SOMETHING HAPPENS!
SOMETHING? LIKE WHAT?
ANYTHING! GRYPH MIGHT TALK THE STATION GUARDS INTO SELLING HIM THEIR PANTS!
I HAD THE MOOMOS GRAB HIM OFF THE STREETS OF CHANDRILA TO USE IN THE TARIS OP--AND THAT TURNED INTO A DISASTER!

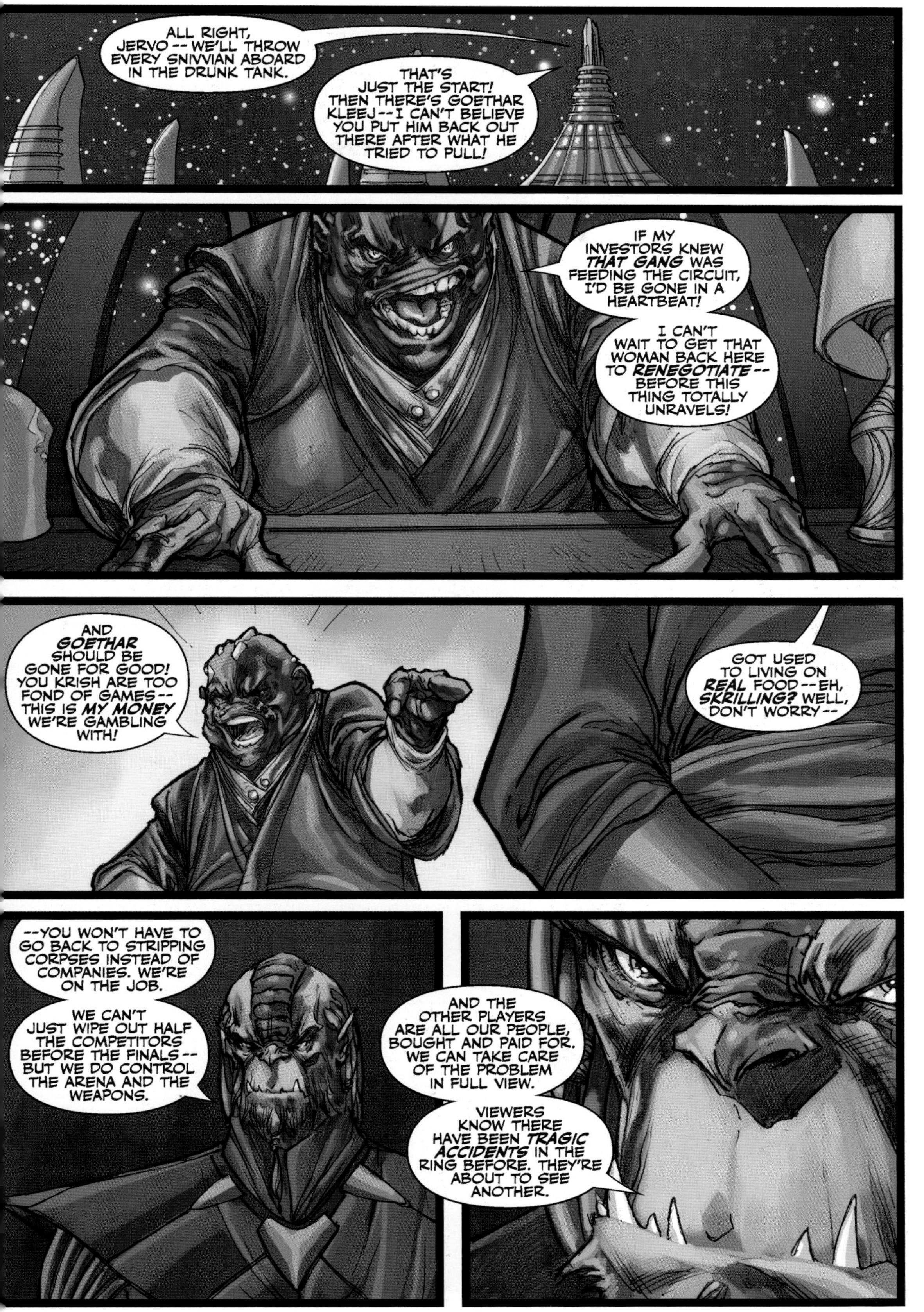

ALL RIGHT, JERVO--WE'LL THROW EVERY SNIVVIAN ABOARD IN THE DRUNK TANK.
THAT'S JUST THE START! THEN THERE'S GOETHAR KLEEJ--I CAN'T BELIEVE YOU PUT HIM BACK OUT THERE AFTER WHAT HE TRIED TO PULL!
IF MY INVESTORS KNEW *THAT GANG* WAS FEEDING THE CIRCUIT, I'D BE GONE IN A HEARTBEAT!
I CAN'T WAIT TO GET THAT WOMAN BACK HERE TO *RENEGOTIATE*--BEFORE THIS THING TOTALLY UNRAVELS!
AND *GOETHAR* SHOULD BE GONE FOR GOOD! YOU KRISH ARE TOO FOND OF GAMES--THIS IS *MY MONEY* WE'RE GAMBLING WITH!
GOT USED TO LIVING ON *REAL* FOOD--EH, *SKRILLING?* WELL, DON'T WORRY--
--YOU WON'T HAVE TO GO BACK TO STRIPPING CORPSES INSTEAD OF COMPANIES. WE'RE ON THE JOB.
WE CAN'T JUST WIPE OUT HALF THE COMPETITORS BEFORE THE FINALS--BUT WE DO CONTROL THE ARENA AND THE WEAPONS.
AND THE OTHER PLAYERS ARE ALL OUR PEOPLE, BOUGHT AND PAID FOR. WE CAN TAKE CARE OF THE PROBLEM IN FULL VIEW.
VIEWERS KNOW THERE HAVE BEEN *TRAGIC ACCIDENTS* IN THE RING BEFORE. THEY'RE ABOUT TO SEE ANOTHER.

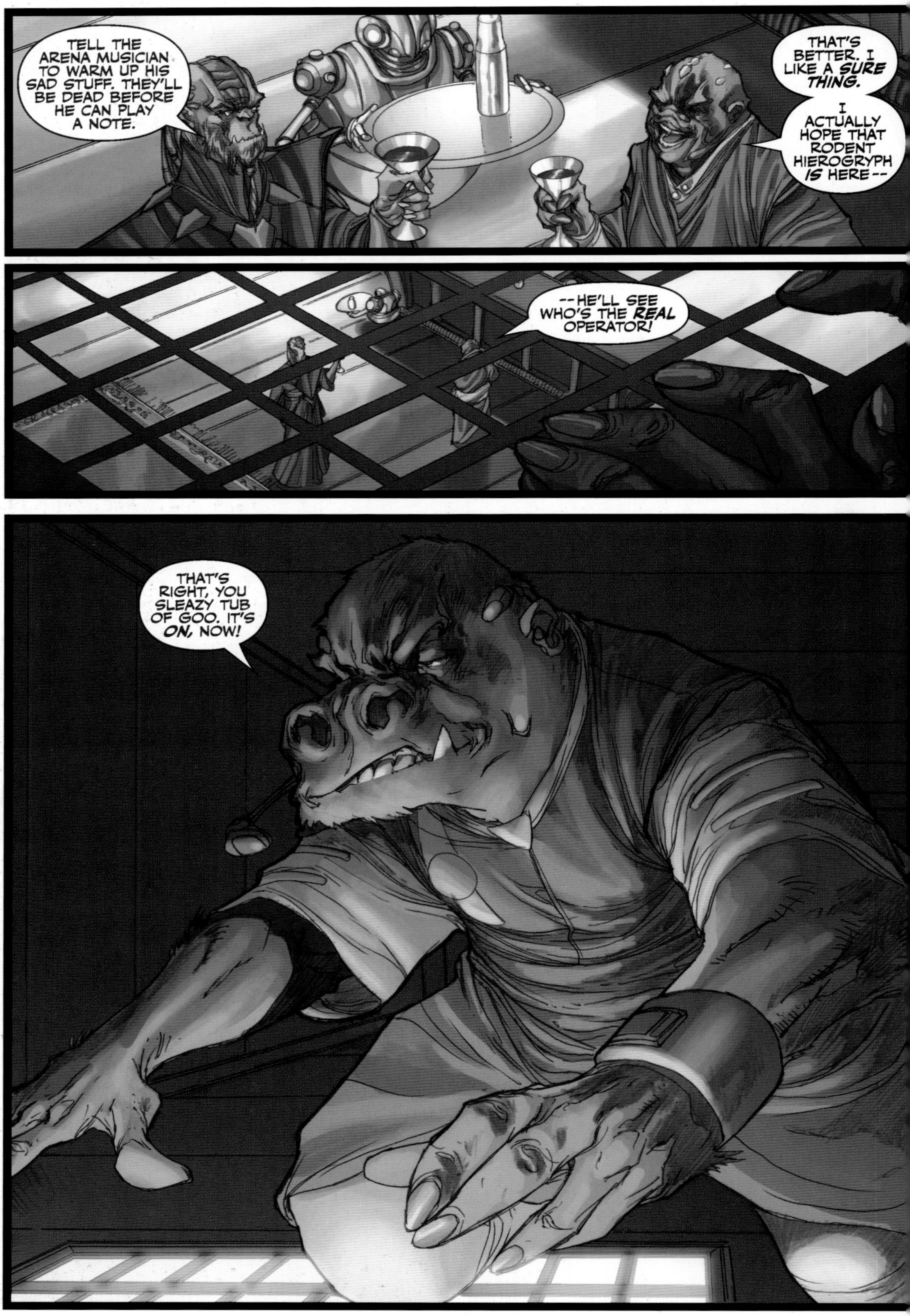
TELL THE ARENA MUSICIAN TO WARM UP HIS SAD STUFF. THEY'LL BE DEAD BEFORE HE CAN PLAY A NOTE.
THAT'S BETTER. I LIKE A *SURE THING.*
I ACTUALLY HOPE THAT RODENT HIEROGRYPH *IS* HERE--
--HE'LL SEE WHO'S THE *REAL* OPERATOR!
THAT'S RIGHT, YOU SLEAZY TUB OF GOO. IT'S *ON,* NOW!

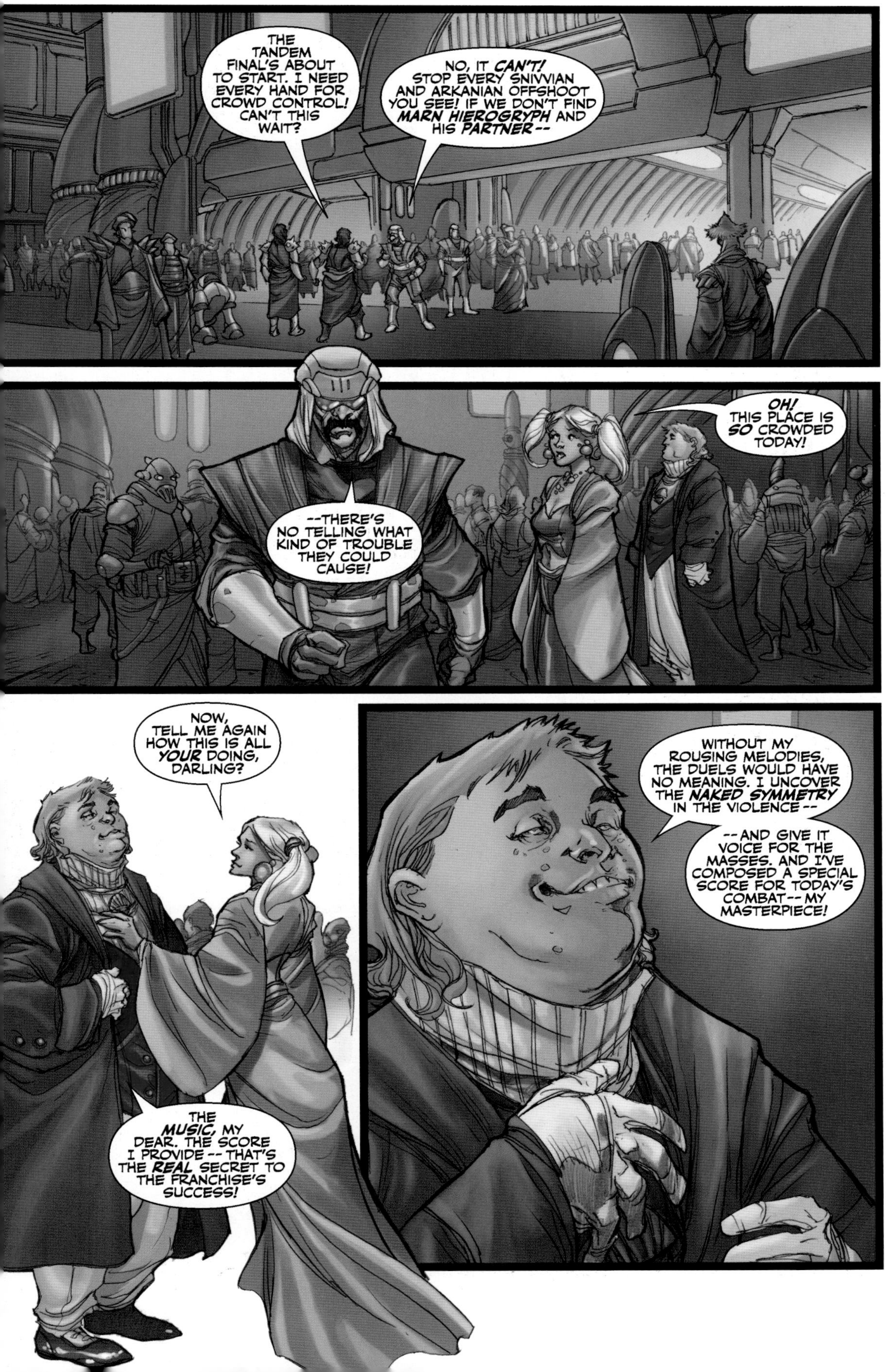
THE TANDEM FINAL'S ABOUT TO START. I NEED EVERY HAND FOR CROWD CONTROL! CAN'T THIS WAIT?
NO, IT CAN'T! STOP EVERY SNIVVIAN AND ARKANIAN OFFSHOOT YOU SEE! IF WE DON'T FIND MARN HIEROGRYPH AND HIS PARTNER--
OH! THIS PLACE IS SO CROWDED TODAY!
--THERE'S NO TELLING WHAT KIND OF TROUBLE THEY COULD CAUSE!
NOW, TELL ME AGAIN HOW THIS IS ALL YOUR DOING, DARLING?
THE MUSIC, MY DEAR. THE SCORE I PROVIDE -- THAT'S THE REAL SECRET TO THE FRANCHISE'S SUCCESS!
WITHOUT MY ROUSING MELODIES, THE DUELS WOULD HAVE NO MEANING. I UNCOVER THE NAKED SYMMETRY IN THE VIOLENCE --
--AND GIVE IT VOICE FOR THE MASSES. AND I'VE COMPOSED A SPECIAL SCORE FOR TODAY'S COMBAT-- MY MASTERPIECE!

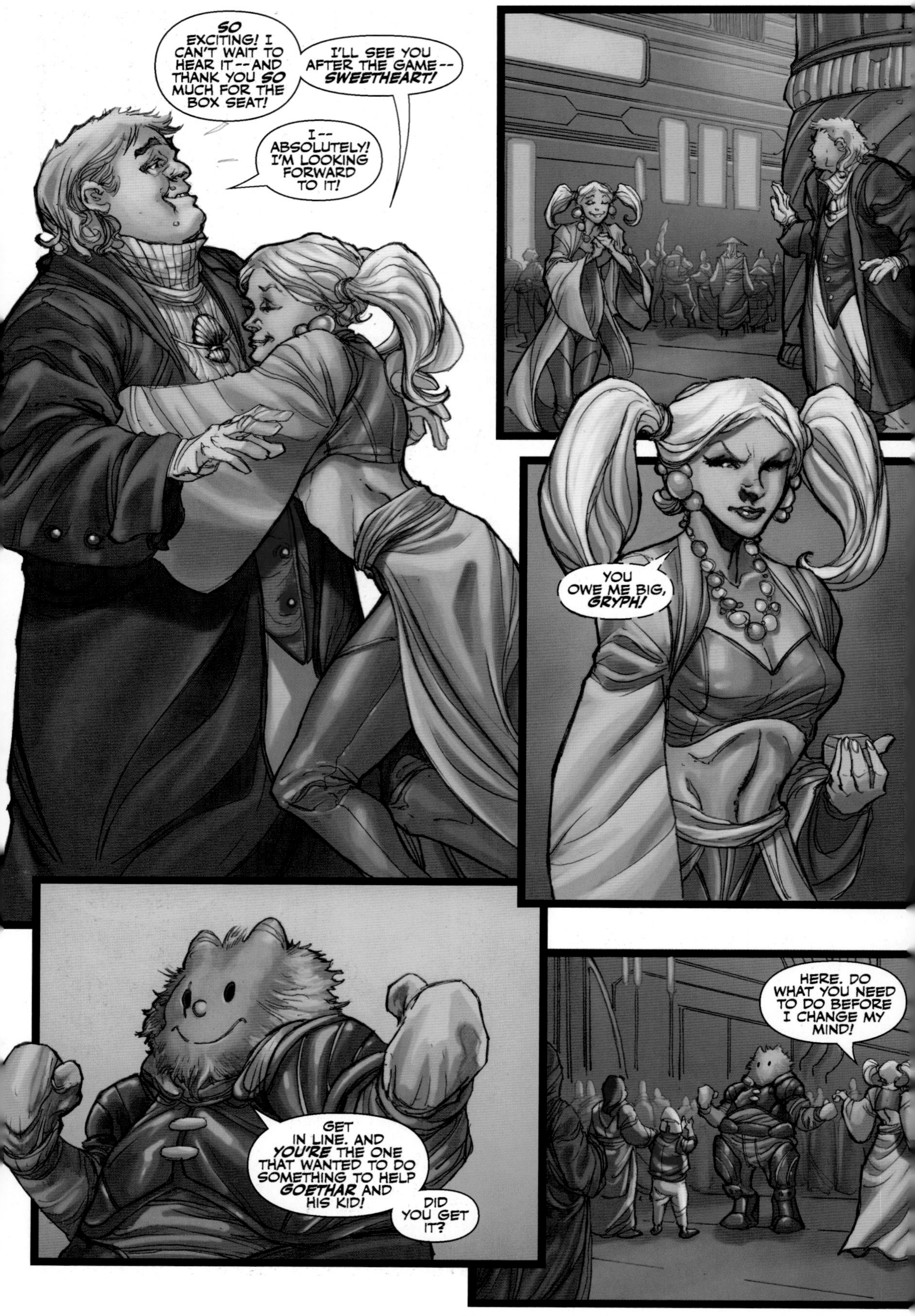
SO EXCITING! I CAN'T WAIT TO HEAR IT--AND THANK YOU SO MUCH FOR THE BOX SEAT!
I'LL SEE YOU AFTER THE GAME-- SWEETHEART!
I-- ABSOLUTELY! I'M LOOKING FORWARD TO IT!
YOU OWE ME BIG, GRYPH!
GET IN LINE. AND YOU'RE THE ONE THAT WANTED TO DO SOMETHING TO HELP GOETHAR AND HIS KID!
DID YOU GET IT?
HERE. DO WHAT YOU NEED TO DO BEFORE I CHANGE MY MIND!

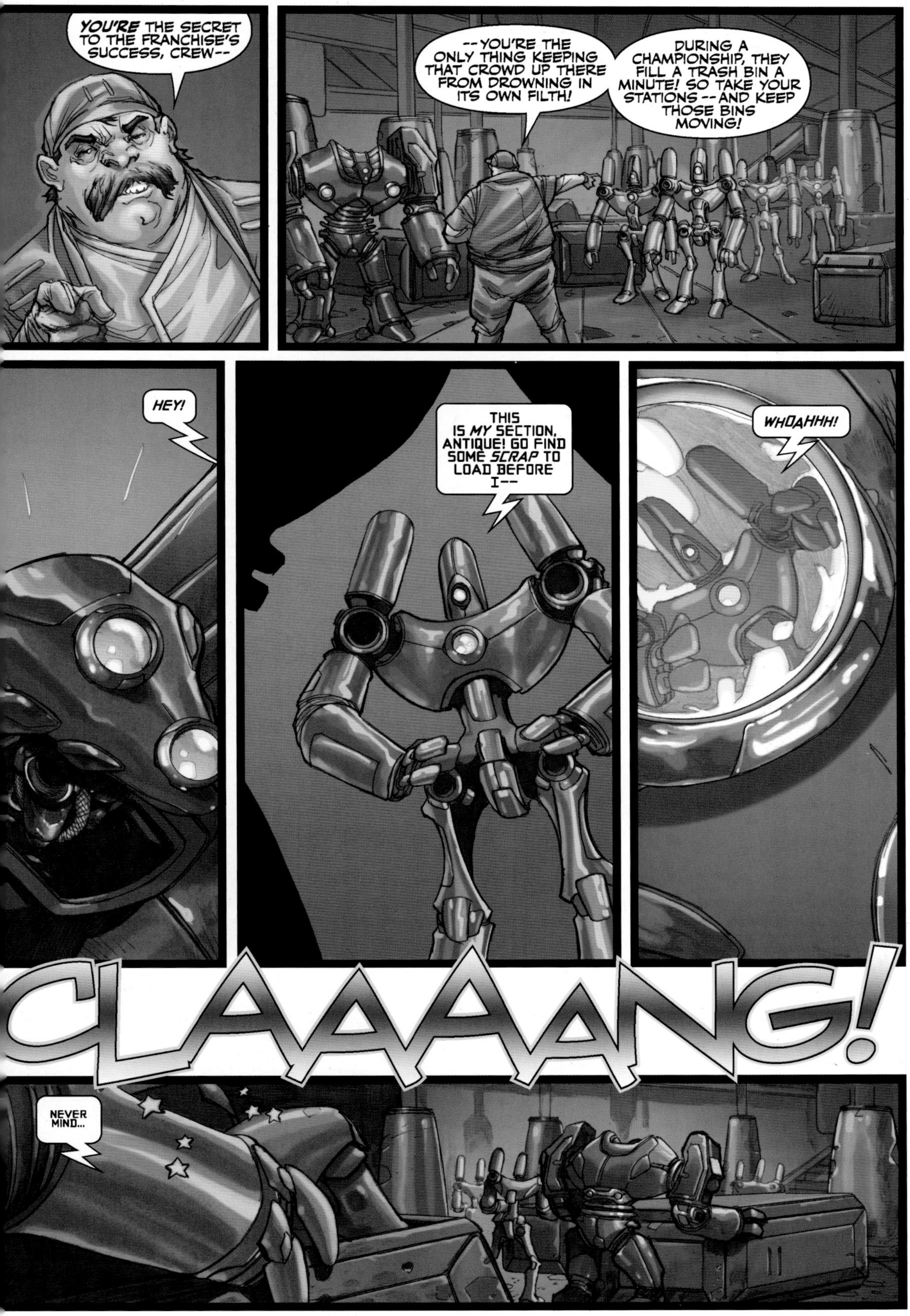
YOU'RE THE SECRET TO THE FRANCHISE'S SUCCESS, CREW--
--YOU'RE THE ONLY THING KEEPING THAT CROWD UP THERE FROM DROWNING IN ITS OWN FILTH!
DURING A CHAMPIONSHIP, THEY FILL A TRASH BIN A MINUTE! SO TAKE YOUR STATIONS--AND KEEP THOSE BINS MOVING!
HEY!
THIS IS MY SECTION, ANTIQUE! GO FIND SOME SCRAP TO LOAD BEFORE I--
WHOAHHH!
CLAAAANG!
NEVER MIND...

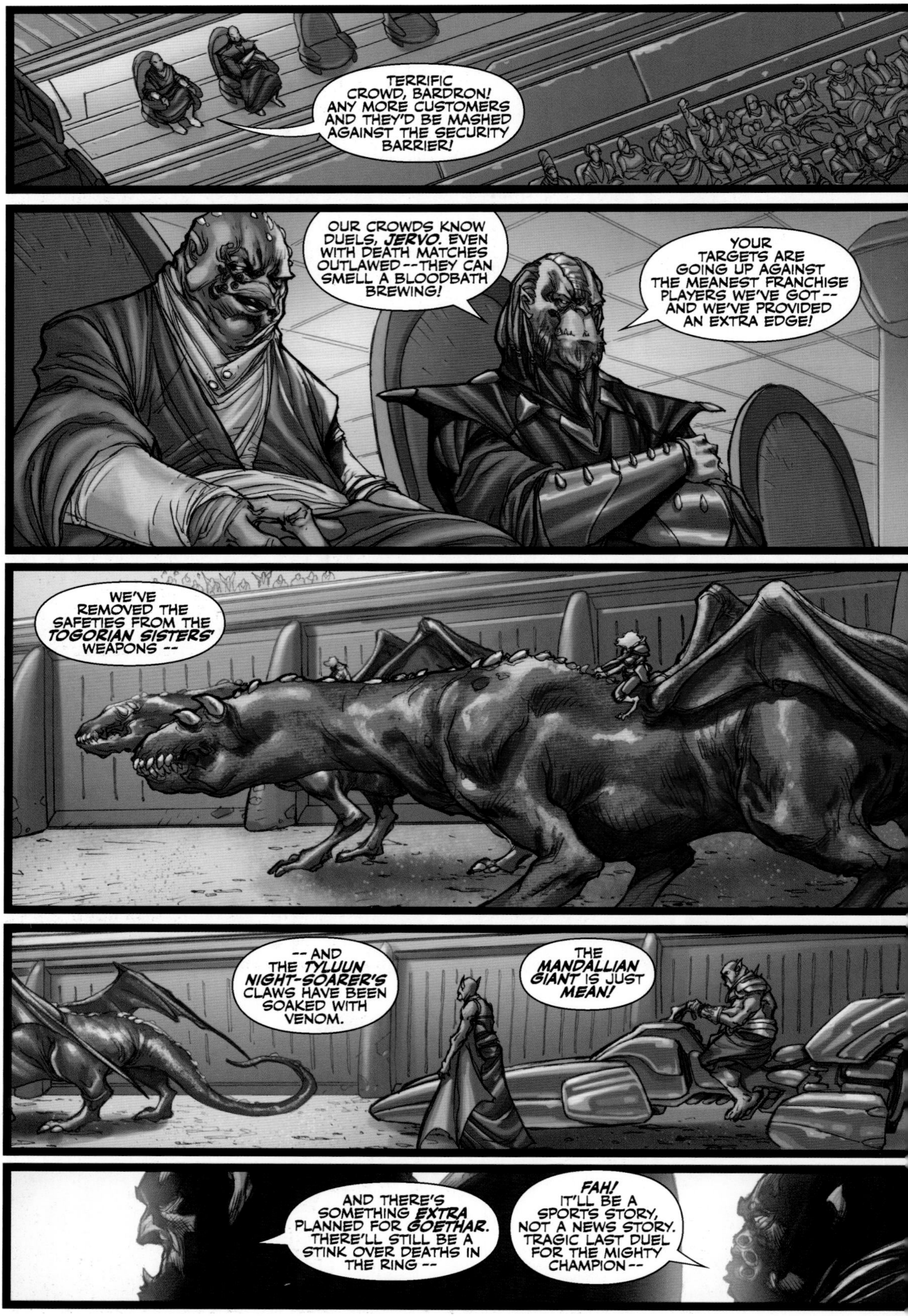
TERRIFIC CROWD, BARDRON! ANY MORE CUSTOMERS AND THEY'D BE MASHED AGAINST THE SECURITY BARRIER!
OUR CROWDS KNOW DUELS, JERVO. EVEN WITH DEATH MATCHES OUTLAWED--THEY CAN SMELL A BLOODBATH BREWING!
YOUR TARGETS ARE GOING UP AGAINST THE MEANEST FRANCHISE PLAYERS WE'VE GOT -- AND WE'VE PROVIDED AN EXTRA EDGE!
WE'VE REMOVED THE SAFETIES FROM THE TOGORIAN SISTERS' WEAPONS --
-- AND THE TYLUUN NIGHT-SOARER'S CLAWS HAVE BEEN SOAKED WITH VENOM.
THE MANDALLIAN GIANT IS JUST MEAN!
AND THERE'S SOMETHING EXTRA PLANNED FOR GOETHAR. THERE'LL STILL BE A STINK OVER DEATHS IN THE RING --
FAH! IT'LL BE A SPORTS STORY, NOT A NEWS STORY. TRAGIC LAST DUEL FOR THE MIGHTY CHAMPION --

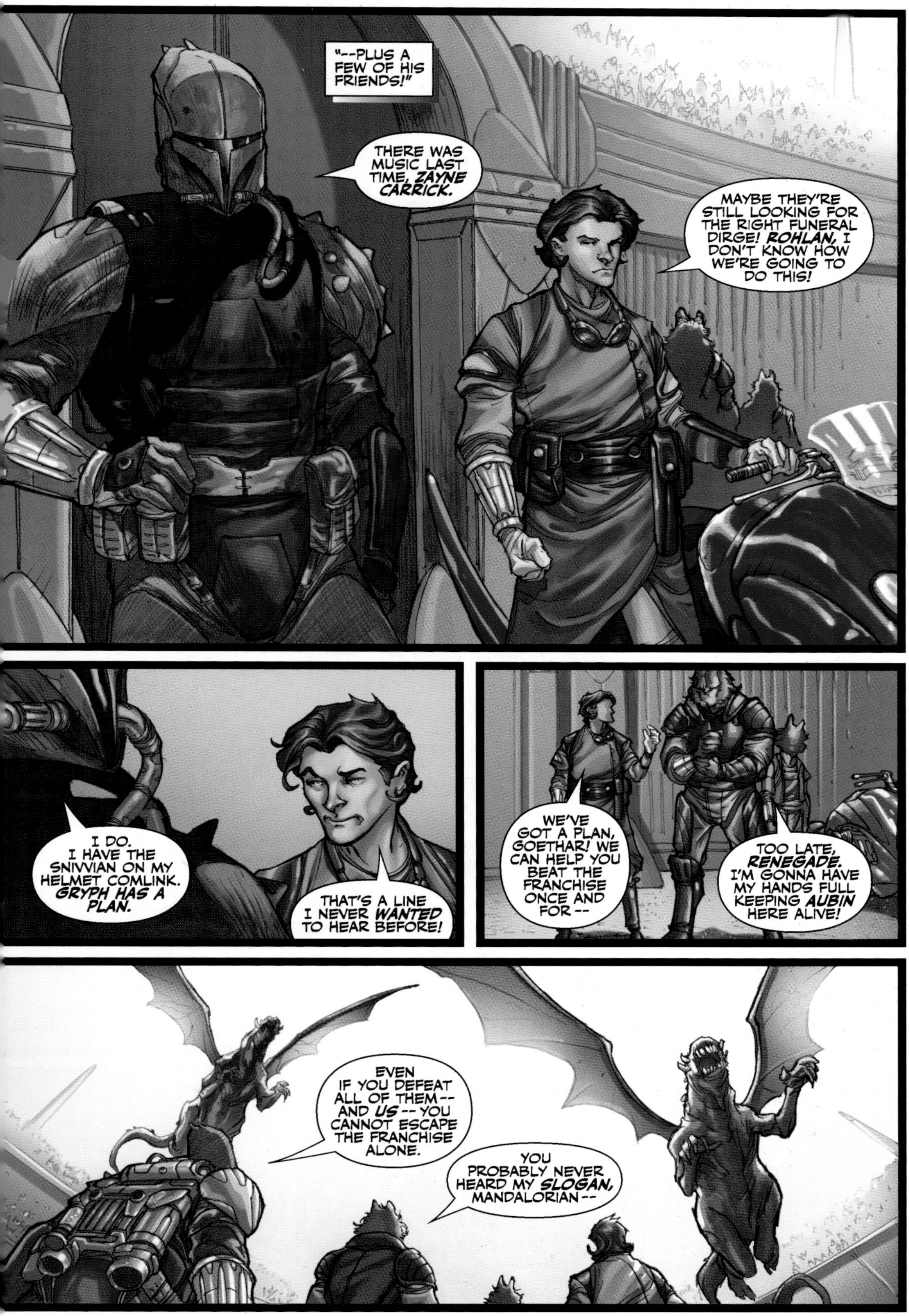
"--PLUS A FEW OF HIS FRIENDS!"
THERE WAS MUSIC LAST TIME, ZAYNE CARRICK.
MAYBE THEY'RE STILL LOOKING FOR THE RIGHT FUNERAL DIRGE! ROHLAN, I DON'T KNOW HOW WE'RE GOING TO DO THIS!
I DO. I HAVE THE SNIVVIAN ON MY HELMET COMLINK. GRYPH HAS A PLAN.
THAT'S A LINE I NEVER WANTED TO HEAR BEFORE!
WE'VE GOT A PLAN, GOETHAR! WE CAN HELP YOU BEAT THE FRANCHISE ONCE AND FOR --
TOO LATE, RENEGADE. I'M GONNA HAVE MY HANDS FULL KEEPING AUBIN HERE ALIVE!
EVEN IF YOU DEFEAT ALL OF THEM -- AND US -- YOU CANNOT ESCAPE THE FRANCHISE ALONE.
YOU PROBABLY NEVER HEARD MY SLOGAN, MANDALORIAN --

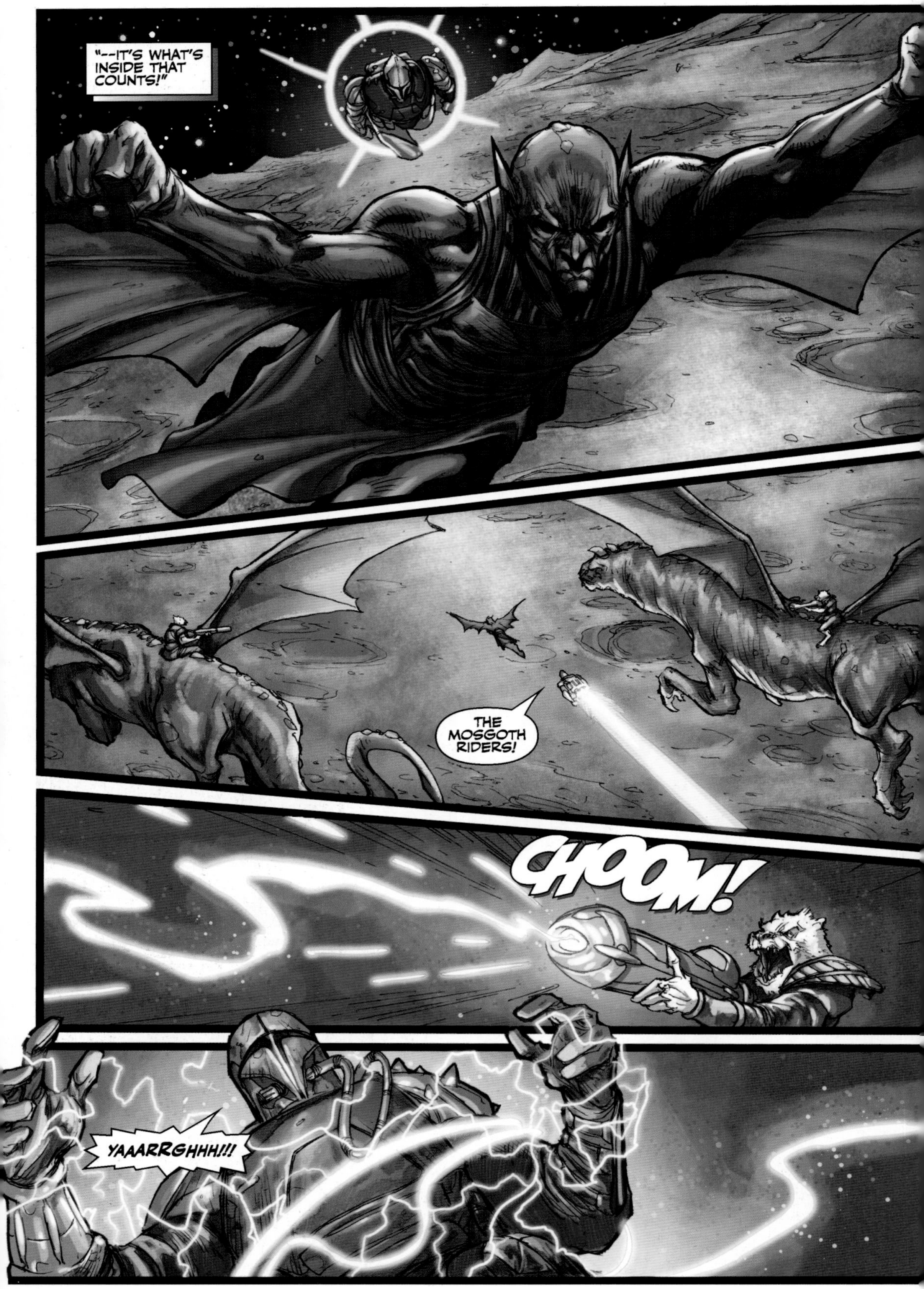
"--IT'S WHAT'S INSIDE THAT COUNTS!"
THE MOSGOTH RIDERS!
CHOOOM!
YAAARRGHHH!!!

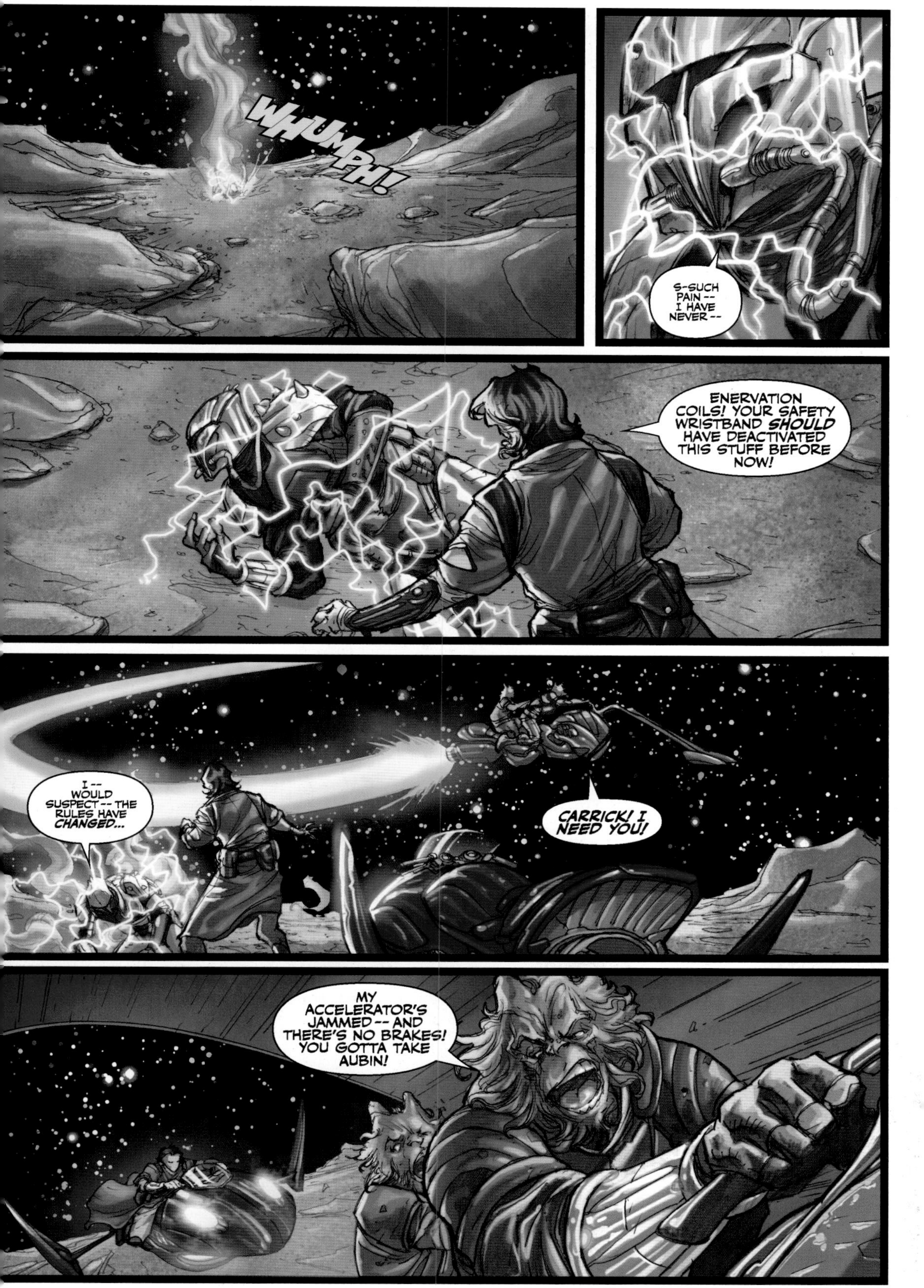
WHUMPH!
S-SUCH PAIN -- I HAVE NEVER --
ENERVATION COILS! YOUR SAFETY WRISTBAND SHOULD HAVE DEACTIVATED THIS STUFF BEFORE NOW!
I -- WOULD SUSPECT -- THE RULES HAVE CHANGED...
CARRICK! I NEED YOU!
MY ACCELERATOR'S JAMMED -- AND THERE'S NO BRAKES! YOU GOTTA TAKE AUBIN!

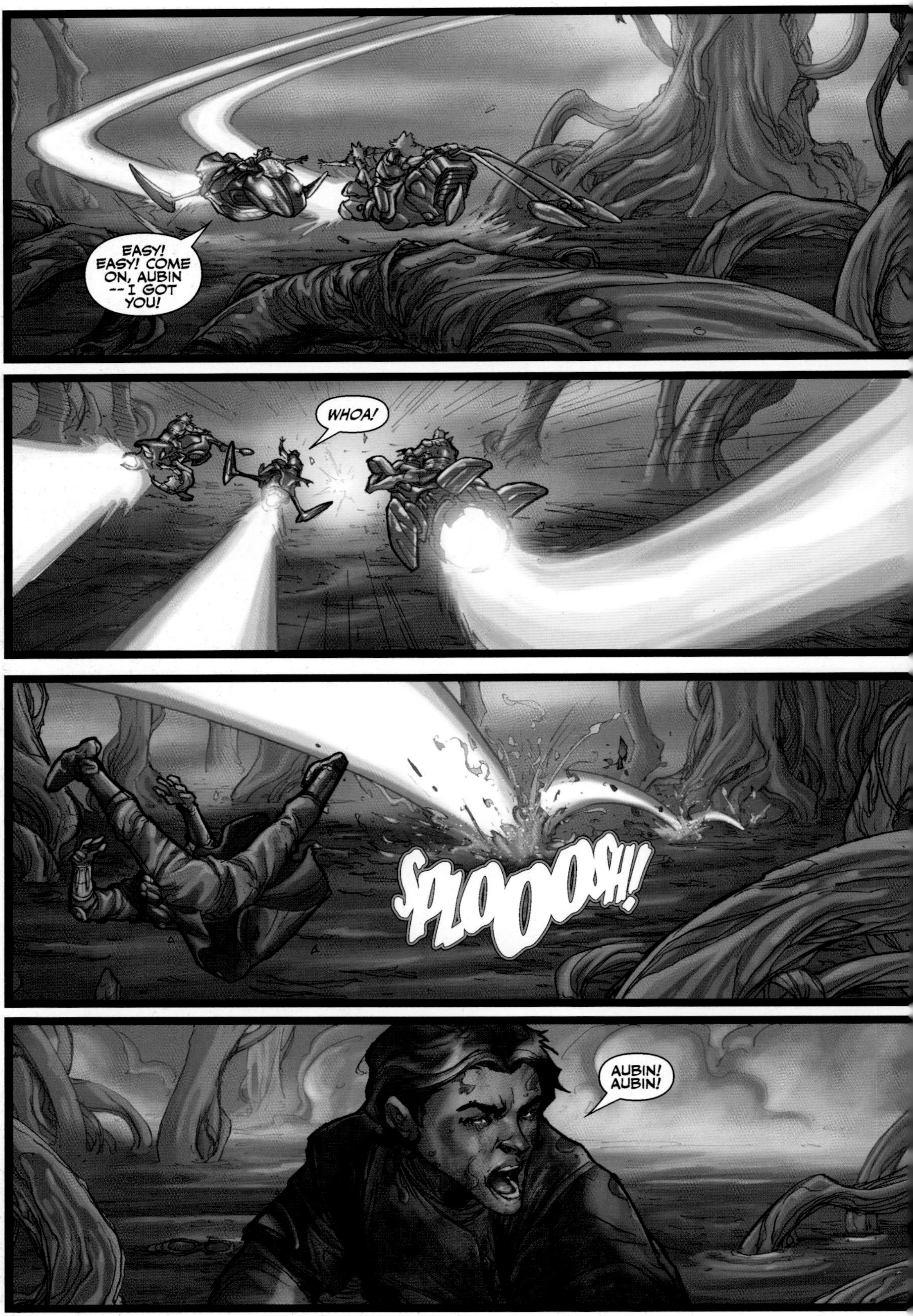
EASY! EASY! COME ON, AUBIN --I GOT YOU!
WHOA!
SPLOOOSH!
AUBIN! AUBIN!

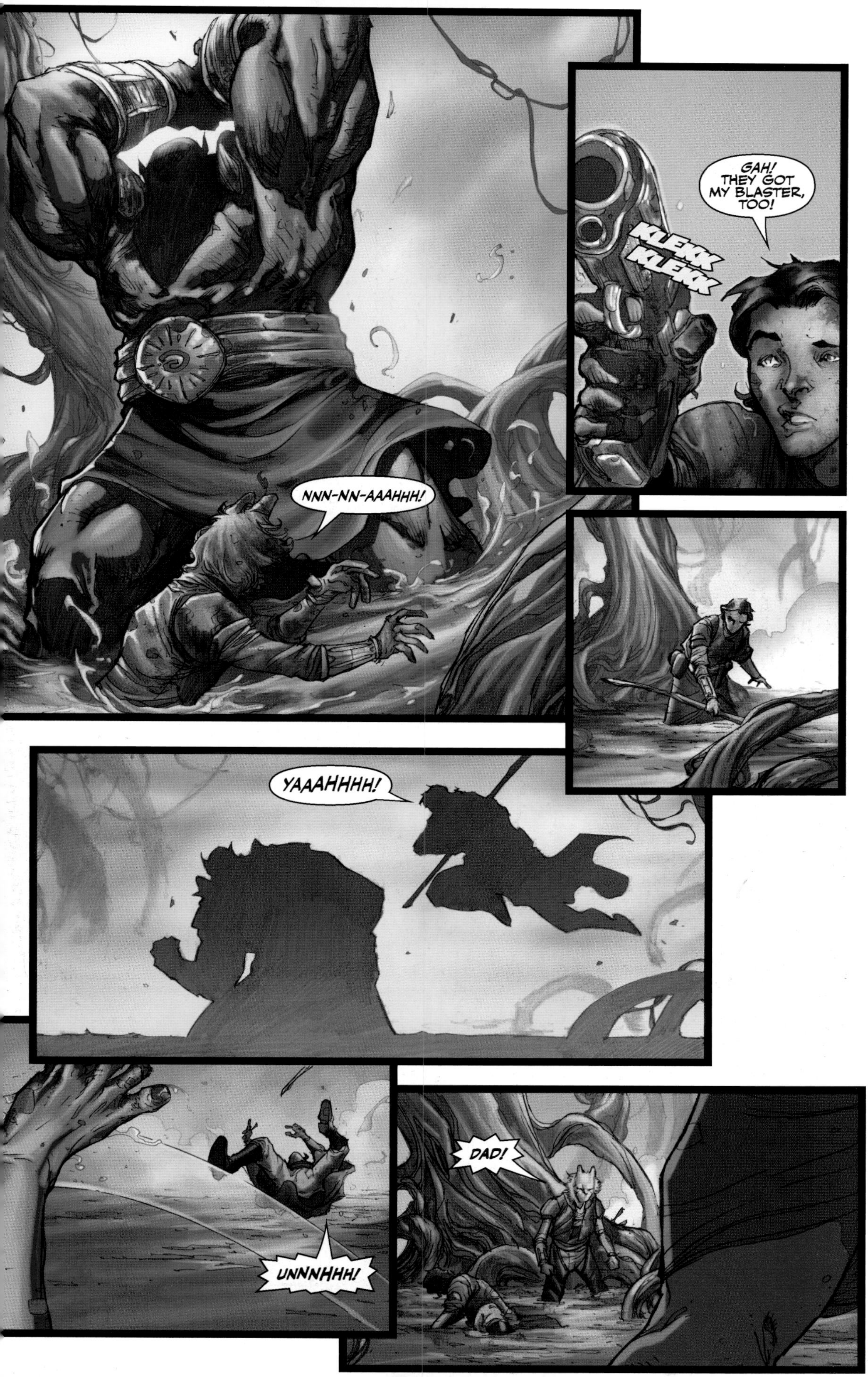
NNN-NN-AAAHHH!
GAH! THEY GOT MY BLASTER, TOO!
KLEKK KLEKK
YAAAHHHH!
UNNHHH!
DAD!

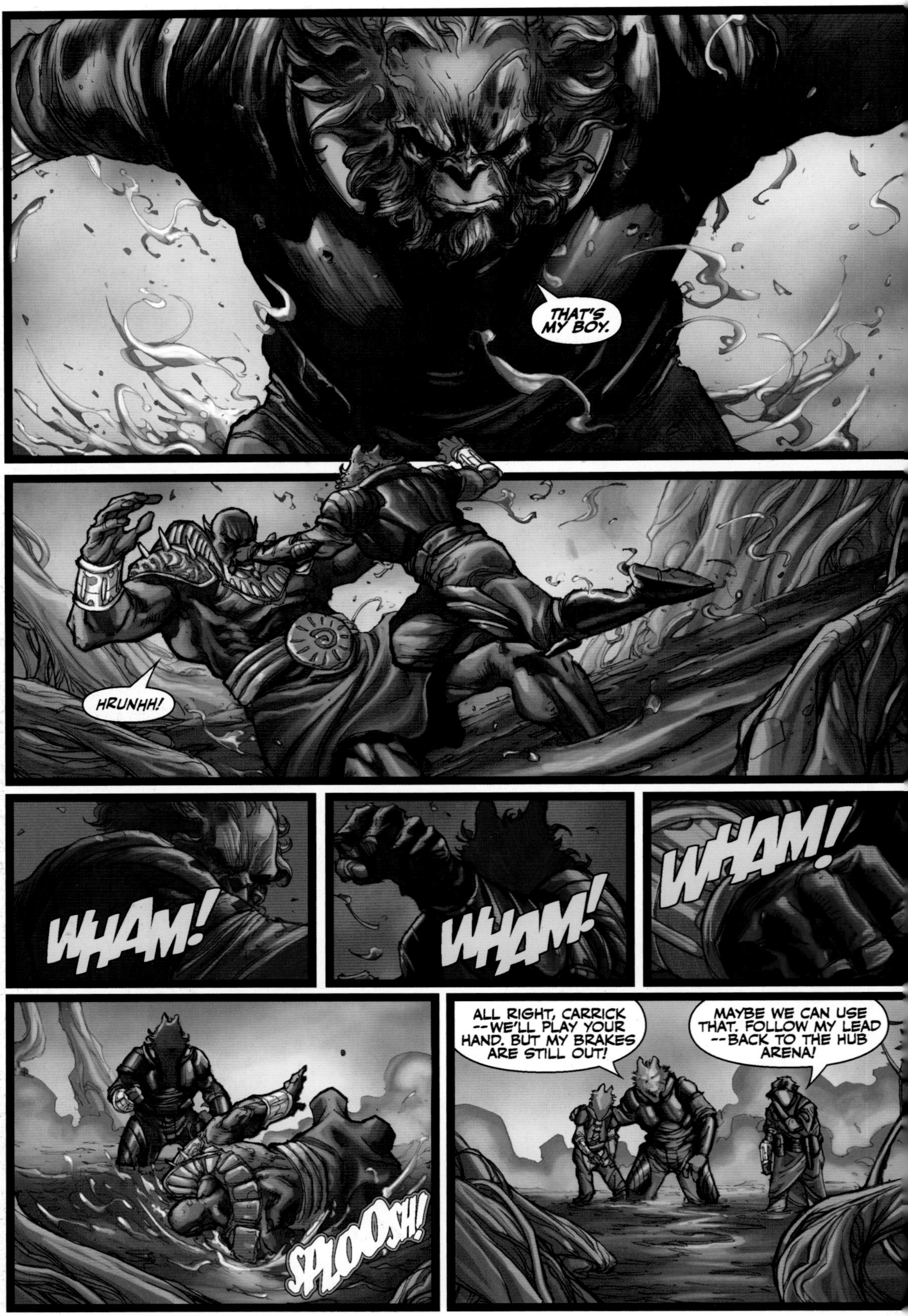
THAT'S MY BOY.
HRUNHH!
WHAM!
WHAM!
WHAM!
SPLOOSH!
ALL RIGHT, CARRICK --WE'LL PLAY YOUR HAND. BUT MY BRAKES ARE STILL OUT!
MAYBE WE CAN USE THAT. FOLLOW MY LEAD --BACK TO THE HUB ARENA!

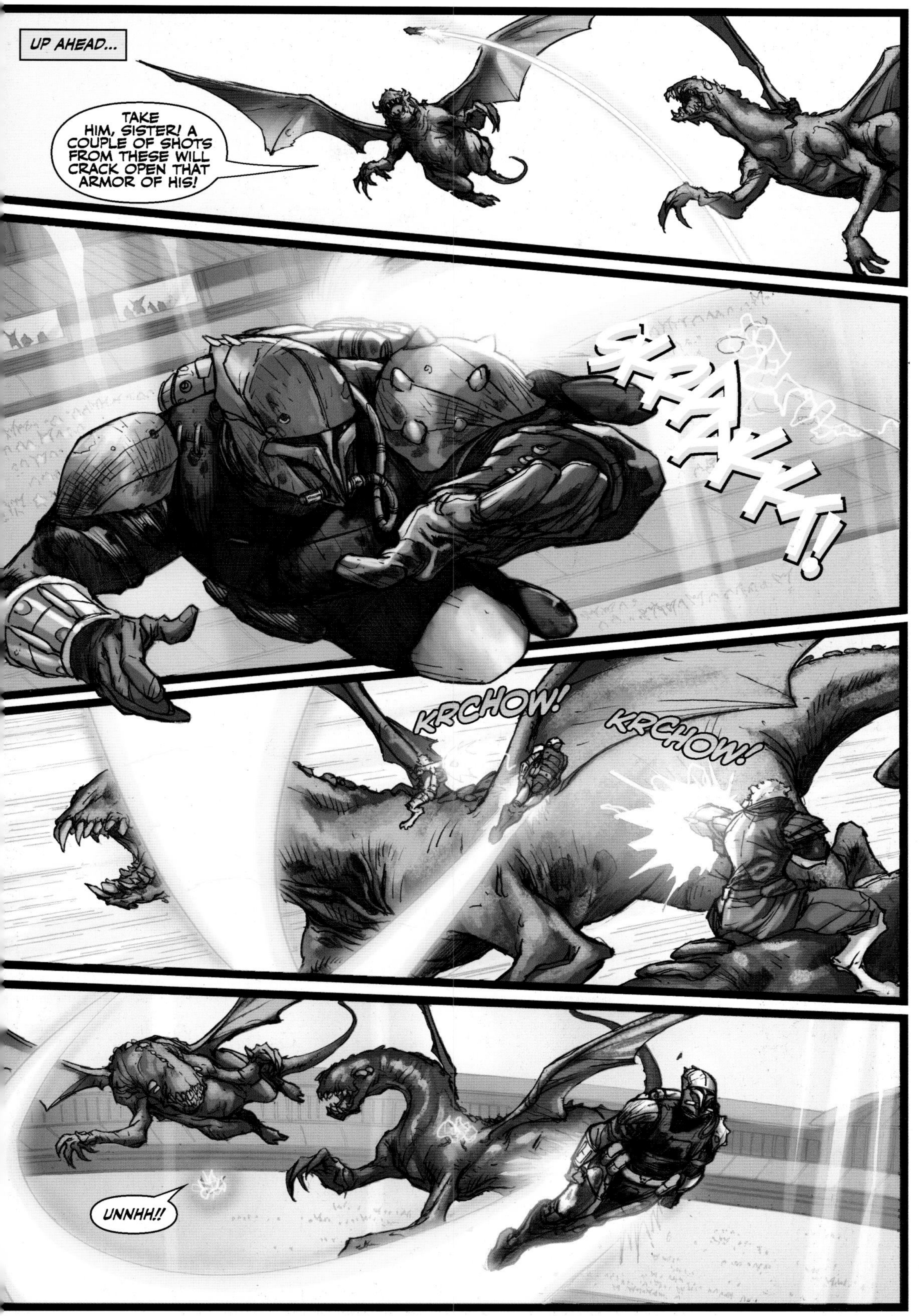
UP AHEAD...
TAKE HIM, SISTER! A COUPLE OF SHOTS FROM THESE WILL CRACK OPEN THAT ARMOR OF HIS!
SKRAKKT!
KRCHOW!
KRCHOW!
UNNHH!!

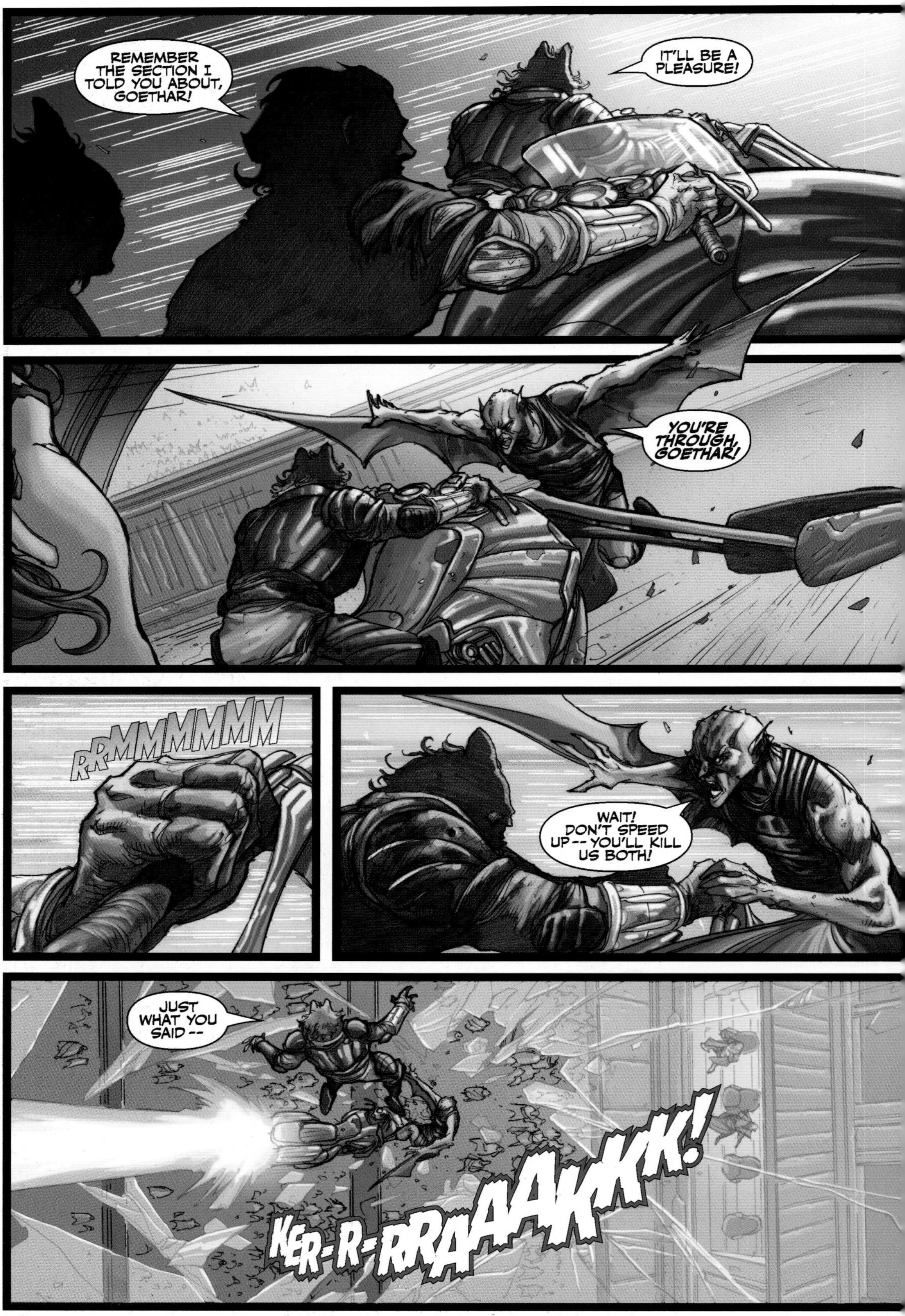
REMEMBER THE SECTION I TOLD YOU ABOUT, GOETHAR!
IT'LL BE A PLEASURE!
YOU'RE THROUGH, GOETHAR!
RRMMMMMMM
WAIT! DON'T SPEED UP -- YOU'LL KILL US BOTH!
JUST WHAT YOU SAID --
KER-R-RRAAAKKK!

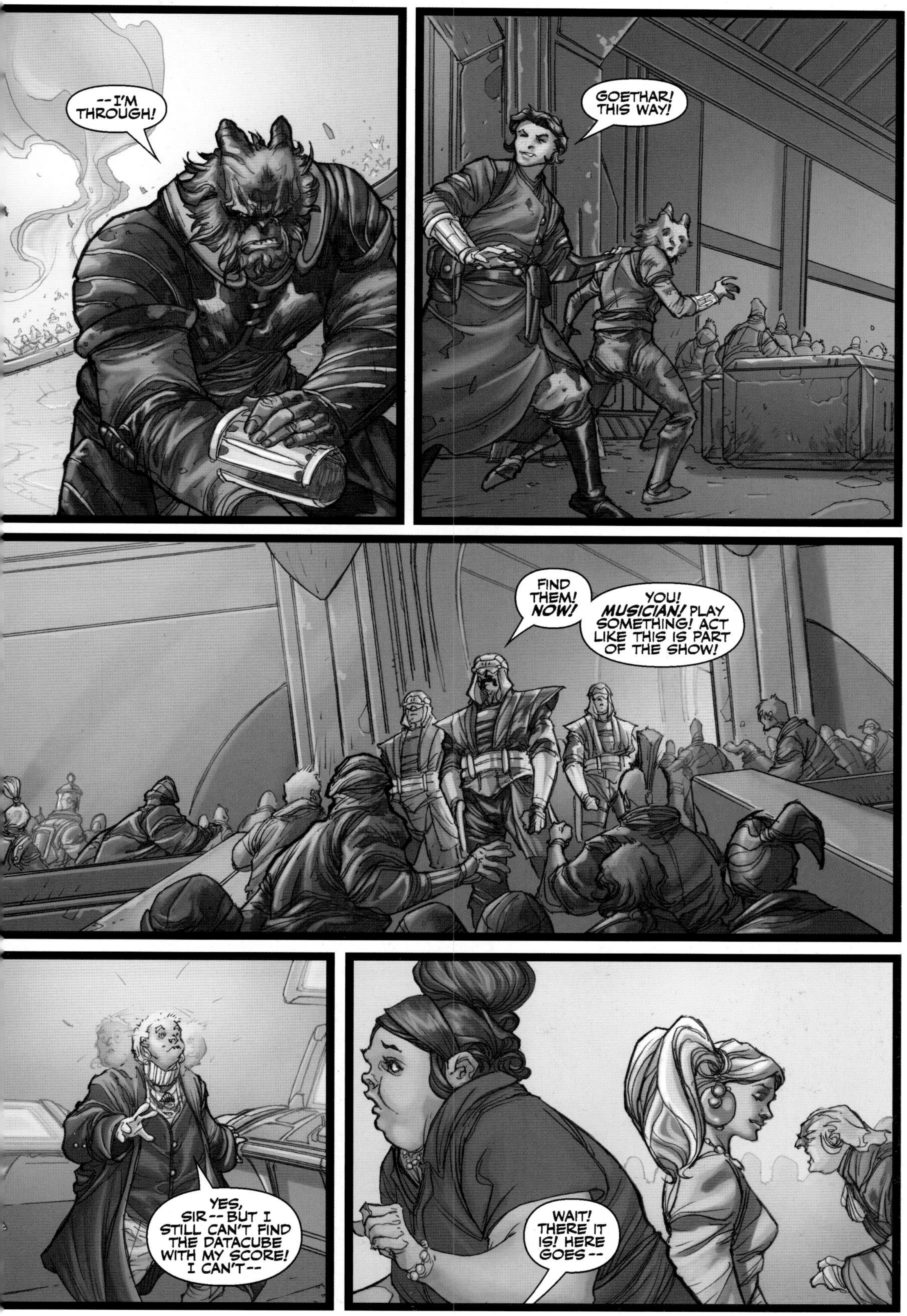
--I'M THROUGH!
GOETHAR! THIS WAY!
FIND THEM! NOW!
YOU! MUSICIAN! PLAY SOMETHING! ACT LIKE THIS IS PART OF THE SHOW!
YES, SIR--BUT I STILL CAN'T FIND THE DATACUBE WITH MY SCORE! I CAN'T--
WAIT! THERE IT IS! HERE GOES--

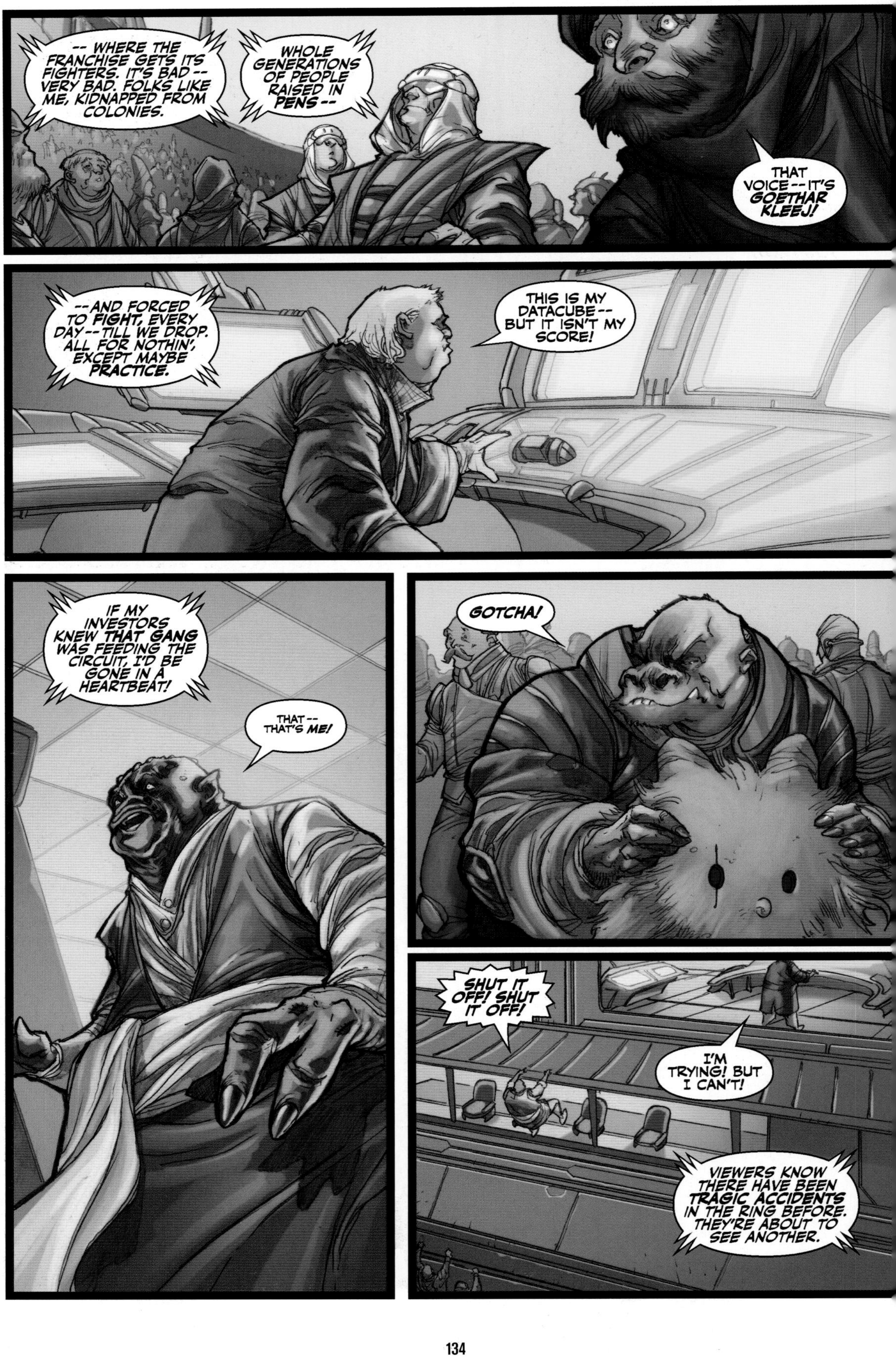
-- WHERE THE FRANCHISE GETS ITS FIGHTERS. IT'S BAD -- VERY BAD. FOLKS LIKE ME, KIDNAPPED FROM COLONIES.
WHOLE GENERATIONS OF PEOPLE RAISED IN PENS --
THAT VOICE -- IT'S GOETHAR KLEEJ!
--AND FORCED TO FIGHT, EVERY DAY--TILL WE DROP. ALL FOR NOTHIN', EXCEPT MAYBE PRACTICE.
THIS IS MY DATACUBE -- BUT IT ISN'T MY SCORE!
IF MY INVESTORS KNEW THAT GANG WAS FEEDING THE CIRCUIT, I'D BE GONE IN A HEARTBEAT!
THAT -- THAT'S ME!
GOTCHA!
SHUT IT OFF! SHUT IT OFF!
I'M TRYING! BUT I CAN'T!
VIEWERS KNOW THERE HAVE BEEN TRAGIC ACCIDENTS IN THE RING BEFORE. THEY'RE ABOUT TO SEE ANOTHER.

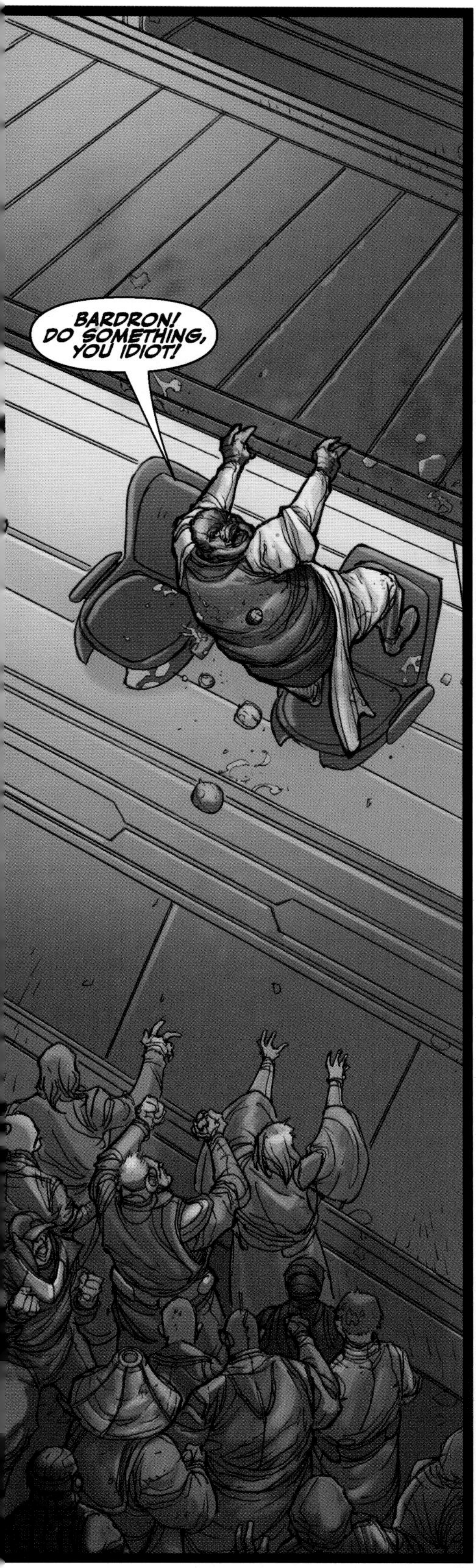
BARDRON! DO SOMETHING, YOU IDIOT!

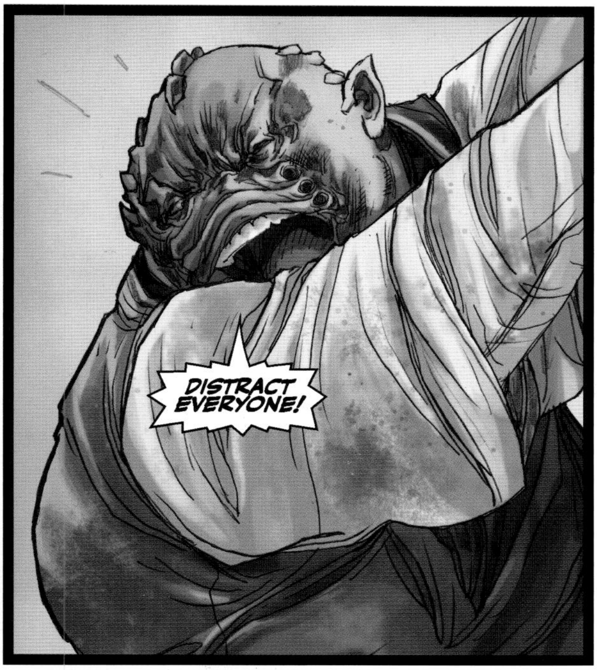
DISTRACT EVERYONE!

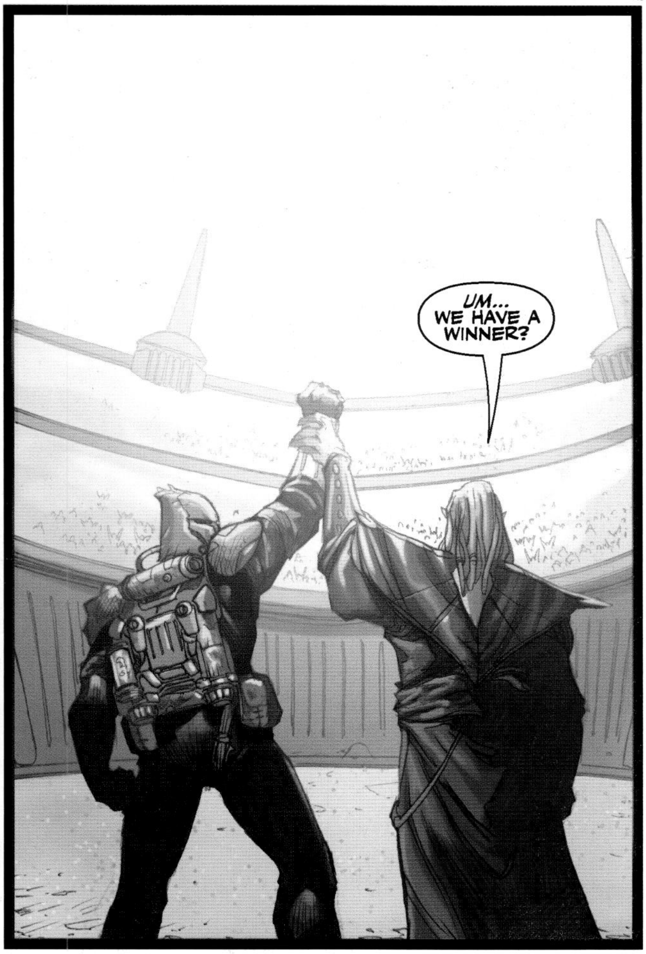
UM... WE HAVE A WINNER?

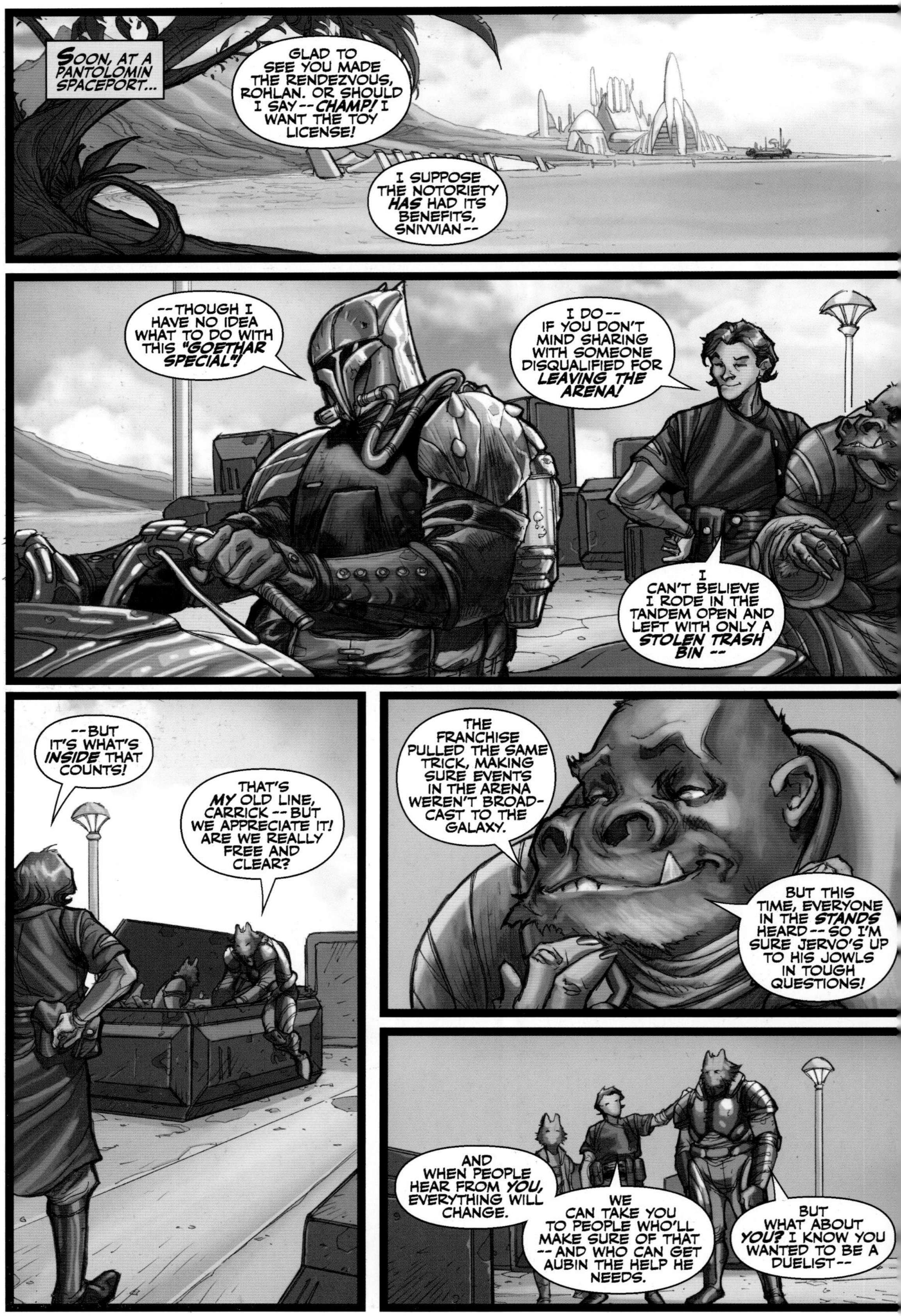

SOON, AT A PANTOLOMIN SPACEPORT...
GLAD TO SEE YOU MADE THE RENDEZVOUS, ROHLAN. OR SHOULD I SAY--CHAMP! I WANT THE TOY LICENSE!
I SUPPOSE THE NOTORIETY HAS HAD ITS BENEFITS, SNIVVIAN--
--THOUGH I HAVE NO IDEA WHAT TO DO WITH THIS "GOETHAR SPECIAL"!
I DO--IF YOU DON'T MIND SHARING WITH SOMEONE DISQUALIFIED FOR LEAVING THE ARENA!
I CAN'T BELIEVE I RODE IN THE TANDEM OPEN AND LEFT WITH ONLY A STOLEN TRASH BIN --
--BUT IT'S WHAT'S INSIDE THAT COUNTS!
THAT'S MY OLD LINE, CARRICK--BUT WE APPRECIATE IT! ARE WE REALLY FREE AND CLEAR?
THE FRANCHISE PULLED THE SAME TRICK, MAKING SURE EVENTS IN THE ARENA WEREN'T BROADCAST TO THE GALAXY.
BUT THIS TIME, EVERYONE IN THE STANDS HEARD--SO I'M SURE JERVO'S UP TO HIS JOWLS IN TOUGH QUESTIONS!
AND WHEN PEOPLE HEAR FROM YOU, EVERYTHING WILL CHANGE.
WE CAN TAKE YOU TO PEOPLE WHO'LL MAKE SURE OF THAT--AND WHO CAN GET AUBIN THE HELP HE NEEDS.
BUT WHAT ABOUT YOU? I KNOW YOU WANTED TO BE A DUELIST--

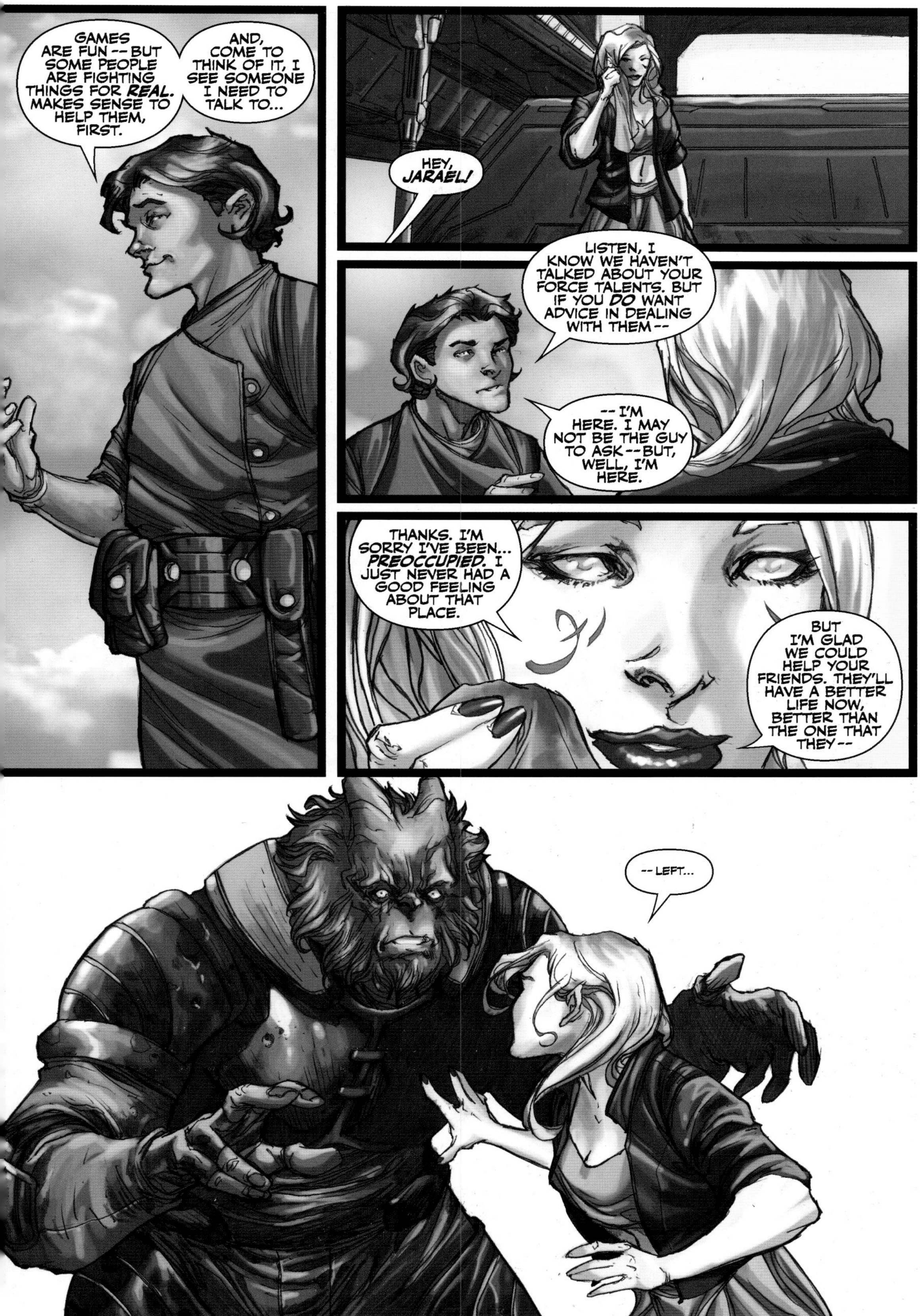
GAMES ARE FUN -- BUT SOME PEOPLE ARE FIGHTING THINGS FOR *REAL*. MAKES SENSE TO HELP THEM, FIRST.
AND, COME TO THINK OF IT, I SEE SOMEONE I NEED TO TALK TO...
HEY, *JARAEL!*
LISTEN, I KNOW WE HAVEN'T TALKED ABOUT YOUR FORCE TALENTS. BUT IF YOU *DO* WANT ADVICE IN DEALING WITH THEM--
-- I'M HERE. I MAY NOT BE THE GUY TO ASK--BUT, WELL, I'M HERE.
THANKS. I'M SORRY I'VE BEEN... *PREOCCUPIED.* I JUST NEVER HAD A GOOD FEELING ABOUT THAT PLACE.
BUT I'M GLAD WE COULD HELP YOUR FRIENDS. THEY'LL HAVE A BETTER LIFE NOW, BETTER THAN THE ONE THAT THEY--
-- LEFT...

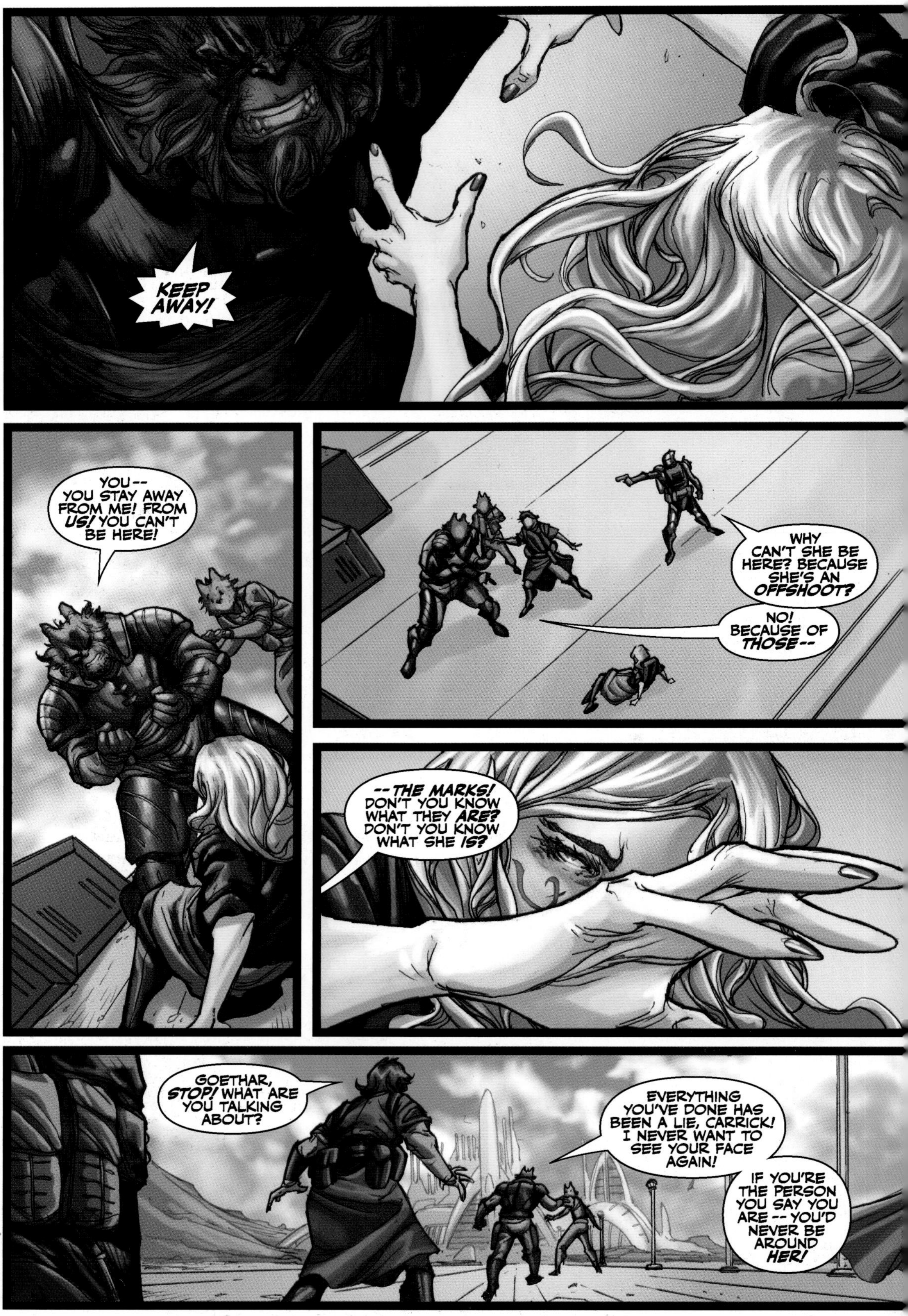
KEEP AWAY!
YOU-- YOU STAY AWAY FROM ME! FROM US! YOU CAN'T BE HERE!
WHY CAN'T SHE BE HERE? BECAUSE SHE'S AN OFFSHOOT?
NO! BECAUSE OF THOSE--
--THE MARKS! DON'T YOU KNOW WHAT THEY ARE? DON'T YOU KNOW WHAT SHE IS?
GOETHAR, STOP! WHAT ARE YOU TALKING ABOUT?
EVERYTHING YOU'VE DONE HAS BEEN A LIE, CARRICK! I NEVER WANT TO SEE YOUR FACE AGAIN!
IF YOU'RE THE PERSON YOU SAY YOU ARE -- YOU'D NEVER BE AROUND HER!

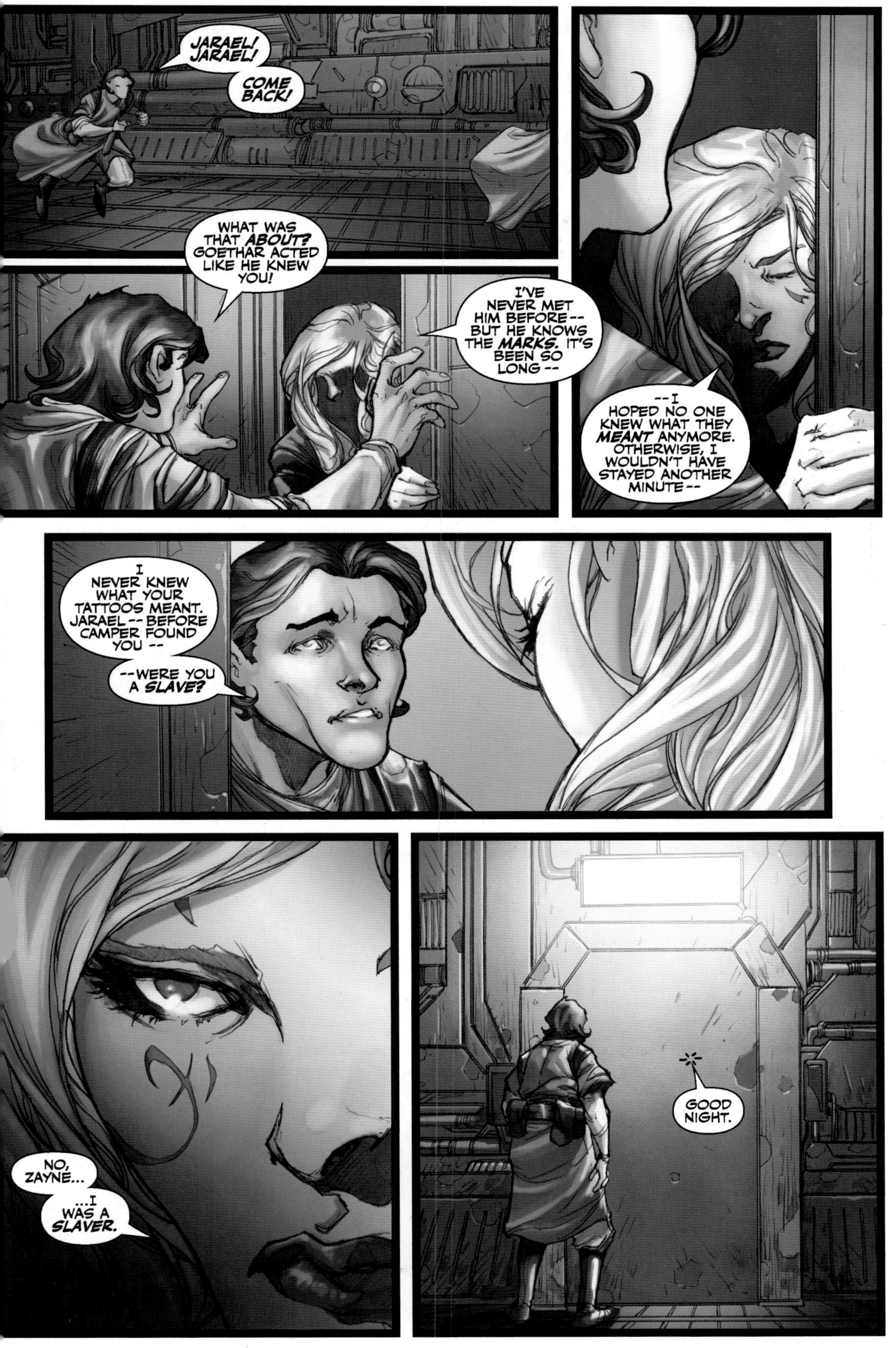
JARAEL! JARAEL!
COME BACK!
WHAT WAS THAT ABOUT? GOETHAR ACTED LIKE HE KNEW YOU!
I'VE NEVER MET HIM BEFORE-- BUT HE KNOWS THE MARKS. IT'S BEEN SO LONG --
--I HOPED NO ONE KNEW WHAT THEY MEANT ANYMORE. OTHERWISE, I WOULDN'T HAVE STAYED ANOTHER MINUTE--
I NEVER KNEW WHAT YOUR TATTOOS MEANT. JARAEL-- BEFORE CAMPER FOUND YOU --
--WERE YOU A SLAVE?
NO, ZAYNE...
...I WAS A SLAVER.
GOOD NIGHT.

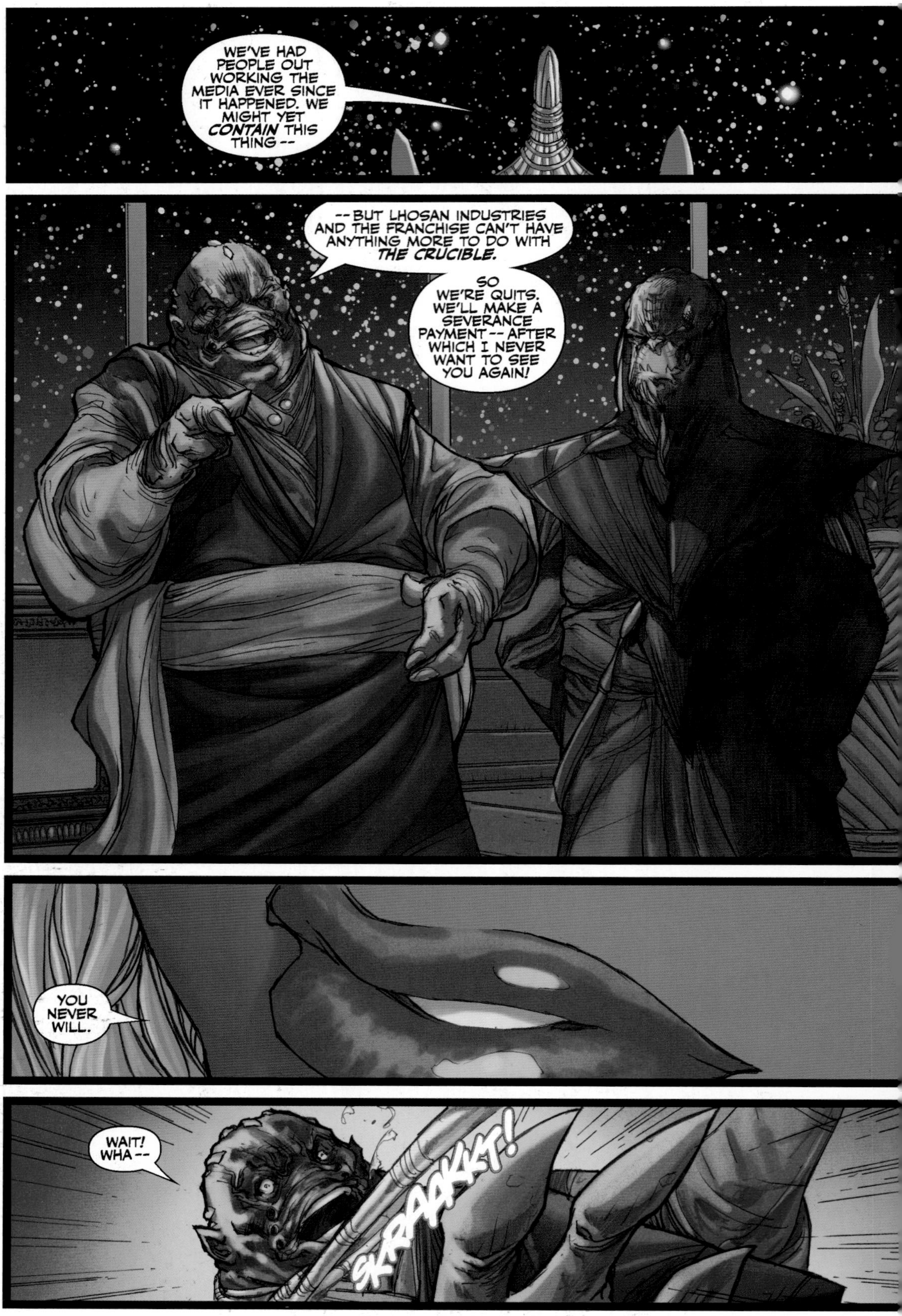
WE'VE HAD PEOPLE OUT WORKING THE MEDIA EVER SINCE IT HAPPENED. WE MIGHT YET CONTAIN THIS THING--
--BUT LHOSAN INDUSTRIES AND THE FRANCHISE CAN'T HAVE ANYTHING MORE TO DO WITH THE CRUCIBLE.
SO WE'RE QUITS. WE'LL MAKE A SEVERANCE PAYMENT--AFTER WHICH I NEVER WANT TO SEE YOU AGAIN!
YOU NEVER WILL.
WAIT! WHA--
SKRAAKKT!

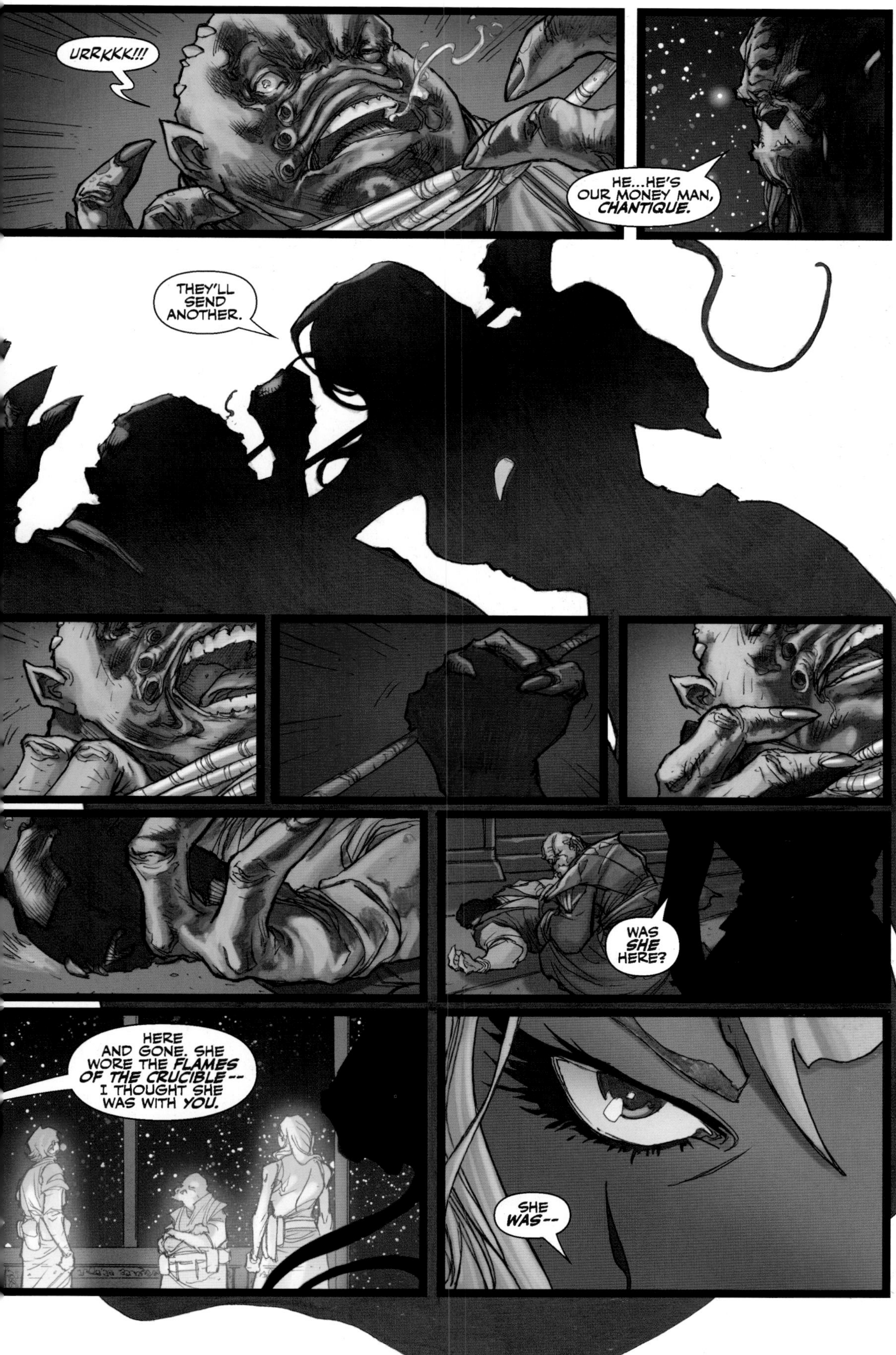
URRKKK!!!
HE...HE'S OUR MONEY MAN, CHANTIQUE.
THEY'LL SEND ANOTHER.
WAS SHE HERE?
HERE AND GONE. SHE WORE THE FLAMES OF THE CRUCIBLE-- I THOUGHT SHE WAS WITH YOU.
SHE WAS--

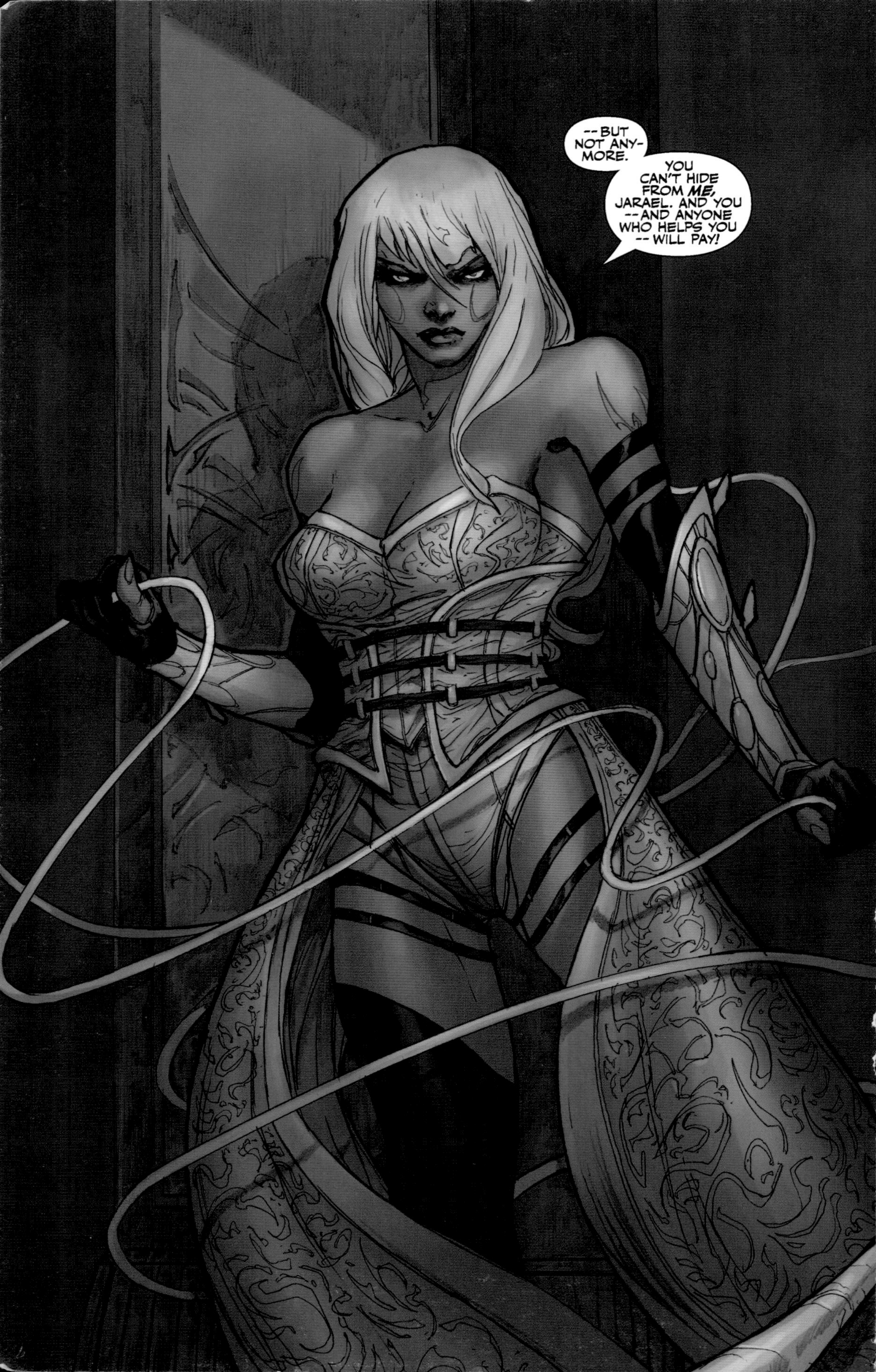
--BUT NOT ANY-MORE.
YOU CAN'T HIDE FROM *ME,* JARAEL. AND YOU --AND ANYONE WHO HELPS YOU --WILL PAY!

PUBLISHER
MIKE RICHARDSON

EXECUTIVE VICE PRESIDENT
NEIL HANKERSON

CHIEF FINANCIAL OFFICER
TOM WEDDLE

VICE PRESIDENT OF PUBLISHING
RANDY STRADLEY

VICE PRESIDENT OF BUSINESS DEVELOPMENT
MICHAEL MARTENS

VICE PRESIDENT OF MARKETING, SALES, AND LICENSING
ANITA NELSON

VICE PRESIDENT OF PRODUCT DEVELOPMENT
DAVID SCROGGY

VICE PRESIDENT OF INFORMATION TECHNOLOGY
DALE LaFOUNTAIN

DIRECTOR OF PURCHASING
DARLENE VOGEL

GENERAL COUNSEL
KEN LIZZI

EDITORIAL DIRECTOR
DAVEY ESTRADA

SENIOR MANAGING EDITOR
SCOTT ALLIE

SENIOR BOOKS EDITOR, DARK HORSE BOOKS
CHRIS WARNER

EXECUTIVE EDITOR
DIANA SCHUTZ

DIRECTOR OF DESIGN AND PRODUCTION
CARY GRAZZINI

ART DIRECTOR
LIA RIBACCHI

DIRECTOR OF SCHEDULING
CARA NIECE

STAR WARS
VECTOR

An event with repercussions for every era and every hero in the *Star Wars* galaxy begins here! For anyone who never knew where to start with *Star Wars* comics, *Vector* is the perfect introduction to the entire *Star Wars* line! For any serious *Star Wars* fan, *Vector* is a must-see event with major happenings throughout the most important moments of the galaxy's history!

VOLUME ONE
(*Knights of the Old Republic* Vol. 5; *Dark Times* Vol. 3)
ISBN 978-1-59582-226-0 | $17.95

VOLUME TWO
(*Rebellion* Vol. 4
ISBN 978-1-59582

KNIGHTS OF THE OLD REPUBLIC
Volume One: Commencement
ISBN 978-1-59307-640-5 | $18.95

Volume Two: Flashpoint
ISBN 978-1-59307-761-7 | $18.95

Volume Three: Days of Fear, Nights of Anger
ISBN 978-1-59307-867-6 | $18.95

Volume Four: Daze of Hate, Knights of Suffering
ISBN 978-1-59582-208-6 | $18.95

Volume Six: Vindication
ISBN 978-1-59582-274-1 | $19.95

Volume Seven: Dueling Ambitions
ISBN 978-1-59582-348-9 | $18.95

REBELLION
Volume One: My Brother, My Enemy
ISBN 978-1-59307-711-2 | $14.95

Volume Two: The Ahakista Gambit
ISBN 978-1-59307-890-4 | $17.95

Volume Three: Small Victories
ISBN 978-1-59582-166-9 | $12.95

LEGACY
Volume One: Broken
ISBN 978-1-59307-716-7 | $17.95

Volume Two: Shards
ISBN 978-1-59307-879-9 | $19.95

Volume Three: Claws of the Dragon
ISBN 978-1-59307-946-8 | $17.95

Volume Four: Alliance
ISBN 978-1-59582-223-9 | $15.95

Volume Five: The Hidden Temple
ISBN 978-1-59582-224-6 | $15.95

DARK TIMES
Volume One: The Path to Nowhere
ISBN 978-1-59307-792-1 | $17.95

Volume Two: Parallels
ISBN 978-1-59307-945-1 | $17.95

darkhorse.com
AVAILABLE AT YOUR LOCAL COMICS SHOP OR BOOKSTORE.
REA, CALL 1-888-266-4226
On the web: darkhorse.com
ne: 1-800-862-0052 Mon.–Fri.
04–2009 Lucasfilm Ltd. & ™ (BL8005)